M000309543

The First Way of Wa

This book explores the evolution of early Americans' first ways of making war to show how war waged against enemy noncombatant populations and agricultural resources ultimately defined Americans' military heritage. Grenier explains the significance of Americans' earliest wars with both Indians and Europeans, from the seventeenth-century conflicts with the Indians of the Eastern Seaboard, through the imperial wars among England, France, and Spain in the eighteenth century, to frontier Americans' conquest of the Indians of the Transappalachian West in 1814. This sanguinary story of Americans' inexorable march across the first frontiers helps demonstrate how they embraced warfare shaped by extravagant violence and focused on conquest. Grenier provides a major revision in understanding the place of warfare directed at noncombatants in the American military tradition, and his conclusions are relevant to understanding U.S. "special operations" in the War on Terror.

John Grenier is an Air Force officer and Associate Professor of History at the United States Air Force Academy.

The First Way of War

American War Making on the Frontier, 1607–1814

John Grenier

CAMBRIDGE
UNIVERSITY PRESS

CAMBRIDGE UNIVERSITY PRESS
Cambridge, New York, Melbourne, Madrid, Cape Town, Singapore,
São Paulo, Delhi, Dubai, Tokyo, Mexico City

Cambridge University Press
32 Avenue of the Americas, New York, NY 10013-2473, USA

www.cambridge.org
Information on this title: www.cambridge.org/9780521732635

First published 2005
First paperback edition 2008
6th printing 2010

A catalog record for this publication is available from the British Library.

Library of Congress Cataloging in Publication Data

Grenier, John, 1967–
The first way of war : American war making on the frontier, 1607–1814 / John Grenier.
p. cm.
Includes bibliographical references and index.
ISBN 0-521-84566-1 (hardback : alk. paper)
1. Indians of North America – Wars – 1600–1750. 2. Indians of North America – Wars
– 1750–1815. 3. Indians of North America – History – Colonial period, ca. 1600–1775.
4. Indians of North America – History – Revolution, 1775–1783. 5. United States –
Politics and government – To 1775. 6. United States – Politics and government –
1775–1783. 7. United States – Politics and government – 1783–1865. I. Title.
E82.G74   2005
355′.00973′0903–dc22   2004052547

ISBN 978-0-521-84566-3 Hardback
ISBN 978-0-521-73263-5 Paperback

For Molly and Sophia

They were no colonists; their administration was merely a squeeze, and nothing more, I suspect. They were conquerors, and for that you want only brute force – nothing to boast of, when you have it, since your strength is just an accident arising from the weakness of others. They grabbed what they could get for the sake of what was to be got. It was just robbery with violence, aggravated murder on a great scale, and men going at it blind – as is very proper for those who tackle a darkness. The conquest of the earth, which mostly means the taking it away from those who have a different complexion or slightly flatter noses than ourselves, is not a pretty thing when you look into it too much.

Joseph Conrad, *The Heart of Darkness*

Contents

Figures and Maps

Figures

Maps

Preface

This book is an attempt to understand better the evolution of an early American way of war that condoned the use of violence against enemy noncombatants. As a serving officer in the United States Air Force, I have tried to focus on a larger audience than colonial historians. As such, I hope this book will encourage military professionals to think about the other sides of our martial culture. Military leaders should look at all the ways, even if they seem brutal and out of character, that we wage war. Similarly, there remains little doubt that a significant part of the future for the American soldier will involve the challenges, in their modern manifestations, that early American soldiers faced. Especially to my colleagues in the profession of arms, therefore, I suggest that relevant lessons abound in a study of early American military history.[1]

Attributing names to the various groups involved in the conflicts that shaped early American history is a difficult task. I have made an effort to distinguish systematically among the different participants in seventeenth- through early-nineteenth-century American wars. First, important differences existed among "Englishmen," "Britons," "Anglo-Americans," and "Americans." "Englishmen" refers to natives of England and Wales; I use "Britons" to describe the same peoples, together with the Scots, after 1707. "Anglo-American" describes Europeans born in England's or Great Britain's North American colonial possessions or those individuals who immigrated to North America. North American–born colonists or immigrants were not called "Americans" until the 1740s and generally did not think of themselves as such until after the War of Independence. However,

---

1 John M. Dederer has observed that the colonial era remains the least studied area of American military history: "the optimum word is *relevance*, or, to be more precise, a lack thereof. Many specialists of nineteenth- and twentieth-century American history seem to feel that there is little significance gained in studying seventeenth- and early-eighteenth-century military affairs." See Dederer, "Colonial Forces, 1607–1776," *A Guide to the Sources of United States Military History: Supplement IV*, ed. Robin Higham and Donald J. Mrozek (New Haven, CT: Archon Books, 1998), 28.

rather than switch from "Anglo-American" to "American" when the narrative reaches the Revolutionary period, I use "American" to describe both creoles and immigrants before the War of Independence and the same groups after 1775. I use "English," "French," and "Spanish" to describe language groups, as well as the Old and New World subjects of their respective European monarchs. When referring to the native European inhabitants of New France, I employ "Canadian." Naming the indigenous peoples of North America is even more difficult. "Native American" could apply to either indigenous peoples or any creole of the Americas. I prefer "Indian." I have distinguished among Indian peoples by tribal designations, although those designations describe more linguistic than political differentiation.[2] The specific names for Indian individuals present another bevy of choices. I have chosen to refer to them by the names by which Americans knew them. But in an attempt to honor their cultural identity, I have placed their Indian name, where possible, after the first citation of their English name. I have assigned places (forts, rivers, regions, etc.) the names their possessors gave them.

No less a problem than naming people and places is deciding to what degree to modernize or translate the prose and speech of seventeenth-through early-nineteenth-century English and French speakers. Authors, especially in their diaries and personal or public correspondence, rarely followed standardized rules of punctuation, capitalization, and spelling. Though their words carry a sense of the age in which they lived, I have opted to adopt the "Modernized Method" outlined in the *Harvard Guide to American History* to clarify obsolete spelling and erratic punctuation.[3] I have translated most quotations taken from French primary sources, with only the occasional exception of short phrases or individual words that seem clear, into English.

---

2 For the use of tribal designations, see Richard White, *The Middle Ground: Indians, Empires, and Republics in the Great Lakes Region, 1650–1815* (New York: Cambridge University Press, 1991), xiv.
3 Frank Freidel, ed., *The Harvard Guide to American History*, rev. ed., 2 vols. (Cambridge, MA: Harvard University Press, 1974), 1: 31–36.

Acknowledgments

In writing this book I have become indebted to many teachers, friends, and academic and military colleagues. A list of all of them would be too lengthy to include here, but I hope all will accept my heartfelt gratitude for the support, assistance, and encouragement they selflessly gave me. I would be grossly remiss, however, if I did not single out Fred Anderson for special thanks. Fred, above all others, shaped this book as both a mentor and a friend. I also would like to offer special thanks to Virginia DeJohn Anderson, Richard Beringer, Don Higginbotham, Todd Laughman, Gloria Main, Mark Pittenger, and Arthur Worrall. Of course, my appreciation goes to Frank Smith, the editorial staff, and the readers at Cambridge University Press for agreeing to take on this project.

Several organizations provided financial support and access to their collections. I thank the William L. Clements Library at the University of Michigan; the Henry E. Huntington Library in San Marino, California; the Massachusetts Historical Society in Boston; the Nova Scotia Archives and Records Management (formerly known as the Public Archives of Nova Scotia) in Halifax; the Norlin Library at the University of Colorado at Boulder; and the Colorado College Tutt Library in Colorado Springs.

Last, but certainly not least, my love and thanks go to my wife, Molly, and my daughter, Sophia. I will never be able to express how much they have meant to me, and I thank them for the innumerable sacrifices they have made in supporting both my career in the Air Force and this book. It is to them that I dedicate all my efforts.

Abbreviations

ASPIA	U.S. Congress. *American State Papers, Class II, Indian Affairs.* 2 vols. Washington, DC: Gales and Seaton, 1832–1834.
ASPMA	U.S. Congress. *American State Papers, Class V, Military Affairs.* 7 vols. Washington, DC: Gales and Seaton, 1832–1861.
Baxter MSS	James Phinney Baxter, ed. *Collections of the Maine Historical Society, Second Series, Documentary History of the State of Maine, Vols. 4, 9–12, Containing the Baxter Manuscripts.* Portland: Brown, Thurston & Company, 1889 (Vol. 4) and LeFavor-Tower Company, 1907–1908 (Vols. 9–12).
CO 5	Great Britain. Public Records Office. Colonial Office, Class 5 Papers.
CSPC	Great Britain. Public Records Office. *Calendar of State Papers, Colonial Series, America and the West Indies.* Edited by J. W. Fortescue et al. 45 vols. to date. London: HMSO, 1860–.
CSPI	Great Britain, Public Records Office. *Calendar of State Papers Relating to Ireland, of the Reign of Charles I, 1633–1647.* Edited by Robert Pentland Mahaffy. 4 vols. 1900–1903. Reprint, Nendeln, Liechtenstein: Kraus Reprint Corporation, 1979.
CTBP	Great Britain. Public Records Office. *Calendar of Treasury Books and Papers, 1729–1745.* Compiled by William A. Shaw et al. 5 vols. 1897. Reprint, Nendeln, Liechtenstein: Kraus Reprint, 1974.
CVSP	William Palmer et al., eds. *Calendar of Virginia State Papers and Other Manuscripts.* 11 vols. 1875–1893. Reprint, New York: Kraus Reprint Corporation, 1968.
DCB	*Dictionary of Canadian Biography.*
GHQ	*Georgia Historical Quarterly.*

HBP	Henry Bouquet. *The Papers of Colonel Henry Bouquet.* Edited by Sylvester K. Stevens. Harrisburg: Pennsylvania Historical Commission, 1941–1943.
Hist. Stats.	U.S. Bureau of the Census. *Historical Statistics of the United States, Colonial Times to 1957.* Washington, DC: GPO, 1960.
HNAI	William C. Sturtevant et al., eds. *Handbook of North American Indians.* 20 vols. planned. Washington, DC: Smithsonian Institution, 1978–.
(O)IEAHC	(Omohundro) Institute of Early American History and Culture, Williamsburg, VA.
JAH	*Journal of American History.*
JSAHR	*Journal of the Society for Army Historical Research.*
<Kappler/>	<http://digitial.library.okstate.edu/kappler/vol2/treaties> for Charles J. Kappler, Jr., ed. *Indian Affairs: Laws and Treaties.* 5 vols. Washington, DC: GPO, 1904–1941.
LO	Earl of Loudoun MSS, Henry E. Huntington Library, San Marino, CA.
LOMBC	Massachusetts. *Laws and Orders of Massachusetts Bay Colony.* Buffalo, NY: W. S. Hein, 1987. 736 microfiches.
MHSC	*Massachusetts Historical Society Collections.*
NC Records	William L. Saunders and Walter Clark, comps. and eds. *The State Records of North Carolina.* 30 vols. 1886–1914. Reprint, New York: AMS Press, 1968–1978.
NEHGR	*New England Historical and Genealogical Register.*
NSARM	Nova Scotia Archives and Records Management (formerly the Public Archives of Nova Scotia), Halifax.
NYCD	Edmund B. O'Callaghan and Berthold Fernow, eds. and trans. *Documents Relative to the Colonial History of the State of New York.* 15 vols. Albany, NY: Weed, Parsons and Company, Printers, 1856–1887.
SAL	William Walter Hening, ed. and comp. *The Statutes at Large; Being a Collection of All the Laws of Virginia, from the First Session of the Legislature in the Year 1619.* 13 vols. 1819–1832. Reprint, Charlottesville: Published for the Jamestown Foundation of the Commonwealth of Virginia by the University Press of Virginia, 1969.
Terr. Papers	Clarence Edwin Carter, comp. and ed. *The Territorial Papers of the United States.* 12 vols. Washington, DC: GPO, 1934–1945.
TJP	Thomas Jefferson. *The Papers of Thomas Jefferson.* Edited by Julian P. Boyd et al. 29 vols. to date. Princeton, NJ: Princeton University Press, 1950–.

WJP	William Johnson. *The Papers of Sir William Johnson.* Edited by James Sullivan et al. 14 vols. Albany: University of the State of New York, 1921–1965.
WMQ	*William and Mary Quarterly*, 3d ser.
WO 34	Great Britain. War Office. Class 34 Papers.

Introduction

This study began as an attempt to address one of early American military history's most perplexing ambiguities and contradictions: the place and relationship between what we today know as unlimited war and what eighteenth-century writers termed *petite guerre* (little war) in the American military tradition. Unlimited war, in both its modern and earliest American manifestations, centers on destroying the enemy's will or ability to resist by any means necessary, especially by focusing attacks on civilian populations and the infrastructure that supports them. Military theorists now use several different terms in place of *petite guerre*, including "irregular," "guerrilla," "partisan," "unconventional," or "special" operations.[1] Today's United States military places those kinds of wars under the rubric of "low-intensity conflict." But no matter what we call it or how we define it today, early Americans understood war to involve disrupting enemy troop, supply, and support networks; gathering intelligence through scouting and the taking of prisoners; ambushing and destroying enemy detachments; serving as patrol and flanking parties for friendly forces; operating as advance and rear guards for regular forces; and, most important, destroying enemy villages and fields and killing and intimidating enemy noncombatant populations.[2]

---

1 French military theorists began to speak of *petite guerre* in the middle of the eighteenth century. During the duke of Wellington's Peninsular Campaign in the Napoleonic Wars, Anglophones replaced *petite guerre* with the Spanish term *guerrilla* to describe the practice of "irregular" warfare. See *The Stanford Dictionary of Anglicized Words and Phrases*, 1964 ed., s.v. "La Petite Guerre" and "Guerrilla." George Smith, *An Universal Military Dictionary, A Copious Explanation of the Technical Terms &c.* (1779: reprint, Ottawa: Museum Restoration Service, 1969), 202, described the practitioners of *petite guerre* as "partisans." "Unconventional" is a term that theorists developed in the twentieth century to address aspects of modern warfare that fall outside "regular" (state-on-state or army-on-army) forms of war making.

2 United States Army, *Field Manual 7–85 Ranger Unit Operations* (Washington, DC: Headquarters, Department of the Army, 1987), states that Army rangers conduct "special military operations" in support of conventional military operations or act independently when conventional forces cannot be used. *FM 7–85* notes that special military operations include "strike operations, usually deep penetration, and special light infantry

1

Military historians long have sought to describe Americans' approach to war. Russell F. Weigley has been the most influential of the scholars to suggest that Americans have created a singular military heritage. Indeed, his seminal book *The American Way of War* established the paradigm that most scholars use to explain the American military tradition. This study offers an alternative understanding to Weigley's, one based on the proposition that war focused on noncombatant populations is itself a fundamental part of Americans' military past, indeed, is Americans' first way of war.

Weigley's argument, and with it the accepted synthesis of American military history, rested on two conceptual pillars, both the products of post-Napoleonic German scholarship. First, he contended that Carl von Clausewitz's *On War* defines in general terms the parameters within which we can understand America's military culture. Clausewitz distinguished between two kinds of war: those that seek the overthrow of the enemy and those that seek merely to achieve a limited victory. Weigley asserted that all of American military history falls in that framework. In America's earliest wars, he argued, English colonists, and later the United States, proved too weak to pursue anything other than limited wars; as time went on and Americans' military might grew, however, Americans increasingly fought unlimited wars to overthrow their enemies. The Civil War, especially William T. Sherman's March to the Sea, symbolized how Americans embraced the Clausewitzian conception of the complete destruction of the enemy as a goal of war.[3]

The second part of Weigley's thesis derived from his understanding of another German military philosopher and historian, Hans Delbrück. Delbrück suggested that there are two kinds of military strategy: the strategy of annihilation, which seeks to erase an enemy's military power in a thunderclap of violence, and the strategy of attrition, which attempts to erode it.[4] Weigley argued that most modern American military strategists have preferred Delbrückian wars of annihilation and closing with the enemy for the "decisive" battle. He suggested that when American

operations. Strike operations include raids, interdiction, and recovery operations" (pp. 1-1-1-2).

3 Russell F. Weigley, *The American Way of War: A History of United States Military Strategy and Policy* (Bloomington: Indiana University Press, 1973), xviii–xxiii.

4 A third strategic option, available to modern soldiers, is that of strategic paralysis. Strategic paralysis originated with the armored warfare theorists (J. F. C. Fuller and B. H. Liddell Hart) of the 1920s and 1930s. Its goal is to weaken and destroy the enemy's ability to resist by focusing on his command and control and sustainment capabilities. Modern airpower theorists, especially those in the United States Air Force, have adopted strategic paralysis as their mantra. Strategic paralysis can be achieved by simultaneous or parallel attacks on an enemy's centers of gravity. Early American soldiers, naturally, did not have the technology that would allow parallel war. Thus, their strategic options necessarily were only attritive or annihilationist.

military resources were slight, Americans accepted the strategy of attrition out of necessity. But the abundance of economic resources characteristic of the United States from the mid-nineteenth century on, coupled with the adoption of Clausewitzian unlimited war aims, created an environment in which the strategy of annihilation became *the* American way of war. Weigley's synthesis of Clausewitz and Delbrück therefore led him to see American military history through a lens that focuses only on the complete destruction of the enemy through annihilation of the enemy's military power.

Two features of Weigley's account limit its explanatory power and range.[5] First, it is disjunctive. Weigley established a demarcation between American wars before and after 1846, similar to the break that we sometimes assume separates colonial from later American history. He saw America's pre–Mexican War conflicts as limited-attritional wars; thereafter, Americans turned to an approach more in line with the unlimited-annihilationist model. Weigley suggested, for example, that a lack of military resources influenced George Washington's and Nathanael Greene's commitment to limited-attritional strategies in the War of Independence. Thus, while crediting Greene with creating an American conception of guerrilla war, he contended, "The later course of American military history, featuring a rapid rise from poverty of resources to plenty, cut short any further American evolution of Greene's type of strategy. He therefore remains alone as an American master developing a strategy of unconventional war."[6] The assumption that colonial military history differed significantly from what followed led Weigley, with his focus on post-mid-nineteenth-century American war, to minimize continuity and evolution in America's military past in favor of an abrupt and "revolutionary" departure from previous norms and institutions.

Weigley's tendency to privilege the affairs of regular armies over the actions and attitudes of nonprofessional soldiers marks the second limiting characteristic of his argument. His subject was primarily the formal entity of the United States Army or, in the case of the colonial period, the British Army. Weigley's approach to military history centered on organizations, major campaigns, doctrinal thinking, and diplomacy. From it, he explained superbly the grand strategy and policy of the United States Army. Americans, however, had served and fought outside professional

---

5 For another critique of Weigley's thesis, see Brian M. Linn, *"The American Way of War Revisited," Journal of Military History* 66 (2002): 501–530. For Weigley's response, see "Response to Brian McAllister Linn by Russell F. Weigley," ibid., 531–533. Note that neither Linn nor Weigley explains how Americans' military experience in the two and a half centuries before the Civil War shaped the parameters of the "American way of war."

6 Weigley, *American Way of War,* 36.

military organizations for nearly 175 years before the Army came into existence in 1775. And while many Americans found their way to both the British and United States Armies, many more fought as Indian fighters as members of ad hoc organizations formed for specific operations and disbanded at their conclusion. Thus, Weigley was unable to provide more than a few incidental insights into the non-Army aspects of the American military experience.

Yet if we look closely at early American military history, we see that it had less to do with grand strategy, the movements of armies, or the clash of nations than with what eighteenth-century writers called *petite guerre*. War in early America among Americans, Indians, Britons, Canadians, Frenchmen, and Spaniards consisted of a multitude of "little wars" and quasi-personal struggles. Although in the 1690s the colonists became embroiled in the century-long series of Anglo–French conflicts that historians sometimes call the Second Hundred Years' War, Americans fought those wars for different ends. While great European armies fought for dynastic and geopolitical goals in Europe, handfuls of colonists waged life-and-death struggles against Indians and Canadians on the American frontier. Without a Sébastien Vauban–style web of fortifications and magazines covering the land, or the massive armies like those engaged at Lützen, Blenheim, and Mollwitz, *petite guerre* reigned supreme.[7] Americans' use of *petite guerre* did not end with the colonial era's wars. A series of small but brutal wars between frontiersmen and Indians ran concurrently with the War of Independence in the Transappalachian West and along the New York frontier. Similarly, the first military operations of the United States in the 1790s were not wars typical of the state-centered struggles occurring in Europe at that time. The American wars were primarily conflicts waged against Indians on the frontier that only

---

7   Of course, there were Vauban-style forts in North America. Louisbourg and San Agustín, for example, would have fit in as middle-sized European forts. The difference was that American forts stood independent of one another, whereas in Europe they belonged to fortification and magazine systems. In fact almost all warfare between regular armies conducted in early America was siege warfare. There were, then, two kinds of military endeavors in colonial North America: siege and fortress war, on the one hand, the province of regular soldiers (British troops or militia formed into provincial regiments); and *petite guerre* on the other, the purview of Indians, rangers, backwoodsmen, and the Troupes de la Marine of New France.
    One could argue that fortifying the frontier with blockhouses – a pared-down version of fortress warfare – was another part of Americans' way of war. Indeed, forts were as ubiquitous in colonial military history after 1675 as rangers. Some of the leading figures of late-seventeenth- and early-eighteenth-century New England society, like the Saltonstalls of Haverhill, Massachusetts, made both names and fortunes for themselves as the builders and organizers of New England's frontier fortification system. For a study that puts forts and garrisons at its center, see Stephen C. Eames, "Rustic Warriors: Warfare and the Provincial Soldier on the Northern Frontier, 1689–1748" (Ph.D. diss., University of New Hampshire, 1989), chaps. 2–3.

occasionally, and usually reluctantly, saw the participation of the United States Army. Even in the 1810s, the period that most historians credit with signaling the birth of a professional American Army, *petite guerre* proved as important as, if not more important than, the operations of that Army in the American conquest of the Old Northwest and Old Southwest. For the first 200 years of our military heritage, then, Americans depended on arts of war that contemporary professional soldiers supposedly abhorred: razing and destroying enemy villages and fields; killing enemy women and children; raiding settlements for captives; intimidating and brutalizing enemy noncombatants; and assassinating enemy leaders.

Why, then, did Weigley not address that ubiquitous albeit darker side of American military history in his analysis? The answer would seem to be that, like the German theorists on whose work he drew, he tended to see professional military behavior and organization as normative.[8] Clausewitz's service on the Russian general staff in 1812, in which he witnessed firsthand the horrifying behavior of the Tsar's Cossacks, led to his repudiation of their methods as an inferior, as well as ineffectual, way to fight.[9] Clausewitz argued that war, rightly understood, was the rational instrument of national policy; he wrote that if "civilized nations do not put their prisoners to death, do not devastate towns and countries, this is because their intelligence exercises greater influence on their mode of carrying on War, and has taught them more effectual means of applying force than these rude acts of mere instinct."[10] Delbrück, on the other hand, was a Prussian nationalist interested in chronicling the nineteenth-century Wars of German Unification. He emphatically shared Clausewitz's belief that war fell within the purview of a legitimate nation-state.[11]

Weigley embedded both Clausewitz's revulsion at indiscriminate violence and Delbrück's focus on national war in his analysis. These biases – for that is what they are – led Weigley to discount the kind of war that early Americans waged as abnormal or unworthy of serious consideration. In the process, Weigley created, like the military theorists who preceded him, an artificial dichotomy between "regular" and "irregular" war and

8 In his essay on "American Strategy from Its Beginnings through the First World War" in *Makers of Modern Strategy: From Machiavelli to the Nuclear Age*, ed. Peter Paret (Princeton, NJ: Princeton University Press, 1986), Weigley briefly assessed the impact of unlimited war on American war making, after which he wrote, "historians may tend to exaggerate the readiness of early Americans to turn toward absolute war." See Weigley, ibid., 409.

9 Peter Paret, "Clausewitz," ibid., 186–213.

10 Carl von Clausewitz, *On War*, ed. Anatol Rapoport (New York: Penguin Books, 1982), 103.

11 Gordon Craig, "Delbrück: The Military Historian," *Makers of Modern Strategy*, 326–353.

organization.[12] In Weigley's paradigm, the frontier wars against Indians are relatively unimportant. He saw American military history following a path of Clausewitzian–Delbrückian evolution from the mid-nineteenth century to its ultimate manifestation in World War II. In reality, the American way of war also traveled an evolutionary route that began with the first days of European settlement in the early seventeenth century and stretched into the early nineteenth century.

Weigley's interpretation bestrides American military historiography like a colossus. Military historians have been unable to move far beyond it and advance a new synthesis on the place of early war making in the broader American military tradition. Most early American military historians, a small group to begin with, have focused their studies on military institutions and organizations. Moreover, the most recent review essays on colonial military history, as well as the definitive bibliography on United States military history, show that the topic of early American war making is bereft of any general study of *petite guerre*.[13] Max Boot's *The Savage Wars of Peace*, for example, discusses America's small wars after the birth of the Federal government; the first small war he addresses is the Barbary War of 1801–1805. Indeed, Boot "focuses strictly on American small wars abroad," most of which "were fought by relatively small numbers of professional soldiers pursuing limited objectives with limited means."[14] *The First Way of War* describes a small war tradition that saw nonprofessional soldiers pursue unlimited objectives, often through irregular means.

One group of historians, nonetheless, has noted that there was something distinctive about war in colonial America. That difference often manifested itself in patterns of extravagant violence and *petite guerre*. For example, Ian Steele argues that Americans built a tradition of war that was an amalgam of both traditional European and Indian methods of war.

---

12 Seventeenth- and eighteenth-century military theorists were the first to divide war making between regular and irregular. Today's United States military uses a "spectrum of conflict" to describe the different kinds of conflicts the army faces. It divides the spectrum into three main areas: low, mid, and high. Low-spectrum conflict includes low-intensity conventional warfare, unconventional war, and terrorism. Mid-spectrum conflict involves primarily minor conventional war and aspects of major conventional war. High-spectrum conflict encompasses other characteristics of major conventional war and nuclear war. Modern-day special operations forces are the progeny of early American rangers' military tradition and are trained, equipped, and tasked to operate primarily in the low and mid spectrums.

13 Wayne Lee, "Early American Ways of War: A New Reconnaissance, 1600–1815," *The Historical Journal* (Cambridge) 44 (2001): 269–289; Don Higginbotham, "The Early American Way of War: Reconnaissance and Appraisal," *WMQ* 44 (1987): 230–273; Wayne Carp, "Early American Military History: A Review of Recent Work," *Virginia Magazine of History and Biography* 94 (1986): 259–284; Robin Higham and Donald J. Mrozek, eds., *A Guide to Sources of United States Military History: Supplement IV* (New Haven, CT: Archon Books, 1998).

14 Max Boot, *The Savage Wars of Peace: Small Wars and the Rise of American Power* (New York: Basic Books, 2002), xiv.

Adam Hirsch similarly contends that the very different military cultures of native and colonizing groups interacted dialectically in seventeenth-century New England. "In the New World, honor was tossed aside – and once the colonists set the precedent, the surrounding Indians followed suit . . . an antecedent of total war had somehow emerged."[15] Ronald Dale Karr, building on Hirsch's argument and focusing on the Pequot War, argues that the "virulent hybridization of military cultures" of which Hirsch wrote resulted from the failure of the English and the Pequots to maintain a reciprocal relationship, a balance of power, in which they mutually defined and agreed upon the limits of permissible battlefield behavior. English failure to see the Pequots as sovereign, Karr suggests, ordained that they would treat the Indians like rebels, heretics, or infidels.[16] Yet, in cases where a rough balance of power existed and the Indians even appeared dominant – as was the situation in virtually every frontier war until the first decade of the nineteenth century – Americans were quick to turn to extravagant violence.

Two other historians have delved into how early Americans viewed their environment and themselves to help illuminate the fundamental characteristics of American war making. John Ferling argues that the wilderness, coupled with racism, imparted a unique "brutality" to early American military history, an experience that led Americans to look toward extirpating Indians. He suggests that while "Europe's wars grew less ferocious, or at least had less drastic impact on the civilian population, American wars tended to become more feral."[17] John Dederer contends that the distinctive characteristic of early American military history centered on Americans' combined experiences of Indian fighting with their reading of histories of antiquity's wars. As a result, Americans forged the ideal of the militarily self-sufficient citizen-soldier in the service of a virtuous republic.[18] Together, Ferling and Dederer are right to suggest that brutality and self-sufficiency in distant locales profoundly shaped early Americans' experience of war.

Guy Chet argues there was little distinctly American in the ways that the colonists fought. He narrowly focuses his analysis on the tactical level of war and the overwhelming majority of his narrative on the seventeenth century. Chet finds that the first colonists remained committed to European tactics and maintained a preference for massed firepower

15 Ian Steele, *Warpaths: Invasions of North America* (New York: Oxford University Press, 1994), 106; Adam J. Hirsch, "The Collision of Military Cultures in Seventeenth-Century New England," *JAH* 74 (1988): 1204.
16 Ronald Dale Karr, "'Why Should You Be So Ferocious?': The Violence of the Pequot War," *JAM*, 85 (1999): 908–909.
17 John Ferling, *A Wilderness of Miseries: War and Warriors in Early America* (Westport, CT: Greenwood Press, 1980), 197.
18 John Dederer, *War in America to 1775: Before Yankee Doodle* (New York: New York University Press, 1990).

and the tactical defense. His aim is to challenge the suggestion that New England militiamen fought "Indian style." But in finding continuity between European and American tactics in the early seventeenth century, he stopped his analysis there and engaged in a cursory narrative of Queen Anne's, King George's, and the Seven Years' Wars. He thereby missed how both American strategy and tactics evolved in the late seventeenth and early eighteenth centuries. Thus, he is correct to observe that Americans conquered the Indians of North America through attrition, but he fails to explain how those attritive wars changed over time and space.[19]

Other historians have focused on how American operations influenced the development of the eighteenth-century British Army's doctrine and practice of war. Daniel Beattie has argued that the British Army in the Seven Years' War used *petite guerre* partially to overcome the problems involved in wilderness campaigning. Eric Robson, Rory Cory, and David Parker have suggested that its experiences in North America during the Seven Years' War and the War of Independence led the British Army to incorporate American-style tactics and organization during the Napoleonic Wars. Peter Russell believes that the tactics that the British Army used against Indians in America during the Seven Years' War originated in the British officer corps' mid-eighteenth-century experience fighting European partisans in Scotland, Flanders, and Central Europe. Taken together, Beattie's, Robson's, Cory's, Parker's, and Russell's interests lie with the British experience with *petite guerre*, an experience that they see had more importance for European than American military developments.[20]

The one area in which historians have come closest to addressing the impact of American conditions on the American military tradition has been in studies of the War of Independence. John Shy has argued that Charles Lee's argument for a "partisan" campaign against the British offered a "radical alternative" to the war conducted by George Washington and the Continental Army. Mark Kwasny shows that the state militias attached to Washington's army indeed fought a partisan war in Connecticut, New York, and New Jersey. Similarly, John Pancake and others who

19 Guy Chet, *Conquering the American Wilderness: The Triumph of European Warfare in the Colonial Northeast* (Amherst: University of Massachusetts Press, 2003).
20 Daniel Beattie, "The Adaptation of the British Army to Wilderness Warfare, 1755–1763," *Adapting to Conditions: War and Society in the Eighteenth Century*, ed. Maarten Ultee (Tuscaloosa: University of Alabama Press, 1986), 56–83; Eric Robson, "British Light Infantry in the Mid-Eighteenth Century: The Effect of American Conditions," *The Army Quarterly and Defense Journal* 43 (1952): 209–222; Rory McKenzie Cory, "British Light Infantry in North America in the Seven Year War" (Ph.D. diss., Simon Fraser University, 1993); David E. Parker, "That Loose Flimsy Order: The Little War Meets British Military Discipline in America 1775–1781" (M.A. thesis, University of New Hampshire, 1985); Peter Russell, "Redcoats in the Wilderness: British Officers and Irregular Warfare in Europe and America, 1740 to 1760," *WMQ* 35 (1978): 629–652.

have written on the Revolution in the South have described it as a partisan and brutal civil war. Wayne Lee's description of how North Carolinians accepted certain kinds of violence (brutality toward Indians who practiced unlimited ways of war and executions for Americans who engaged in unlimited war) as legitimate goes far in explaining the ferocity of the civil war in the South. Shy's essay on "British Strategy for the Southern War," coupled with Sylvia Frey's depiction of the Revolution in the South as a "Triangular" war among patriots, slaves, and British soldiers, especially suggests the distinctive war in the American South during the War of Independence.[21]

Yet in none of those works can we put the first way of war of the Revolutionary era in both the context of its development from the previous colonial wars and its impact on the development of the American military tradition that followed. Instead, the War of Independence appears as a militarily self-contained unit, with only tenuous ties to trends that came before it and none with patterns that followed it.[22] Thus, these accounts, like Weigley's, are essentially disjunctive and similarly limited in explanatory power.

The break in the military historiography between the colonial era and the Age of the Early Republic is striking. Many fine studies exist that discuss the carryover of military institutions from the colonial period to the 1790s and early 1800s (e.g., the transformation of the Continental Army into the United States Army) or address the specifics of individual

21 John Shy, "American Strategy: Charles Lee and the Radical Alternative," *A People Numerous and Armed: Reflections on the Military Struggle for American Independence*, rev. ed. (Ann Arbor: University of Michigan Press, 1990); Mark Kwasny, *Washington's Partisan War, 1775–1783* (Kent, OH: Kent State University Press, 1996); John Pancake, *This Destructive War: The British Campaign in the Carolinas, 1780–1782* (Tuscaloosa: University of Alabama Press, 1985); Wayne E. Lee, *Crowds and Soldiers in Revolutionary North Carolina: The Culture of Violence in Riot and War* (Gainesville: University Press of Florida, 2001); Shy, "British Strategy for Pacifying the Southern Colonies, 1778–1781," *A People Numerous and Armed*; Sylvia Frey, *Water from the Rock: Black Resistance in a Revolutionary Age* (Princeton, NJ: Princeton University Press, 1991).
22 The historical practice of *petite guerre* outside the American military experience has received the attention of several scholars. In 1896, Colonel Charles E. Calwell of the British Army published his classic *Small Wars: Their Principles and Practice* (London: HMSO, 1896). Calwell was most interested in providing a military treatise for British army officers in Africa and Central Asia to use in combatting "opponents who will not meet them in the open field" (p. 21). Walter Laqueur's *Guerrilla: A Historical and Critical Study* (Boston: Little, Brown and Company, 1976) examined guerrilla and terrorist theory throughout history. Laqueur focused on examining the doctrine and actions of twentieth-century European partisans and the place of guerrilla warfare in "Third World Wars of National Liberation." Robert Aspery's *War in the Shadows: The Guerrilla in History*, 2d ed. (New York: William Morrow and Company, Inc., 1994), like Laqueur's study, focuses on twentieth-century guerrillas. Aspery, however, included material on guerrilla warfare as a phenomenon of both ancient and early-modern warfare.

conflicts like the Old Northwest Indian War of 1789–1795 or the War of 1812. Few works, however, contextualize the American art of war as it evolved out of the colonial period, through the 1790s, and into the 1810s. Indeed Armstrong Starkey's recent book, *European and Native American Warfare*, is one of the few attempts to trace patterns of American war making from the late seventeenth century and the first two-thirds of the eighteenth century into the early nineteenth century. The centerpiece of Starkey's analysis, however, is his explanation of how, from 1675 to 1815, regular warfare, primarily because Americans were incompetent at Indian-style fighting, inexorably came to dominate frontier warfare. Like Weigley, Starkey favors *grande guerre* over *petite guerre*, and as a result, the place of nonregular warfare in American military history remains ambiguous and unclear.[23]

This book therefore seeks to examine the whole of the early American military experience from 1607 through 1814 by addressing a series of questions. First, and centrally, how did Americans develop a way of war that was both unlimited in its ends and irregular in its means, and how did that way of war change over time? Second, what cultural, social, and military experiences and perceptions informed Americans' understanding and practice of war making? Similarly, which groups within American society participated in those wars, and why did they choose, or feel required, to do so? Finally, how and in what ways was early American war making distinctive?

The answers to those questions comprise my central argument: early Americans created a military tradition that accepted, legitimized, and encouraged attacks upon and the destruction of noncombatants, villages, and agricultural resources. Most often, early Americans used the tactics and techniques of *petite guerre* in shockingly violent campaigns to achieve their goals of conquest. In the frontier wars between 1607 and 1814, Americans forged two elements – unlimited war and irregular war – into their first way of war.

Military history is passé in most academic circles, and its practitioners often are derided as the "drum and bugle corps." More often than not, critics see military history as litanies of orders of battle, the movements of regiments, or the deeds of the Great Captains. I have therefore tried to approach the writing of military history in such a way as to address the criticisms that many have levied against it. My approach is that of the so-called new military historians, who have tried to contextualize warfare by examining its social, cultural, and economic dimensions. In addition, however, I have tried always to bear in mind the essence of war

---

23 Armstrong Starkey, *European and Native American Warfare, 1675–1815* (Norman: University of Oklahoma Press, 1999).

for the soldier: to kill the enemy and destroy his means of resistance. I therefore also concentrate, like traditional military historians, on how early Americans used the first way of war to strike at their enemies, and how they forged a martial tradition from the materials at hand. Most important, this study is not about war in the abstract. It is about the essence of war: killing and destruction.

This study seeks to trace the evolutionary path of the first way of war across two centuries. Each of its seven chapters focuses on a unique point in the development of American war making; in that sense, each can stand alone as an argument addressing a specific issue in early American military history. The sum of the chapters, however, is intended to form a narrative greater than its individual parts. As a whole, this book addresses three unresolved issues in early American history.

First, and most obviously, this study's story line points to the importance of the first way of war in early American military history. It shows that it was Americans' "first" way of war both temporally and in terms of preference. Attacking and destroying Indian noncombatant populations remained Americans', particularly frontiersmen's, preferred way of waging war from the early sixteenth through early nineteenth centuries, even after the formation of the regular American Army and its attempts to move toward the eighteenth-century European norm of limited war.

Second, it seeks to explain the extravagant violence of the American–Indian conflicts and their tendency to become unrestrained struggles for the complete destruction of the enemy.[24] Most explanations for the Indian wars' brutality focus on racism. Americans' racism toward Indians, however, did not solidify until the middle of the eighteenth century, and their first extirpative wars occurred nearly a generation before Americans' negative racial views of Indians began to emerge.[25] Many early American

---

24 Harold E. Selesky correctly observes that in colonial America, "men acted without hesitation to do the things they thought were necessary to achieve their goals and worried only afterward about their consciences and other men's opinions." See Selesky, "Colonial America," *The Laws of War: Constraints on Warfare in the Western World*, ed. Michael Howard, George J. Andreopoulos, and Mark R. Shulman (New Haven, CT: Yale University Press, 1994), 59.

25 The literature on racism in early America is voluminous. Scholars now agree that racial attitudes took time to develop. In the most clear explanation of the gradual development of Americans' racial attitudes toward Indians, Daniel Richter observes, "Whites and Indians had to *learn* to hate each other – had even to learn that there were such clear-cut 'racial' categories as 'White' and 'Indian' – before the 'westward expansion' across a steadily advancing 'frontier' could become the trajectory for a nation that was itself a belated result of the same learning process." See Richter, *Facing East from Indian Country: A Native History of Early America* (Cambridge, MA: Harvard University Press, 2001), 2. Alan Gallay, in his *The Indian Slave Trade: The Rise of the English Empire in the American South, 1670–1717* (New Haven, CT: Yale University Press, 2002), similarly notes that in the late seventeenth century, "Indians, Africans, and Europeans had many identities, but membership in a 'race' was not one of them" (p. 9). Nonetheless,

soldiers in fact admired Indians and the ways they fought; the two "races" often fought alongside one another as allies.[26] Thus, an explanation that complements, not supplants, that of race centers on the uncontrollable momentum of violence that the first way of war fueled. Instead of racism leading to violence, in early America violence led to racism. From both military necessity and hands-on experience, successive generations of Americans, both soldiers and civilians, made the killing of Indian men, women, and children a defining element of their first military tradition and thereby part of a shared American identity. Indeed, only after seventeenth- and early-eighteenth-century Americans made the first way of war a key to being a white American could later generations of "Indian haters," men like Andrew Jackson, turn the Indian wars into race wars.

Third, this book shows how the first way of war became Americans' preferred tool of conquest. Both contemporaries and students of early American history have observed that the first settlers were an imperialistic lot.[27] They, at times methodically and at other times haphazardly, conquered the Indian peoples of the Eastern seaboard and the French, Spanish, and Indians in the marchlands of Nova Scotia and Georgia; aided Great Britain's conquest of the French in Canada; and subjugated the Indians of the Transappalachian West. The one constant roadblock to the settlers' expansion into the interior of the continent was always the Indians. Thus, if they could eliminate the Indians, the settlers could make North America their own. Limited wars like those conceived by European dynastic states (including Great Britain), however, did little to drive the Indians from their lands. Americans thus chose the most effective means of subjugating the Indians they faced. They sent groups of men, sometimes a dozen, sometimes hundreds, to attack Indian villages and homes, kill Indian women and children, and raze Indian fields.

Chapter 1 discusses the American experience of war through roughly 1730. Long before significant numbers of British troops arrived in the

by the middle of the eighteenth century, racial attitudes were well developed, in part because Indians started to think of themselves as different from Europeans. See Gregory Evan Dowd, *War Under Heaven: Pontiac, the Indian Nations and the British Empire* (Baltimore: Johns Hopkins University Press, 2002).

26 Joyce Chaplin notes that colonists who lived along the frontier wanted "to be *like* the enemy but not *as* him. In this manner, colonists styled themselves as counterparts of Indians, not so as to express sympathy with them, however, but to fight and kill them." See Chaplin, *Subject Matter: Technology, the Body, and Science on the Anglo-American Frontier, 1500–1676* (Cambridge, MA: Harvard University Press, 2001), 82.

27 For seventeenth-, eighteenth-, and early-nineteenth-century "American imperialism" as a construct for better understanding early American history, see Fred Anderson and Andrew R. L. Cayton, "War and Trade, Empires and Revolutions: Rethinking Early American History, 1500–1917" (paper presented at the second annual conference of the Institute of Early American History and Culture, Boulder, CO, May 1996), 1 and their forthcoming (as of summer 2004) *Dominion of War*.

colonies, Americans had improvised their own way of war. This chapter addresses the challenges of fighting Indians that confronted seventeenth- and early-eighteenth-century Americans and describes how they directed their military energies toward killing noncombatants and destroying agricultural resources. It traces the colonists' embrace of the three practices – extirpative war making, the creation of specialized units for Indian fighting (rangers), and the use of scalp hunters to motivate privatized, commercialized campaigns through the issuance of scalp bounties – that provided the pillars upon which the first war of war rested.[28] This chapter argues that by 1730 Americans had created a way of war centered often on individual action, focused primarily on Indian fields, food supplies, and civilian populations.

That American way of war intersected with military practice that differentiated between Old World and New World ways of war in the 1740s. In the North American Wars of King George II (1733–1755), a small cadre of British soldiers and administrators became deeply involved in fighting Indians and quickly discovered the inadequacy of their European approaches to making war. Chapter 2 therefore focuses on the importance of the first way of war to British success in the early Wars of King George II – the War of Jenkins' Ear, King George's War, and the obscure conflict in Nova Scotia that preceded the Seven Years' War – an episode I have called Father Le Loutre's War. Chapter 2 focuses on how American rangers' operations in the marchland provinces of Georgia and Nova Scotia marked both a continuation and a refinement of the first way of war. Just as important, Chapter 2 explains how, with British commanders' use of American rangers to pacify the hinterlands of Great Britain's North American frontier, the eighteenth-century wall between British war making and Americans' first way of war began to crumble.

Since colonial Americans were part of a larger British Empire, and since it would be specious to suggest that their art of war developed in a vacuum of North America, Chapter 3 examines European irregular warfare – the kind of war most analogous to Americans' first way of war. It describes the European interaction between regular and irregular operations, compares traditions of irregular war in continental Europe with those of Britain and Ireland, and clarifies differences in theory and practice among European models of *petite guerre*. It shows that European soldiers, including the British soldiers who served in Ireland and Scotland, had by the middle of the eighteenth century created a corpus of knowledge on irregular war that

---

28 Englishmen probably first used "ranger" near the start of the fourteenth century. During the late Middle Ages, "range" was a common verb to describe the act of patrolling specific areas by military and law enforcement bodies. See *A Dictionary of Americanisms on Historical Principles*, 1951 ed., s.v. "Ranger."

was rooted in both experience and theory. The European model of *petite guerre*, however, differed from the American variety in one crucial way. In Britain, *petite guerre* was the bastard child of a military culture that found it useful within limits but so distasteful as to be unworthy of acknowledgment as an acceptable mode of military operations. In America, it was a key component to the primary means of waging war. Thus, Chapter 3 seeks to show how American war making eventuated in a martial culture strongly shaped by North American circumstances, and thus quite different from the model upon which professional British soldiers operated.

Chapter 4 explains how the Seven Years' War (1754–1763) legitimized Americans' first way of war within British military circles. In the late 1750s, the British government, for the first time, sent large numbers of regulars to North America. Faced with a shortage of Indian allies, and in most cases disdaining the ones who presented themselves, the British soon turned to American rangers to fight the French Troupes de la Marine (the colonial regulars of New France who had mastered Indian-style warfare) and New France's Indian allies. By describing how and why the British Army ultimately accepted Americans' first way of war, Chapter 4 argues that by the end of the Seven Years' War, Americans and Britons alike had acknowledged the first way of war as a legitimate endeavor.

Chapter 5 details the role of the first way of war in the frontier wars that spanned the era of American Revolution. It examines how during the Revolutionary period, the first way of war remained Americans' preferred approach to fighting Indians on the frontier. By focusing on the Indian wars instead of the affairs of the Continental Army and the well-trodden partisan war in the Southern and Middle Colonies, Chapter 5 gives us an alternative vantage point from which to view the first years of United States military history. From it, we can see the Revolutionary period not so much as a beginning of a new American way of war, but as another chapter in the history of the first way of war. It puts the Revolutionary period's military history in context with the years that preceded 1775 and followed 1783.

Chapter 6 traces the evolutionary path of the first way of war into the Federalist Era. Most studies of military affairs in that era focus on civil–military affairs and the creation of the United States Army. Historians normally dismiss backcountry settlers' burning of Indian villages and fields as a sideshow to the Army's attempt to mold itself into a force like those found in Europe. Yet the wars in the Upper Ohio Valley and on the Tennessee and western Georgia frontiers are vitally important to understanding the evolution of Americans' military heritage. It is significant that as the federal government and the Army failed to secure the 1790s frontier, backcountry settlers, tiring of what they saw of governmental and Army incompetence, focused their energies on destroying Indian villages and food supplies. They were unabashed in declaring that their intentions were to drive the Indians from lands on the western side of the Appalachian range and claim those lands as their own, whether the nation-state of the United States wanted them to do so or not. Chapter 6 therefore details the germinal contribution that the first way of war made in the United States' conquest of its first frontier, as well as its permanence among frontiersmen during the very time that the United States Army was attempting to define its identity as a professional, regular military force.

Chapter 7 follows the first way of war to its apogee in the 1810s, describing how it shaped Americans' approach to the Indian wars in the Old Northwest and Old Southwest. For the second time in as many generations, American frontiersmen wearied of the Army's inability and unwillingness to drive the Indians from the lands of the Transappalachian West and took matters into their own hands. They unleashed a final spasm of extreme violence that crushed the Indians. Chapter 7 suggests that the frontiersmen who won the West were the inheritors of Americans' first military tradition, one that had its origins in the early seventeenth century.

The Epilogue puts the argument of this study in a broader context. The first way of war lost its central place in American war making after 1814. No longer needing it to conquer the Indian peoples of the eastern half of the continent, Americans could embark on the path that led to a second way of war, the one that we today call the "American way of war." Still, Americans must not forget that the first way of war has remained part of their military heritage. Whether in the Indians wars of the nineteenth century, the Civil War, the strategic bombing campaigns against Nazi Germany and Japan in World War II, or the Vietnam War, Americans often blurred or even erased the boundaries between combatants and noncombatants. That has been less a part of a Clausewitzian–Delbrückian synthesis than a living legacy of the first way of war.

If we, both students of history and practitioners of the profession of arms, hope to understand completely the nature of our martial culture, we must begin by acknowledging the centrality of the first way of war to America's military past. By seeing that it has served as both a component and a unique part of the American martial culture from the start, we may acquire a better grasp of how Americans have waged and possibly will wage war. I hope this study will illuminate an uncharted region in early American military history and fill the gaps in Weigley's masterful yet incomplete interpretation of our military past. I believe our attempts to find the roots of modern American war making can then begin with our earliest military experiences. From there, we will be able to identify rather than merely presume elements of continuity and change across the entire course of American military history.

1

The First Way of War's Origins in Colonial America

In July 1779 Thomas Jefferson wrote to William Phillips explaining the treatment of Lieutenant Governor Henry Hamilton, a British officer held prisoner of war by the state of Virginia. In an earlier letter Phillips, who had been Hamilton's superior at Detroit, protested Jefferson's insistence that Hamilton remain in "strict confinement." Tradition as well as several written agreements on the treatment of prisoners of war dictated that captors had the responsibility to either exchange officer prisoners quickly or parole them.[1] However, when his captors brought him from Illinois to Williamsburg, Jefferson authorized them to shackle Hamilton in irons and lock him in a prison cell. Phillips, upon receiving word of this seeming ill treatment, requested that Jefferson "put a claim for this British Officer Lieutenant Governor Hamilton being set at liberty and considered a prisoner of war."[2]

Jefferson refused to intervene on Hamilton's behalf. Instead, he sent Phillips an impassioned argument against granting Hamilton parole or exchange. "Governor Hamilton's conduct," Jefferson wrote, "has been such as to call for exemplary punishment on him personally." He reminded Phillips that the "general nature of the service he [Hamilton] undertook at Detroit and the extensive exercise of the cruelties, which that involved" justified his refusal to either parole Hamilton or exchange him for an American officer held in Phillips's custody.[3]

---

1 The Convention of Écluse, for instance, signed by Great Britain and France during the Seven Years' War, read, "All prisoners . . . were to be returned fifteen days after capture, or sooner if possible, either by exchange or ransom." See Reginald Savory, "The Convention of Écluse, 1759–1762: The Treatment of Sick and Wounded, Prisoners of War, and Deserters of the British and French Armies during the Seven Years' War," *JSAHR* 42 (1964): 68. Eighteenth-century officers, in principle at least, could expect treatment more benevolent than that which Henry Hamilton received.
2 Phillips to Jefferson, July 5, 1779, *TJP*, 3: 27.
3 Jefferson to Governor of Detroit [Phillips], July 22, 1779, *CVSP*, 1: 322. In October 1780, Jefferson paroled Hamilton and allowed him to travel to New York. However, in January of the next year, Jefferson refused the request of Chevalier Charles-François, Dubuysson des Hayes, a French officer in American service held captive by the British,

What in Hamilton's conduct at Detroit was so reprehensible as to make Jefferson forbid him the privileges normally accorded officer prisoners of war? Although by the summer of 1779 the War of Independence had been in progress for four years and had destroyed thousands of lives, the parole and exchange of enemy officers had remained a common practice. Jefferson, however, viewed Hamilton not as a prisoner of war but as a war criminal. For in Jefferson's mind Hamilton had committed the most grievous transgression imaginable to an early American: he had unleashed the horrors of "Indian warfare" against settlers on the frontier. As Jefferson told Phillips,

> The known rule of warfare with the Indian Savages is an indiscriminate butchery of men women and children. These Savages under this well known character are employed by the British Nation as allies in the War against the Americans. Governor Hamilton undertakes to be the conductor of the war. In the execution of that undertaking he associates small parties of whites under his immediate command with large parties of the Savages, & sends them to act, not against our Forts or armies in the field, but farming settlements on our frontiers. Governor Hamilton then is himself the butcher of men women and children. I will not say to what length the fair rules of war would extend the right of punishment against him: but I am sure that confinement under its strictest circumstances as a retaliation for Indian devastation & Massacre must be deemed Lenity.[4]

Eighteen months after Jefferson lectured Phillips on Hamilton's atrocious behavior, his correspondence again touched on cruelties perpetrated against women and children on the frontier. In a letter from Arthur Campbell, the commander of a Virginia army operating in western North Carolina, Jefferson learned that raiders had put frontier settlements to the torch and targeted noncombatants. In that instance, however, Campbell's men, not Indians, were responsible for the killings and pillage.

Campbell spent the winter of 1780–1781 with a 700-man Virginian army ravaging the Cherokee country. Campbell related to Jefferson with evident satisfaction that the sight of American columns converging on

---

to be exchanged for Hamilton. See Henry Hamilton's Parole, October 10, 1780, *TJP*, 4: 24–25; Theodorick Bland to Jefferson, January 29, 1781, ibid., 4: 462.

4 Jefferson to Phillips, July 22, 1779, *CVSP*, 1: 322. Jefferson's condemnation of Hamilton resembled his indictment of King George III in the Declaration of Independence, in which he accused the King of endeavoring "to bring on the inhabitants of our frontiers, the merciless Indian Savages, whose known rule of warfare, is an undistinguished destruction of all ages, sexes, and conditions."

their homes had sent the Cherokees "flying in consternation."[5] Indeed, the Cherokees had good reason to flee. On Christmas Day in 1780, Campbell wrote that one of his detachments "surprised a party of Indians, took one scalp, and Seventeen Horses loaded with clothing and skins and House furnishings." The same day, Campbell detailed one of his company commanders, a certain Captain Crabtree, "with 60 men to burn the Town of Chilhowee; he succeeded in setting fire to that part of it, situated on the South side of the river, although in time he was attacked by a superior force. He made his retreat good."[6]

The Americans relentlessly pursued the Cherokees. The day after Crabtree's attack on Chilhowee, Campbell sent a troop of 150 mounted men under Major John Tipton to sack Tilassee. Major Christen Gilbert's 150 infantry also returned to Chilhowee to continue the work that Captain Crabtree's men had started but had been unable to finish the previous day. Campbell reported that unlike Crabtree's men, "this Party did their duty well, killed three Indians and took nine prisoners."[7]

The campaign in Cherokee country was a resounding success. Campbell told Jefferson that the Americans'

> whole loss on this Expedition was one man killed by the Indians, and two wounded by accident. By the Returns of the Officers of different detachments, we killed 29 men, and took 17 Prisoners, mostly women and children, the number of wounded is uncertain. The Towns of Chote, Scittigo, [illegible], Chilhowee Togue, Micliqua, Kai-a-tee, Sattoogo, Telico, Hiwassee, and Chistowee, all principal Towns, besides some small ones, and several scattering settlements, in which were upwards of one thousand Houses, and not less than fifty thousand Bushels of Corn, and large quantities of other kinds of provisions, all of which after taking sufficient subsistence for the army whilst in the Country and on its return, were committed to the flames, or otherwise destroyed.[8]

Considering Campbell's frank account of his men's actions, what should we make of Jefferson's refusal of parole to Hamilton? Of course, there was a difference in Jefferson's mind between Hamilton's and Campbell's actions. Hamilton encouraged Indians to kill Americans; Campbell encouraged Americans to kill Indians. Nonetheless, simple hatred of the Cherokees or political expediency in excoriating the British cannot alone

---

5   Campbell to Jefferson, January 15, 1781, *CVSP*, 1: 434.
6   Ibid.
7   Ibid., 435.
8   Ibid., 436.

explain what seems to be Jefferson's duplicitous condemnation of Hamilton. Rather, Campbell simply described a campaign that was little more than an outgrowth of long-held American practices of waging war on enemy noncombatants and agricultural resources. Jefferson knew that American soldiers regularly put Indian settlements to the torch. Jefferson also knew that both Americans and Indians had over the course of the previous 150 years ranged across the frontier, killed enemy civilians, and burned enemy towns with devastating regularity. Indeed, both Americans and Indians often resorted to the "indiscriminate butchery of men women and children."

If Americans acted like Indians and regularly burned villages and fields of crops and killed women and children, what then was early Americans' "known rule of warfare?" Jefferson's letters suggest that colonial Americans knew two kinds of warfare: Americans' "civilized" warfare and Indians' "savage" warfare.[9] Jefferson's correspondence with Phillips also implies that the American and Indian approaches to war were mutually exclusive. Indeed, Jefferson's depiction of the colonial military scene was dichotomous. American methods of war occupied one pole in which soldiers discriminated between combatants and noncombatants, and by implication fought within state-sponsored armies. Indian ways of war occupied the opposite pole, in which all enemies, regardless of age or sex, were fair game.

In fact, colonial era Americans, in response to the varied ways that Indians waged war, created a military tradition that resembled in detail the "savage" campaigns that Jefferson decried. The pillars of that tradition – extirpative war, ranging, and scalp hunting – had been built during the seventeenth and early eighteenth centuries; by the late 1720s, they supported Americans' first way of war.[10]

---

9   Jill Lepore has noted Montaigne's observation that "each man calls barbarism whatever is not his own practice." She writes that between the narrow path of virtue, piety, and mercy that Americans traveled were the ways of war of the "cruel" Spaniards and the "savage" Indians. See Lepore, *The Name of War: King Philip's War and the Origins of American Identity* (New York: Alfred A. Knopf, 1998), xiv.

10 Rather than narrate the course of the colonial wars so well described by historians, this chapter addresses how the first way of war shaped the early American culture of war making. For the colonial wars, see Ian Steele's *Warpaths: Invasions of North America* (New York: Oxford University Press, 1994); Douglas Leach, *Arms for Empire: A Military History of the British Colonies in North America, 1607–1763* (New York: Macmillan, 1973); Howard H. Peckham, *The Colonial Wars 1689–1762* (Chicago: University of Chicago Press, 1964); and Edward P. Hamilton, *The French and Indian Wars: The Story of Battles and Forts in the Wilderness* (Garden City, NY: Doubleday & Company, Inc., 1962). For summaries of America's wars before King George's War, see Francis Parkman, especially his *Count Frontenac and New France* (Boston: Little, Brown and Company, 1877) and the first volume of his two-volume *A Half-Century of Conflict* (Boston: Little, Brown and Company, 1892). Despite his Anglocentric biases, his narratives of the wars between Americans and Indians and between Americans and

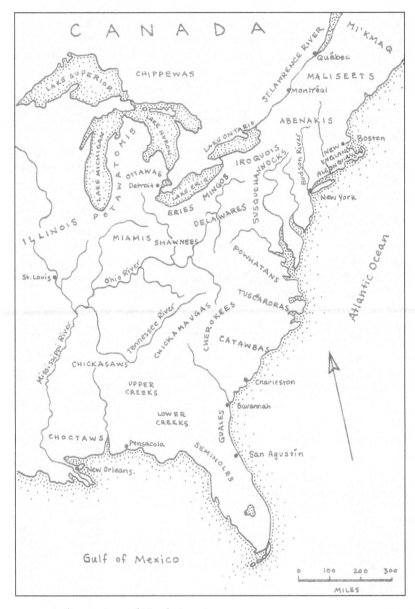

Indian nations of North America

I. Extirpative War Comes to English North America, 1607–1646

Military men figured prominently in the leadership of the first English colonies in North America and, as one would expect, brought with them to the New World their European-derived conceptualization of unlimited war.[11] The mercenaries who led the first colonies' small armies – John Smith in Virginia, Myles Standish at Plymouth, John Mason in Connecticut, and John Underhill in Massachusetts – were products of Wars of Religion that had ravaged Europe from the mid-sixteenth to the mid-seventeenth centuries. The conflicts in which they learned their craft were brutal affairs. Fueled by the passions of the Reformation and Counter Reformation, late-sixteenth- and early-seventeenth-century European soldiers had little compunction about, and some would say almost a preference, for putting towns to the torch and noncombatants to death. Tragically for the Indian peoples of the Eastern seaboard, the mercenaries unleashed a similar way of war in early Virginia and New England.

Military necessity, the colonists believed, demanded that they turn to extirpative war, what today's soldiers term unlimited warfare, manifested by the destruction of enemy noncombatants and their agricultural resources. Over the course of nearly four decades, the English colonists of Virginia embraced increasingly harsher measures for dealing with their Indian neighbors, until by 1646 they had made the killing of Indian noncombatants their preferred strategy and tactic.

In Virginia in 1607, the Jamestown colonists were at a loss over how to deal with Powhatan warriors who stealthily moved through the woods, attacked working details, and then, John Smith wrote, "by the nimbleness of their heels escaped."[12] Smith, as the individual responsible for the colony's defense, responded with a crash training program to teach the settlers "to march, fight, and skirmish in the woods [so that they] were

---

French Canadians remain informative, engaging, and beautifully written narratives in the grand style. For a contemporary's view of New England's colonial wars, see Samuel Niles's *A Summary Historical Narrative of the Wars in New-England with the French and Indians, in the Several Parts of the Colony*. The Massachusetts Historical Society published it in its *MHSC* in two parts, the first in 3d ser., 6 (1837): 154–279 and the second in 4th ser., 5 (1861): 311–589.

11   In the first Virginia Assembly formed in 1619, for instance, 9 of the 22 members had military titles. Even if leaders did not actually have military experience, they felt a military title gave them an air of authority. A Reporte of the Manner of Proceeding in the General Assembly Convented in James City, July 30–31, 1619, *The Records of the Virginia Company of London*, ed. Susan Myra Kingsbury, 4 vols. (Washington, DC: GPO, 1906–1935), 3: 153–154.

12   John Smith, "The Proceedings of the English Colonie in Virginia," *The Complete Works of Captain John Smith*, ed. Philip L. Barbour, 3 vols. (Chapel Hill: University of North Carolina Press for IEAHC, 1986), 1: 206.

better able to fight."[13] He abandoned that course, however, when he realized it had done little to turn Englishmen into effective woodland warriors. Smith then turned to what he and his men knew best.

Noting that "if they assaulted us, their Towns they cannot defend," Smith engaged the Powhatans in a "feedfight," or the destruction of Powhatan fields and villages. The feedfight had worked well for the English in Ireland, but in North America it was a dangerous gamble.[14] The English were dependent on the Indians for food, and if any group were to starve in Virginia because soldiers had destroyed crops and fields, it would be the settlers. Needing therefore to do more than burn Indian fields to secure victory, Smith warned "King" Powhatan that if his subjects attacked English foragers, the colonists would seek ghastly retribution against the Indians' wives and children. Smith learned that making good on such threats worked. When, for example, the Indians refused to return several Englishmen they had taken captive, Smith and his men sallied forth "and burnt their Towns, and spoiled, and destroyed, what they could, but they brought our men and freely delivered them."[15]

The extirpation of Indians, rather than just a feedfight, became the order of the day when full-fledged war between the English and Powhatans erupted in August 1609. After a year of inconclusive skirmishing in which the English found themselves virtually trapped in Jamestown, Virginia's Governor Thomas Gates, in August 1610, ordered a full-scale mobilization of the colony's meager military resources under George Percy, a veteran of the Wars of Religion in the Netherlands. Percy was "to take Revenge" and destroy the Paspaheghs.[16] Their extirpation, Gates and Percy hoped, would serve as a powerful deterrent for other Indian villages that might join Powhatan's war with the English.

Few contemporary accounts relate the depths of ferocity of the settlers' extirpative war better than George Percy's *A Trewe Relacyon*. Upon arriving at a Paspahegh village, Percy recalled, he and his men "beset the savages' houses that none might escape." Upon his signal, the English

> fell in upon them, put some fifteen of sixteen to the Sword and Almost all the rest to flight, Whereupon I caused my drum to beat and drew all my Soldiers to the Colors. My Lieutenant

13   Smith, "A True Relation of Such Occurances and Accidents of Note, as Hath Hapened in Virginia," ibid, 1: 85.
14   Ibid., 1: 87. William L. Shea, *The Virginia Militia in the Seventeenth Century* (Baton Rouge: Louisiana State University Press, 1983), 20, contends that the feedfight originated in North America. Armstrong Starkey, in *European and Native American Warfare, 1675–1815* (Norman: University of Oklahoma Press, 1999), 41–42, suggests, rightly, that it originated with the English experience in Ireland. See chapter 3, note 45, for support of Starkey's side of the argument.
15   Smith, "A True Relation of Such Occurances," 89.
16   George Percy, "'A Trewe Relacyon': Virginia from 1609 to 1612," *Tyler's Quarterly Historical and Genealogical Magazine* 3 (1922): 260.

bringing with him the Queen and her Children and one Indian prisoner for which I taxed him because he had Spared them, his Answer was that having them now in my Custody I might do with them what I pleased. Upon the same I caused the Indian's head to be cut off. And then disposed my files Appointing my Soldiers to burn their houses and to cut down their Corn growing about the Town, And after we marched with the queen And her Children to our Boats again, where being no sooner well shipped my soldiers did begin to murmur because the queen and her Children were spared. So upon the same a Council being called it was Agreed upon to put the Children to death, the which was effected by Throwing them overboard and shooting out their Brains in the water. Yet for all this Cruelty the Soldiers were not well pleased.[17]

Only after the return to camp was the soldiers' bloodlust satisfied. The colonists, genuinely fearing all Indians and eager to expropriate the natives' lands, proved uninterested in granting quarter of any kind to their Indian enemies. Thus, a certain Captain Davis, Percy related, believed that it was "best to Burn" the "queen" of the Paspaheghs. Percy, however, determined to "give her A quicker dispatch. So turning myself from Captain Davis he did take the queen with two soldiers Ashore and in the woods put her to the Sword."[18]

Similarly, extirpative war became the colonists' modus operandi during the misnamed First Indian War of 1622–1632. The "massacre" of 1622 in which the Powhatan Confederacy under Opechancanough, King Powhatan's brother and successor, attacked virtually every English settlement along the James River hardened the settlers' attitudes toward the Indians. Although a friendly Indian warned the English of the impending attack, nearly 350 of the colony's settlers perished, or almost 30 percent of the European population.[19] George Wyatt, upon learning of the slaughter, advised his son Francis, then Governor of Virginia, that the settlers'

> Game are the wild and fierce Savages haunting the Deserts and woods. Some are to be taken in Nets and Toils alive, reserved to be made tame and serve to good purpose. The most bloody to be rendered to due revenge of blood and cruelty, to teach them that our kindnesses harmed are armed.[20]

17 Ibid., 271–272.
18 Ibid., 272–273.
19 William S. Powell, "Aftermath of the Massacre: The First Indian War, 1622–1632," *Virginia Magazine of History and Biography* 66 (1958): 44.
20 George Wyatt quoted in J. Frederick Fausz and John Kukla, "A Letter of Advice to the Governor of Virginia," *WMQ* 34 (1977): 127.

Smith, speaking for many victims of the attack, wrote from London, "now we have just cause to destroy them by all means possible."[21]

When they proved incapable of catching and extirpating Opechancanough's people, the English fell back on the feedfight and destroyed the Indians' provisioning grounds as a means of subjugating them. John Martin, a planter who sought to use the Indians as slaves, suggested that the English could starve the Indians into submission by denying them access to their food supplies. To that end, Martin proposed to use 200 soldiers to torch Indian fields and destroy fishing weirs. During the summer months, Martin advised, English shallops should patrol the waterways and kill Indians attempting to fish. At the same time, the government should forbid all trade in corn between settlers and Indians, even those Indians friendly to the settlers. With the Indians thus weakened, he argued, settlers could enslave them and take their land for the cultivation of hemp, flax, and silk. In June 1622, the Virginia Council embraced Martin's plan and began the systematic destruction of the Powhatans' agricultural resources. In that month the colony's small army set "upon the Indians in all places," and "slain divers, burnt their Towns, destroyed their Wears [weirs] & Corn."[22] The campaigns continued the next year. A survey of the colony's military rosters shows that of the 180 men fit for military duty in 1623, 80 took up "carrying corn," that is, destroying Powhatan fields.[23] In 1624, the Virginia Council created a special company of "60 fighting men (whereof 24 were employed only in the Cutting down of Corn)" to destroy Indian crops. In the ensuing operations against maize and legumes, the settlers deemed each field destroyed a "great Victory" and relished how the Indians "gave over fighting and dismayedly, stood most ruefully looking on while their Corn was Cut down."[24] The raids, nonetheless, proved quite dangerous; the 1624 operations alone cost the English 16 casualties. Such losses, however, were acceptable since, as Governor Wyatt observed, the colonists had destroyed as much corn "as would have sustained 400 men for a twelvemonth."[25]

After 12 years of peace that saw English control of the Tidewater grow, and unable to drive them from Virginia, Opechancanough must have hoped to reestablish an English–Indian balance of power in which Indians

21 Smith, "The Generall Historie of Virginia, New-England, and the Summer Isles," *Works of Captain John Smith*, 2: 298.
22 John Martin, The Manner Howe to Bringe the Indians Into Submission, *Records of the Virginia Company*, 3: 704–706; Council Report, ibid., 4: 9.
23 Council in Virginia to Company in London, January 20, 1623, ibid., 4: 12; George Sandys to Samuel Wrote, March 28, 1623, ibid., 4: 67.
24 Letter from the Council in Virginia to the Earl of Southampton and the Council and Company of Virginia, ibid., 3: 507.
25 Sir Francis Wyatt and Council of Virginia to Henry Early of Southampton and the Council and Company of Virginia, December 2, 1624, *CSPC, 1574–1660*, 70–71.

could maintain independence and initiative. Thus began the Tidewater War of 1644–1646. As in the Massacre of 1622, the Powhatans attacked the English settlements. Rather than cowing the colonists into dealing with them as coequals, the Massacre of 1644 only enraged the English.

The colonists' reaction to what they perceived as the most recent example of Indian nefariousness was a total embrace of extirpative war. The House of Burgesses raised five times the number of men as it had for the 1622 campaigns.[26] The Tidewater War involved no single event that we rightly can call a "battle." Instead, it consisted of two years of unrelenting English raids on Indian villages and fields that starved nearly every Indian out of the James Valley. When this was added to the capture and murder of the septuagenarian Opechancanough, the few remaining Indians of the Tidewater had little option but to accept total English dominance in eastern Virginia.

The Tidewater War's end ushered in 30 years of peace for Virginians and made extirpative war their preferred and primary form of warfare.[27] Whereas the English originally had room for some Indians among them – they needed Indians to provide food and labor – as the number of first European indentured servants and then African slaves increased in Virginia, English use for Indians disappeared. Thus, by 1646, after two generations of extirpative war and exposure to European diseases had devastated most of the tribes of the Tidewater, the victors displaced the survivors to reserves set away from European settlements and seized their lands, a policy with which the colonists had first experimented in the wake of the Massacre of 1622.[28] While some tribes, like the Piscataways of Maryland, managed to avoid total dislocation by accepting demeaning tributary status, as far as the English were concerned they had sufficiently abandoned their Indian ways. The English would tolerate Indians

26 Virginia Assembly, "Acts of the Virginia Assembly, Indian War of 1644," *Virginia Magazine of History and Biography* 23 (1915): 231–232.
27 Virginians occasionally conducted minor actions against both tributary and "foreign" Indians after 1646. For example, in 1655, 700 Richahecrian Indians established a community near present-day Richmond. In response, the House of Burgesses authorized Colonel Edward Hill to lead 100 militia and friendly "neighboring Indians" to "remove" the Richahecrians. Hill's party murdered five chiefs who had come to parley under a flag of truce. In the action's one large skirmish, the Richahecrians routed the poorly trained Virginia militia and killed most of its Indian auxiliaries. Yet the Richahecrians then unexpectedly abandoned their settlement and ended the war. See *SAL*, 1: 402–403. Later, the Richahecrians migrated to the Savannah River, where they became known as the Westos.
28 Edmund S. Morgan, in *American Slavery American Freedom: The Ordeal of Colonial Virginia* (New York: W. W. Norton & Company, 1975), describes the transition from Indian labor to indentured servant and slave labor in early Virginia. Alden T. Vaughan, "'Expulsion of the Salvages': English Policy and the Virginia Massacre of 1622," *Roots of American Racism: Essays on the Colonial Experience* (New York: Oxford University Press, 1995), 105–127.

within and near their settlements provided that they essentially neither saw nor heard them. Of course, in the struggle to find a path "between total war and complete capitulation," Indians like the Piscataways managed to maintain elements of their cultural identity.[29] Similarly, as Englishmen constructed their new identity as the conquerors and overlords of Virginia, they made extirpative war the defining part of their culture of war making.

Peaceful relations, with only minor exceptions, created an environment of coexistence between Englishmen and Indians in early New England.[30] Unlike the Jamestown colony, located in the middle of the territory controlled by the most powerful Indian confederacy on the Atlantic seaboard, a disastrous epidemic of European diseases between 1617 and 1619 had destroyed perhaps 80 percent of the Indian population of New England. As a result, New England's Indians, at least in the early days of settlement, seemed more tractable to English interests. Yet when war broke out in 1636, the Puritans ignored the years of peace, leaped over the feedfight, and moved directly to the extirpation of their Indian enemies.

Indians villages, and therefore noncombatants, were the main target of the English in the Pequot War, New England's first large-scale military conflict.[31] In response to English attempts to kidnap Pequot women and children to stand as hostages for the Indians' good behavior, the Pequots attacked English settlements on the lower Connecticut River. John Endicott and 90 Massachusetts men countered with a raid on the Pequots' village on Block Island, which they burned with its surrounding fields. After Endicott retreated, the Pequots laid siege to Connecticut's Fort Saybrook. That siege and the ensuing months of Indian raids showed the colonists how vulnerable they were to Indian attacks and made clear

29 "Between total war": James H. Merrell, "Cultural Continuity among the Piscataway Indians of Colonial Maryland," *WMQ* 36 (1979): 549.

30 A treaty of friendship between Massasoit, a Wampanoag sachem, and colonial leaders defused early hostilities between the Pilgrims and the Indians. Tensions between the English and other Indians occasionally boiled near the point of war, including those in the winter of 1622–1623, when a colony led by Thomas Weston on Massachusetts Bay seemed to be on the brink of disintegrating into chaos. To "save" that colony, Plymouth's Captain Standish assassinated several Indian leaders and, according to John Mason, "spread a Terror over all the Tribes of Indians round about him, from the Massachusetts to Martha's Vineyard, and from Cape-Cod harbor to Narragansett." See Mason, *A Brief History of the Pequot War* (1736; reprint, *MHSC*, 2d ser., 8 [1826]): 121.

31 For the causes of the Pequot War, see Alfred A. Cave, *The Pequot War* (Amherst: University of Massachusetts Press, 1996), and Neal Salisbury, *Manitou and Providence: Indians, Europeans, and the Making of New England, 1500–1643* (New York: Oxford University Press, 1982). John Winthrop, *Winthrop's Journal "History of New England," 1630–1649*, ed. James K. Hosmer, 2 vols. (New York: Charles Scribner's Sons, 1908), 1: 191; John Underhill, *News from America; Or, A New and Experimentall Discoverie of New England* (1638; reprint, *MHSC*, 3d ser., 6 [1837]): 6.

the need for direct, concerted action against the Pequots. Connecticut thereupon commissioned its resident mercenary, Captain John Mason, to subjugate the Pequots.[32]

In May 1637, Mason led 90 Connecticut soldiers, with the assistance of 70 Massachusetts troops under John Underhill, against the Indian "fort" on the Mystic River. While there were in fact two main Pequot forts – one with mainly warriors in it and one with women, children, and old men – Mason prudently selected the latter as his troops' target.

The English destruction of the Mystic River fort stands as the most infamous event in the early military history of New England, as well as a striking example of the place extirpative warfare occupied in early Americans' military culture. As soon as the English attack began, some Pequots retreated to their wigwams to barricade themselves inside, others tried to flee the fort, and still others took cover under their beds to hide from the English attackers who broke in to shoot and stab defenseless Pequot women and children. Mason and Underhill led the way in the slaughter and showed their men by personal example what they expected of them. Coming upon some Pequots in a lane between two rows of wigwams, Mason and a party of troops chased them to the end of the lane, backed them into a corner, and dispatched them with swords. Mason then came upon two English soldiers standing idly by watching the massacre. Upbraiding them – "We [the English] should never kill them after that manner" – an inspiration struck him: "We must Burn them."[33] He thus stepped into a wigwam, removed a firebrand, and set the structure afire. Underhill, seeing what Mason had done, kindled a fire on the other side of the compound. The two fires spread quickly, joined, and soon engulfed the entire compound in flames, "to the extreme Amazement of the Enemy, and a great Rejoicing of our selves." Two other officers then joined Mason in setting the wigwams aflame while the shocked "Indians ran as Men most dreadfully Amazed."[34]

The Puritans of New England had set loose a way of war unfamiliar to the Indians. The precontact Indian culture of war making among the Eastern Woodland Indians often was a mix of a highly evolved and ritualized system of limited war and the quest for individual glory. Within the Indian conceptualization of "mourning war," particularly among Iroquoian peoples, vanquished foes and captives often "replaced" losses in native communities. Indian raiding parties would venture forth, take captives, return to the war party's home village with those captives, and

---

32 J. Hammond Trumbull and Charles J. Hoadly, eds., *Public Records of the Colony of Connecticut*, 15 vols. (Hartford: Connecticut Historical Society, 1850–1890), 1: 10.
33 Mason, *Pequot War*, 139.
34 Underhill, *News from America*, 25. Mason, *Pequot War*, 139.

apportion them among grieving clans. At that point, the elder women of the clan determined the fate of the captive: males usually suffered death by excruciating torture; the captors most often incorporated women and children into their society.[35] The Narragansetts therefore joined the English in hopes of reaping a large harvest of prisoners, booty, and glory. But as the Narragansetts observed after the fact, the English ways were "too furious" and "slays too many men."[36] Although the scale of the slaughter shocked even him, Underhill contended that it was necessary. "Should not Christians have more mercy and compassion?" he asked. "Sometimes," he answered, "the Scripture declare the women and children must perish with their parents."[37]

The slaughter at the Mystic River village was only the first act of Connecticut's war of extirpation. Many New Englanders believed that the way to preserve the security of their homes, especially since they had made the Pequots an intractable enemy, was to complete the extirpation of the Pequots that they began on the Mystic River. They therefore embarked on a campaign in which they and the Narragansetts pursued the surviving Pequots, "ranging the country until they destroyed many of them, and the rest were so scattered and dispersed."[38] On one such expedition, Mason and 40 Englishmen came upon 200 old men, women, and children holed up in a swamp. With the Pequots destroyed as a military power, Mason was "loath to kill Women and Children." Instead, he put the men to the sword and "spared" the remaining 180 women and children by enslaving them.[39]

The few remaining bands of Pequots, near starvation and lacking either the strength or the will to fight, found themselves at the mercy of the colonists. When the Pequot sachems sued for peace and prostrated

35 Daniel Richter, *Ordeal of the Longhouse: The Peoples of the Iroquois League in the Era of European Colonization* (Chapel Hill: University of North Carolina Press for IEAHC, 1992), 32–38. Harry Holbert Turney-High [*Primitive War: Its Practice and Concepts* (Columbia: University of South Carolina Press, 1949): 147] argued that the quest for individual glory more than the security of the village or nation defined Indian war making. The result, Turney-High wrote, "was disastrous for the military efficiency of the American Indian." See also Leroy V. Eid, "National War among the Indians of Northeastern America," *Canadian Review of American Studies* 16 (1985): 125–154. Geoffrey Parker, in *The Military Revolution: Military Innovation and the Rise of the West* (New York: Cambridge University Press, 1988), 118, points out that there was an important difference between Europeans who sought to kill and native peoples who fought more often to capture. That focus on killing was an integral component of Parker's "Military Revolution" of 1500–1800.
36 Underhill, *News from America*, 27, 25.
37 Ibid., 25.
38 Philip Vincent, *A True Relation of the Late Battle Fought in New England, between the English and Pequet Salvages* (1638; reprint, *MHSC*, 3d ser., 6, [1837]): 39. Niles, *Wars in New-England, MHSC*, 3d ser., 6 (1837): 173.
39 Mason, *Pequot War*, 147–148.

themselves before the English and Narragansetts at Hartford, all that remained of a nation that had totaled at least 2,000 souls at the beginning of the war was 180 to 200 half-starved survivors.[40] Seeing that total victory was in their grasp, the Puritans apportioned the surviving Pequots among their Narragansett and Mohegan allies as slaves and then forbade the Pequots to inhabit their native lands or even to maintain the name Pequot. Connecticut, weighing the "several Inconveniences that might ensue" from a Pequot "revival," then sent Mason and 40 men to burn the Pequots' remaining wigwams and destroy their cornfields.[41]

Connecticut's decisive victory over the Pequots served as an ominous harbinger to the other Indians of southern New England. When tensions over English encroachments on Indian lands almost erupted into open conflict between the settlers and the Narragansetts in 1643 and 1644, for example, New Englanders responded quickly. Plymouth gave Captain Myles Standish command of a small army, while Massachusetts prepared for war by designating 30 percent of each militia company to be prepared to take the field within half an hour's notice.[42] The Narragansetts, seeing the settlers' preparations and recalling the fate of the Pequots when they had fought the English, appealed to King Charles I for redress. In the early 1640s, however, Charles I faced issues more pressing than the abuse of Indian rights perpetrated by his subjects in Boston. Thus in the summer of 1645 the Narragansetts, who had come to understand that war against the New Englanders could lead to apocalypse, agreed to a treaty in which they accepted tributary status. The threat of extirpation at the hands of the English had come to hang like a Damoclean sword over the heads of Southern New England's Indians.

II. Americans Adopt Ranging and Scalp Hunting, 1675–1711

By 1675, English colonists faced a new military situation. English settlements that had expanded into what a generation earlier had been Indian lands needed protection.[43] Assuming that the Indians who lived among

---

40 Estimates of the Pequot population before the 1617–1619 epidemics vary between 2,200 and 4,000. See Bert Salwen, "Indians of Southern New England and Long Island: Early Period," *HNAI*, Vol. 15, *Northeast*, 169.
41 Mason, *Pequot War*, 149.
42 Nathaniel B. Shurtleff, ed., *Records of the Colony of New Plymouth in New England*. 12 vols. (Boston: Press of William White, 1856–1861), 2: 45–46; Shurtleff, ed., *Records of the Governor and Company of the Massachusetts Bay in New England*. 5 vols. (Boston: Press of William White, 1853–1854), 3: 41, hereafter *Massachusetts Records*.
43 Between 1630 and 1675, the non-Indian population of English North America increased from 26,634 to 151,507. *Hist. Stats.*, 756.

them were not a major threat, the colonists directed their defensive efforts at creating a system of blockhouses to defend against "external" attacks. Their plan revolved around the idea that in times of war, settlers could fortify themselves in blockhouses and ride out Indian attacks. Therefore, success in the Pequot War and models of European siege warfare, not a consideration that the Indians with whom they shared the backcountry would and could make the surrounding countryside uninhabitable for English farmers and traders, set the English up for a disaster in the next war.

When King Philip's War erupted in 1675, the Indians avoided the blockhouses and instead hit isolated farms.[44] The English, secure in their blockhouses, could do little more than watch as the Indians devastated their farms. "Flushed with these exploits," Captain Benjamin Church of the Plymouth militia observed, the Indians "grew yet bolder and skulking everywhere in the bushes, shot all passengers and killed many that ventured abroad."[45]

Of greater significance than the Indians' hit-and-run attacks was their adoption of English-style extirpative war. Whereas the Pequots had fought the English constrained by their understanding of limited warfare, in King Philip's War, Wampanoags and Narragansetts sought to make the frontier an uninhabitable wasteland for the English. Coupled with their adoption of European firearms technology, the scope and scale of the violence they could inflict on the English increased dramatically.[46]

One case is indicative of the new Indian war-making ethos. On October 5, 1675, a party of local Indians sacked Springfield, Massachusetts. The previous day, Major John Pynchon, a fur trader from Springfield and the commander of its local militia, had acted at the direction of

---

44 For the causes of King Philip's War, see James Drake, *King Philip's War: Civil War in New England, 1675–1676* (Amherst: University of Massachusetts Press, 1999); Lepore, *The Name of War*; Russell Bourne, *The Red King's Rebellion: Racial Politics in New England, 1675–1678* (New York: Athenaeum, 1990); and Douglas Edward Leach, *Flintlock and Tomahawk: New England in King Philip's War* (New York: W. W. Norton & Company, 1966).

45 Benjamin Church, *Diary of King Philip's War 1675–76*, ed. Alan and Mary Simpson (Chester, CT: Pequot Press, 1975), 77.

46 For the changing nature of Indian war making in the late seventeenth century, see Richter, *Ordeal of the Longhouse*, 50; Colin G. Calloway, *New Worlds for All: Indians, Europeans, and the Remaking of Early America* (Baltimore: Johns Hopkins University Press, 1997), chap. 5; Adam J. Hirsch, "The Collision of Military Cultures in Seventeenth-Century New England," *JAH* 74 (1988): 1210. Armstrong Starkey, in *European and Native American Warfare, 1675–1815* (Norman: University of Oklahoma Press, 1998), implies that at around the time of King Philip's War there occurred a "military revolution" in North America as the Indians of New England adopted European weaponry. For the further effects of firearms on war in North America, see Donald E. Worster and Thomas F. Schilz, "The Spread of Firearms among the Indians of the Anglo-French Frontier," *American Indian Quarterly* 8 (1984): 103–115.

the Massachusetts Council and marched his troops away from Springfield to counter a suspected Indian threat.[47] The neighboring but quietly hostile Indians took advantage of the militia's absence to burn the settlement and then escape with impunity. When Pynchon returned to Springfield the next day, he "came to a Lamentable and woeful site." In a letter to his friend John Russell, Pynchon described the destruction of property and the human tragedy that resulted from the Indians' campaign to drive the English from the frontier.

> The Town in flames, not a house or barn standing except Old Gooden Branch's, till we came to my house & then Mr. Glover's. John Hitchcock's and Gooden Stewary's, burnt down with Barns, corn and all they had... My Grist Mill & Corn Mill Burnt down: with some other houses & Barns I had let out to Tenants; all Mr. Glover's library burnt, with all his Corn, so that he has none to live on, as well as myself, & Many more that have not for subsistence they tell me; 32 houses & the Barns belonging to them are Burnt & all the Livelihood of the owners, & what more may meet with the same strokes the Lord only knows.
>
> Many more had their estates Burnt in these houses: So I believe 40 families are utterly destitute of Subsistence; the Lord show mercy to us. I see not how it is Possible for us to live here this winter, & If so the sooner we were helped off, the Better.[48]

By late autumn 1675, Indians had repeated the scene at Springfield across the frontier. The Massachusetts Assembly, although not yet officially at war, advised frontier communities to evacuate their women and children to more settled areas.[49] Five months later, Indian raids to the north forced Rhode Island to make special provisions to shelter the hundreds of refugees who had flooded into the colony and sought protection from the emboldened Wampanoags and Narragansetts. Those settlers who stayed behind to save their homes and fight were, wrote John Sharpe, "in expectation of the enemy every day."[50] Indeed, over the course of the war, Wampanoag and Narragansett war parties, one contemporary postwar report noted, burned over 1,200 of New England's 12,000 houses,

47 J. H. Temple, *History of North Brookfield, Massachusetts. Preceded by an Account of Old Quabaug Indian and English Occupation, 1657–1676; Brookfield Records, 1686–1783* (North Brookfield, n.p., 1887), 109.
48 Major John Pynchon [to Rev. John Russell], October 5, 1675, "Letter on the Burning of Springfield in King Philip's War," *NEHGR* 48 (1894): 317.
49 *Massachusetts Records*, 4: 48.
50 John R. Bartlett, ed., *Records of the Colony of Rhode Island and Providence Plantation. Volume 2. 1664 to 1677* (Providence: General Assembly of Rhode Island, 1856), 533; John Sharpe to Thomas Meekins, January 8, 1676, *NEHGR* 10 (1856): 65.

made one-tenth of its male population casualities of war, and cost the region's colonies £150,000.[51]

The key to the Indians' initial success, like that of the Indians of Virginia, was their ability to capitalize on speed and stealth to strike and retreat out of harm's way, tactics the New Englanders pejoratively called "skulking."[52] William Harris, writing from Rhode Island in 1676, noted that the Narragansetts did "so many mischiefs in a secret sly, skulking way, no man knew well how to find them."[53] Nathaniel Saltonstall described the Narragansetts as "being like Wolves, and other Beasts of Prey, that commonly do their Mischiefs in the Night, or by Stealth, dare not come forth out of the Woods and Swamps, where they lay skulking in small Companies, being so light of Foot that they can run away when they list, and pass Bogs, rocky Mountains and thickets, where we could by no Means pursue them."[54]

One of the obvious ways to counter the skulking Indians was to destroy them before they could destroy the English settlements. Benjamin Church, however, had learned firsthand the difficulty of that task. In the fall of 1675, he and his militia company had engaged the Wampanoags in several skirmishes. The more mobile Indians regularly defeated them. Church also commanded one of the militia companies on the so-called Hunger March that followed the English massacre at the Great Swamp Fight in December 1675, in which they had killed nearly 300 Narragansetts.[55] After their victory, the colonists had hoped to extirpate the Narragansetts and set out for their villages. However, the militia never caught the Narragansetts, who had fled westward. Instead, they found themselves in the middle of enemy territory and without provisions. Their pursuit quickly degenerated into an affair of wilderness survival in which the raiders ate their horses rather than starve.[56]

Church argued that the colonists "must make a business of the war as the enemy did."[57] Although he was still recovering from wounds that

---

51 Extracts from Edward Randolph's Report to the Council of Trade, n.d., *NYCD* 3: 243–244. See also Salisbury, *Manitou and Providence*, 52; Leach, *Flintlock and Tomahawk*, 243, 247.

52 For a study of skulking, see Patrick M. Malone, *The Skulking Way of War: Technology and Tactics Among the New England Indians* (New York: Madison Books, 1991).

53 William Harris to Sir Joseph Williamson, August 12, 1676, "Letter to Sir Joseph Williamson, August 12, 1676," *Rhode Island Historical Society Collections* 10 (1902): 163.

54 Nathaniel Saltonstall, *A New and Further Narrative of the State of New-England, by N.S., 1676*, in *Narratives of the Indian Wars, 1675–1699*, ed. Charles H. Lincoln (New York: Charles Scribner's Sons, 1913), 89.

55 Niles, *Wars in New-England, MHSC*, 3d ser., 6 (1837): 182.

56 Church, *Diary of King Philip's War*, 83–90. Ray Gilbert Hawes, "First American Warriors in Battle," *JAH* 4 (1910): 424.

57 Church, *Diary of King Philip's War*, 106.

he had received at the Great Swamp Fight, Church took it upon himself in early 1676 to learn the Indian way of skulking. He enlisted the support of a group of friendly Indians, selected a handful of hardy settlers who could survive the rigors of winter campaigning, and set out to search for the Narragansetts.[58] Church's company traveled north along the Connecticut River as far as the Nipmuck country (present-day north central Massachusetts). There, Church related in his memoirs, "They had success of killing many of the enemy, until at length, their provisions failing, they returned home."[59] Although the raid was of only limited tactical value, it showed Church that colonists acting in concert with friendly Indians could adapt to the skulking way of war. The "Nipmuck Expedition," however, had greater importance: it inaugurated the American ranger tradition – the second element in the emerging first way of war.

Church's raid into the Nipmuck country convinced his fellow settlers that he was "a person extraordinarily qualified for and adapted to the affairs of war."[60] Indeed, Church and his handful of men were nearly the only Englishmen who had made any offensive endeavors against the Wampanoags and Narragansetts. Church tried to capitalize on his newfound reputation and claim a larger role for himself and his tactics for fighting Indians. He petitioned Governor Edward Winslow for permission to raise a company of 60 to 70 handpicked "scouts" for wilderness warfare. Church and his scouts would "not lie in any town or garrison with them [the militia]," he told Winslow, "but would lie in the woods as the enemy did." To do otherwise, he advised, would "be but to deliver so many men into their hands [the Indians'] to be destroyed."[61]

After initially balking at the costs of his company, Winslow commissioned Church in July 1676 to form America's first ranger force. He directed Church to take 60 Englishmen and 140 friendly Indians to "discover, pursue, fight, surprise, destroy, or subdue" the colony's Indian enemies.[62] The ratio of Englishmen to Indians in Church's company is instructive, for it illustrates the mechanics of Americans' earliest tradition of ranging. In that early stage, even the ablest would-be Indian fighters, like Church, knew that without the help of friendly Indians, they were no match in the woods against Indian warriors. Americans in fact never could have become rangers without the tutelage of Indian allies. Indeed,

---

58 Richard Johnson has argued that from the earliest days of settlement, New Englanders attempted to solve the military problems that Indians posed by incorporating them into the colonial military structure. See Johnson, "The Search for a Usable Indian: An Aspect of the Defense of Colonial New England," *JAH* 44 (1977): 623–651.
59 Church, *Diary of King Philip's War*, 102–104.
60 Ibid., 105.
61 Ibid., 106.
62 Ibid., 128.

until the end of the colonial period, rangers depended on Indians as both allies and teachers.

Church's company began patrolling the frontier, searching for Wampanoags and Narragansetts to ambush and kill, as well as learning how to range. The patrols, however, were not for the fainthearted; the rangers, Thomas Danforth directed Church's subaltern, Charles Frost, were to "in all places & by all ways & means...take, kill, & destroy the enemy without limitation of place or time."[63] The deeper they penetrated into Indian country, the more Church and the other ranger leaders, including Charles Frost and John Gorham II, found themselves in a deadly war of ambushes and skirmishes. Nevertheless, in the hard school of frontier warfare, the rangers learned valuable lessons about small-unit operations, working with Indian scouts, maneuvering, setting and avoiding ambushes, and close-quarters fighting.

It would be an overstatement to give Church's rangers the credit for securing the English victory in 1676. The Indians who chose to attack the colonists in 1675 never stood a chance. Of more importance than any of Church's patrols, at the outbreak of the war in New England, New York's Governor, Sir Edmund Andros, enlisted the nations of the Iroquois League in the first of several military and diplomatic alliances with the English that in time formed the Covenant Chain – the system of treaties that made the Iroquois the primary object of diplomacy in the colonial Northeast.[64] By the summer of 1676, disease, as well as losses to the Mohawks, had devastated the Wampanoags and Narragansetts. Indeed, without Iroquois participation on the side of the colonists, it is difficult to imagine an English victory over King Philip. Still, Church's formation of his rangers was not for naught; he had planted the seed from which the American ranger tradition would grow.

Church was not alone in experimenting with ranging. At about the same time that Church formed his company in New England, Virginians, in the midst of the Susquehannock War, moved toward the creation of a Southern variation on the emerging ranger tradition. Upon being warned in 1676 of a potential Indian war on the frontier, the House of Burgesses enlisted a 125-man mounted force to "range" between the headwaters of the Piedmont's major rivers.[65] Designed more as a screening than an

---

63 Thomas Danforth to Charles Frost, n.d. [probably spring 1676], "Indian War Papers," ed. Charles W. Parsons, *NEHGR* 3 (1849): 24.

64 Richter, *Ordeal of the Longhouse*, 134–142. For the role of the Iroquois League in King Philip's War, see Stephen Saunders Webb, *1676: The End of American Independence* (New York: Alfred A. Knopf, 1984), 367–371. See also Daniel R. Mandell, *Behind the Frontier: Indians in Eighteenth-Century Eastern Massachusetts* (Lincoln: University of Nebraska Press, 1996), 22.

65 *SAL*, 2: 327. During King William's War, when the threat to Virginia originated in raiders from the Ohio country descending upon the Piedmont, the House of Burgesses,

offensive force, the rangers never got the chance to prove their worth. In a repeat of King Philip's War in the North, the Mohawks shattered and then incorporated the Susquehannock bands as they fled into the Virginia backcountry.[66]

The differences between New England's and Virginia's rangers provide credence to the claim that Benjamin Church was the father of American ranging. First, no single Virginian, like Church in New England, emerged as the founder and focus of Southern ranger efforts. Second, the purposes of the two forces were different. Church designed his force primarily to emulate Indian patterns of war. To that end, as noted earlier, he endeavored to learn to fight like Indians from Indians; the Virginia rangers, modeled on European cavalry, stand as another example of how Englishmen could adapt Old World practices to New World conditions.

Despite the absence of a single leader with a vision like Church, the first Virginia rangers nonetheless became an effective fighting force and laid the groundwork for what in time would become a distinctive Southern ranger tradition. While New Englanders never developed cavalry or dragoon forces on a large scale – with the exception of the one-seventh of its militia that Connecticut put in a "flying army" in King William's War (1689–1697)[67] – the Southern rangers depended on their horses. Perhaps because they needed horses to cover the more open areas of the Piedmont, or perhaps because of the influence of Virginians' "horse culture," Southerners remained steadfastly committed to mounted rangers.[68] Whatever

in 1691, 1692, 1693, and 1695, created troops of horse-mounted rangers. See *SAL*, 3: 17, 82–83, 115, 119, 126.

66 Richter, *Ordeal of the Longhouse*, 135–136. Stephen Saunders Webb has written that the Iroquois chose to go against the Susquehannocks because they wanted to "absorb the best of the Susquehanna warriors as the janissaries of the Iroquois." See Webb, *1676*, 374.

67 Harold Selesky observes that the effectiveness of those dragoons is still open to question. See Selesky, *War and Society in Colonial Connecticut* (New Haven, CT: Yale University Press, 1990), 25.

68 The densely wooded forests of New York and New England made cavalry operations difficult. In 1756, for instance, Anthony Van Schaick wrote to the earl of Loudoun that he had made seven trips to the south bay of Lake Champlain "to find a Way, by which a Carriage, or at least a horse might go, but could never find any such." Van Schaick to Loudoun, August 1756, LO 1163. Twenty years later, Major General Charles Lee of the Continental Army noted that in the American South "a body of horse is a *sine qua non*, in a country circumstanced like this." See Lee to the President of Congress, April 19, 1776, Lee Papers, *Collections of the New-York Historical Society* (1871): 434. For the Virginia horse culture, see David Hackett Fischer, *Albion's Seed: Four British Folkways in America* (New York: Oxford University Press, 1989), 359. Virginia DeJohn Anderson, in "Animals into the Wilderness: The Development of Livestock Husbandry in the Seventeenth-Century Chesapeake," *WMQ* 59 (2002): 385, argues that only in the 1670s did the horse population of the Chesapeake expand. If Anderson is correct, the Virginia rangers of the Susquehannock War, organized in cavalry troops, were on the cutting edge of military-technological evolution in North America.

the reason, first Virginians and then other Southerners would carry their style of mounted ranging with them into Kentucky, Tennessee, and the Old Southwest. By the 1810s, the mounted rangers of Kentucky were the most sought-after troops for killing the Indians of the Transappalachian West.

As early as King William's War, the New England rangers proved the only means by which the colonial land forces could strike the French and Indians. In that conflict, the Iroquois, effectively isolated from the English interests by the French and their Algonquian-speaking allies' raids into Iroquoia, refused to join the colonists. New England's and New York's advance up Lake Champlain, meanwhile, was stillborn when the 1,800 Covenant Chain Iroquois the commanders expected never materialized.[69] Although Sir William Phips took Port Royal, Acadia, his army failed to breach the walls of the citadel at Québec and returned to Boston to criticism and recriminations.[70] All the while, Abenaki raiders from present-day Vermont and Maine killed and burned on the frontier.

Benjamin Church took it upon himself to stop those raids. Uninterested in dealing with what most colonists saw as the cause of the Indian attacks on the frontier (the French presence in Canada), and instead focused on the immediate problem of Indian attacks, Church in 1689 led the first of his "Eastward Expeditions" to Maine against the Abenakis. In 1690, 1692, and 1696 he followed with other campaigns into Maine. In each of them, Church's Indian and English rangers skirmished with Abenaki warriors and waged extirpative war on Abenaki villages and the noncombatants they contained.[71]

Like King Philip's War, the Eastward Expeditions offered another laboratory in which Americans could learn firsthand valuable lessons on

---

69   For the details of Iroquois participation in King William's War, see Richter, *Ordeal of the Longhouse*, chap. 7, and Richard White, *The Middle Ground: Indians, Empires, and Republics in the Great Lakes Region, 1650–1815* (New York: Cambridge University Press, 1991), 34.

70   See The Revolutionary Government at New York to the Earl of Shrewsbury, June 23, 1690, *CSPC, 1689–1692*, doc. 955; Thomas Savage, *Expedition Against Quebec, 1690* (1691; reprint *MHSC*, 2d ser., 3 [1845]), 256–259.

71   Letter from Major Benjamin Church, October 7, 1689, *Baxter MSS*, 4: 472. In 1689, colonists had formed at least two combined Indian–ranger companies that consisted of 64 and 34 Indians, respectively. See Joseph Prout to the Governor & Council, September 13–19, 1689, ibid., 458. Daniel Mandell, in *Behind the Frontier*, 51, shows that in 1701 the Massachusetts Assembly gave 190 acres to their Indian allies who had fought in King Philip's and King William's Wars. Records also suggest that Church may have had soldiers of African descent in his army. Silvanus Davis, a captain of the rangers, wrote, "Major Church & his soldiers Both White & Black" arrived at Fort Loyall. See Silvanus Davis to Governor and Council, September 22, 1689, *Baxter MSS*, 4: 455. In 1690, there were an estimated 400 blacks residing in Massachusetts. See *Hist. Stats.*, 756. Stephen C. Eames, "Rustic Warriors: Warfare and the provincial Soldier on the Northern Frontier, 1689–1748" (Ph.D. diss., University of New Hampshire, 1989), 161–163.

ranging. The most important lesson to emerge from the campaigns to the Eastward was the realization that Americans, if necessary, could alone be effective rangers. The opening months of the war proved that if the colonists ever wanted to succeed fully at ranging, they would have to lessen their dependence on what they saw as fickle Indian allies. In 1689, for instance, Church complained to the Governor and Council of Massachusetts that he could progress no further into the wilderness because he lacked Indian scouts who were familiar with and willing to guide him in the land "east" of Casco Bay. Necessity, of course, is the mother of invention, and daring colonists stepped up to replace some of the Indian scouts. Moreover, by the middle of the war the best of Church's rangers – men like John Gorham II and Charles Frost – had learned enough from their Indian teachers, and had gained enough confidence in their abilities, to form ranger companies that they led to the Eastward. The leaders of those first ranger companies were well on their way to building a base of knowledge that would provide the foundation for American ranging well into the next century.

The ranger companies of King William's War in fact became the nurseries for successive generations of New England rangers. By the middle of the 1740s, most New England rangers served in units under officers who had a direct connection to Church. In King Philip's War, for instance, one of Church's subaltern officers was John Gorham I of Barnstable (now Yarmouth), Massachusetts. Gorham died of wounds he received at the Great Swamp Fight, but his son, John Gorham II, served with the ranger company that Church formed in 1676. Twenty years later, in 1696, Gorham II was second in command of the rangers on the Fourth Eastward Expedition. During King George's War, his grandson, John, became commander of Gorham's Rangers. Joseph Gorham, one of John II's other grandsons, commanded Gorham's Rangers and saw combat as a ranger in Nova Scotia, outside Québec, in Cuba, and through the War of Independence.[72]

The military lineage of the Gorham clan suggests an intriguing point about the importance of ranging to the first way of war and early American history. The careers of John Gorham, his son, and grandsons suggest that

---

72 For the genealogical record of the Gorham family, see "Col. John Gorham's 'Wast Book' and the Gorham Family," *New York Genealogical and Biographical Record* 28 (1897): 133–136, 197–201. For a partial summary of the Gorham family's military service, see Frank W. Sprague, "Barnstable Gorhams: The Old House in Which They Lived, and Their Services in the Colonial Wars," *NEHGR* 50 (1896): 32–34, and John Gorham, "Col. John Gorham's 'Wast Book' Facsimiles," ed. Frank W. Sprague, ibid., 52 (1898): 186–192. See also John Gorham, "Col. John Gorham's 'Wast Book' and His Dayly Journal," ed. George Ernest Bowman, *Mayflower Descendent* 2 (1903): 172–180; John Gorham, "Gorham Letters, with Facsimiles," ibid., 3 (1904): 181–184; Anon., "Barnstable, Mass., Vital Records," ibid., 33 (1935): 139–142.

ranging was a way of life for successive generations of New Englanders, among whom a "corporate knowledge" of ranger warfare passed down from generation to generation. John Gorham of King George's War was not born a ranger, but there certainly was something in his family's remembered past that led him to ranging. Who better than Gorham, whose great-grandfather and grandfather both had served with Benjamin Church, to lead the New England rangers of King George's War? Indeed, when the call for rangers went out in 1744, Gorham was one of the first to answer. Undoubtedly, tales of campaigns past must have furnished a store of practical lessons passed down to the younger Gorhams and applied time after time in New England's wars.

The Gorhams were not alone in tracing ranger service across the generations. The Lovewell family, of Dunstable (present-day Nashua), New Hampshire, followed a direct line from Church through the Seven Years' War. John Lovewell I fought alongside Church and Gorham at the Great Swamp Fight. His son, John Lovewell II, became the most famous ranger of Father Râle's (alternatively spelled Rallé or Rasles) War. At the time of his death in 1725, the younger Lovewell's wife, Hannah, was pregnant with their son, Nehemiah. During the Seven Years' War, Captain Nehemiah Lovewell commanded a ranger company for New Hampshire.[73]

From Lovewell's ranger and Indian fighting companies emerged another family that could trace its ranger service across two wars. Although John Lovewell met his end in 1725, two brothers who were members of his company, Eleazer and David Melven, survived "Lovewell's Fight." Both Eleazer and David went on to serve in the provincial army that besieged Louisbourg in 1745 during King George's War. In 1748, they enlisted as New Hampshire rangers. Eleazer became Captain Melven, and his brother became a lieutenant.[74]

Taken together, the military lineages of the Gorhams, Lovewells, and Melvens point to the permanence of ranging on the seventeenth- and eighteenth-century frontier. Within the American military tradition there was more than enough room for rangers, men experienced in Indian fighting. The "experience" of fighting is an important distinction to make. Several thousand young colonists served with provincial armies of units composed of American militia and attached to the regular English or British Army mustered for King William's, Queen Anne's, and King George's Wars. Yet the Americans who most frequently experienced combat before the Seven Years' War, and thus who stamped the colonial military

---

73 Thompson Maxwell, "The Narrative of Major Thompson Maxwell," *Essex Institute Historical Collections* 7 (1865): 98.
74 Eleazer Melven, "Journal of Captain Eleazer Melven," *New Hampshire Historical Society Collections* 5 (1837): 207.

tradition with a force disproportionate to their numbers, were the rangers. Indeed, only men who volunteered to serve as rangers experienced battle with any regularity before large-scale provincial service. As such, they certainly deserve a place as the originators of the first way of war.

Limited numbers of rangers, companies of a few dozen or so men, however, could do only so much to protect the frontier. Even with and perhaps because of Church's, Gorham's, and Frost's companies patrolling the countryside and subjecting Abenaki villages to destruction, Indian war parties continued to burn settlements and kill and capture settlers all along the New England frontier. Indeed, by the end of King William's War, Americans realized that extirpative war waged by the growing but still small corps of frontiersmen skilled in ranging could not guarantee the security of the frontier. Upon surveying the situation that faced them, however, Americans realized that in their tradition of extirpative war and their growing familiarity with ranging lay the potential to strike greater blows directly against their Indian enemies. Colonial governments needed to increase the number of rangers who would take to the frontier. Their answer – state-sponsored scalp hunting – became the third pillar of the first way of war.[75]

Scalp bounties – unlike the bounties placed on Indian heads that Connecticut and Massachusetts had offered in the Pequot War – first appeared in the laws of the American colonies in the mid-1670s. Originally, the bounty was for either Indian captives or their scalps. In the Susquehannock War, for instance, the Virginia House of Burgesses offered a reward of one matchcoat or 20 arm's lengths of tobacco for every Indian captive. In King Philip's War, Plymouth placed a bounty of trucking cloth worth five shillings on each Wampanoag "head skin." For King Philip's scalp, the reward was 100 shillings (£5), although Church and his company received only 30 shillings.[76] In July 1689, at the start of King William's War, Massachusetts declared that each soldier would receive £8 out of the public treasury for each Indian scalp, "and whatever Indian plunder falls into their hands shall be their own."[77]

Yet it was not battle-hardened rangers who brought scalp hunting to the fore of the American consciousness, but the ordeal of a mother on the

---

75 For the origins of scalping, see James Axtell and William C. Sturtevant, "The Unkindest Cut, or, Who Invented Scalping?" *WMQ* 37 (1980): 451–472. Axtell and Sturtevant argue that scalping was a pre-contact Indian practice, but one that Europeans adopted and incorporated into their own cultures of war making.

76 *SAL*, 2: 348. Nathaniel Saltonstall, *The Present State of New-England*, in Lincoln, ed., *Narratives of the Indian Wars*, 34. Church, *Diary of King Philip's War*, 156.

77 Order for Encouraging Volunteers, *Baxter MSS*, 9: 7. The English were not alone in encouraging scalping. In 1688, the Governor of Canada instructed his Indian allies to strike at the English and their Indian allies and "kill all what you can, bring no prisoners but their scalps, and I'll give ten beavers for every one of them." See Examination of Magsigpen, an Indian, September 15, 1688, *NYCD*, 3: 562.

Hannah Dustan bronze statue in Haverhill, Massachusetts

Maine frontier. Indeed, if Benjamin Church stands as the father of American ranging, Hannah Dustan of Haverhill, Massachusetts, is the mother of the American tradition of scalp hunting.

Hannah Dustan became a folk hero for scalping Indians. In March 1697, an Abenaki war party descended on Haverhill and captured Dustan, her newborn child, and her nurse, Mary Neff. Over the course of the next two weeks, 12 Abenakis – 2 men, 3 women, and 7 children – prodded Dustan and Neff 150 miles toward Canada, where they intended to enslave, adopt, or sell them to the French.[78] In the first mile of the

---

78 Ian Steele has shown that during times of peace Indians often sold their captives to French authorities, who in turn either sold them back to the English or exchanged them for French prisoners. During times of war, however, Indians often killed their captives. See Steele, *Betrayals: Fort William Henry and the "Massacre"* (New York: Oxford University Press, 1990), 14–18.

march, Dustan, too weak to carry her baby, passed the child to Neff. Neff, however, soon tired, at which point an Abenaki warrior ripped the child from Neff's arms and "dashed out the Brains of the Infant, against a Tree."[79] Dustan must have resolved to take vengeance on her Abenaki captors, for nearly two weeks after her capture, while still on the march toward Canada, she took a tomahawk from one of her captors while he slept. She waited until just before dawn and then struck at the murderers of her child. She, Neff, and another captive taken from Worcester, Massachusetts, crushed the skulls of the Abenaki men. Only one Indian adult escaped – an old woman whom Dustan wounded with a hatchet blow to the head. One of the children, whom Dustan had planned to transport back to Boston and sell as a slave, awoke in the ruckus and fled into the woods. Dustan then methodically scalped her victims. When she related her tale to the Massachusetts General Assembly and presented it with 10 Indian scalps, it rewarded her with £50.[80]

Many wanted to follow Dustan's example – insofar as it led to a reward. The colonial assemblies were willing to oblige. Governments that did not have the resources to engage in large-scale operations often resorted to privateering.[81] Whereas in port towns colonial governors issued ship captains letters of marque, in frontier communities they commissioned ranger captains on similar terms. The colonial governments had discovered the means to motivate untold numbers of men to take to the field and range against the Indians. In the process, they established the large-scale privatization of war within American frontier communities.

Possessing virtually no army, seeing the Iroquois clinging fast to the neutrality that they had agreed to with New France in 1701, and hearing that New York refused to participate in any campaigns for fear of pushing the Iroquois into the French camp, Massachusetts turned to scalp hunters when Queen Anne's War began on the northern frontier in 1702. Leaders asked little of prospective hunters other than that they enlist in a company sanctioned by the colonial government, one "under a proper officer, to be appointed and commissioned by the captain-general or commander-in-chief."[82] Massachusetts, for example, offered £10 for "every Scalp of an Indian Enemy killed in fight, that is, ten Years of

---

79 Mather, *Decennium Luctuosum*, in Lincoln, ed., *Narratives of the Indian* Wars, 263–266.
80 Anon., "An Historical Sketch of Haverhill, in the County of Essex, and Commonwealth of Massachusetts; with Biographical Notices," *MHSC*, 2d ser., 4 (1846): 129.
81 For naval privateering, particularly in the War of Jenkins' Ear and King George's War, see Carl E. Swanson, "American Privateering and Imperial Warfare, 1739–1748," *WMQ* 42 (1985): 357–382. For the role that offers of plunder had in encouraging men to enlist in provincial land armies, see Eames, "Rustic Warriors," 280.
82 *LOMBC*, October 1704: 558.

age."[83] When that bounty proved too small to attract sufficient numbers of scalp hunters, the General Assembly first increased it to £20 per head and then eventually to £100 for the scalp of each adult Indian male capable of bearing arms. For women above 10 years old the bounty stood at £10. Children under 10 were to be taken captive and then sold into slavery, with the profits from the sale going to the scalp hunters.[84]

"Adult," "capable," and "child," of course, were discretionary terms dependent on the judgment of the scalp hunter. Although graduated by age and sex, the bounties certainly erased the distinction between combatants and noncombatants. Indeed, many a scalp hunter must have faced a financial, though probably not a moral, dilemma. Should he kill and scalp an Indian child under 10 and then claim that the child was capable of bearing arms and collect a guaranteed £20 or £100? Alternatively, should he transport the child to Boston, where he would receive the profits from selling the child into slavery? Of course, not every scalp procured was taken by a hunter in a commissioned body. Thus it is probable, though impossible to prove, that a black market in scalps may have arisen.

Scalp hunting offered American frontiersmen acting as *entrepreneurs de guerre* the potential for an economic windfall.[85] Besides a means of earning replacement income during times of war when frontier settlers otherwise would have evacuated their homes for the protection of the forts, the promise of a bounty of £10 (200 shillings), at a time when the daily wages of laborers rarely exceeded 2 shillings, must have seemed appealing.[86] In the records of the Massachusetts General Assembly, there are numerous samples of the rewards that individuals received for scalps. In 1698, for example, Massachusetts paid Benjamin Wright and 13 of his compatriots £22 for the scalp of an Indian they killed. In 1704, William Southworth and his 40 men each received £4.3s.4d for the four scalps

83 Ibid., October 1703: 32.
84 For Massachusetts' scalp bounties in Queen Anne's War see ibid., September 1703: 530; October 1703: 31–32; March 1704: 44–45; October 1704: 558; August 1706: 594; March 1706–1707: 600.
85 André Corvisier coined the term *entrepreneur de guerre* to describe the condottieri who hired out the services of their personal companies of mercenaries to the Italian city-states during the Renaissance. See Corvisier, *Armies and Societies in Europe, 1494–1789*, trans. Abigail T. Siddal (Bloomington: Indiana University Press, 1979), 42.
86 *Hist. Stats.*, 771. For estimates of the average wages of skilled and farm laborers in New England from 1630 to 1774, see Gloria Main, "Gender, Work, and Wages in Colonial New England," *WMQ* 51 (1994), 48. John J. McCusker and Russell R. Menard, in *The Economy of British North America, 1607–1789* (Chapel Hill: University of North Carolina Press for IEAHC, 1991), 61, show that the average wealth per free white person in New England in 1774 was only £33 (pounds sterling). Even accounting for the deflation that accompanied the conversion of provincial funds into pounds sterling, scalp bounties offered significant sums. For the relative purchasing power of the money received from scalp bounties, see Gloria L. Main and Jackson T. Main, "The Red Queen in New England?" *WMQ* 56 (1999): 129.

they presented to the Assembly. The same year, the Assembly paid Thomas How £10, Samuel Partridge £10, Caleb Lyman £21, and a certain Captain Wells £60 for scalps. In 1709 the Assembly rewarded Captain Wright and his company of nine men, "having lately made a march to Canada against the Indian Enemy, and have had the good Success to Kill (as they suppose) seven or eight of said Enemy, One of whose Scalps they recovered & brought in," with £66.[87] Even in times of peace, the colonial governments continued to honor bounties on both Indian and French scalps. The Privy Council in London, for instance, issued a report detailing how in 1750 – two years after King George's War ended in the Peace of Aix-la-Chapelle – colonists paraded French scalps through the streets of New York City. The Indians who had brought in the scalps were "handsomely treated by the Council and gentlemen of this City, and afterwards by the Assembly."[88]

By embracing scalp hunting, American society, besides commercializing war, had made the killing of noncombatants a legitimate act of war. Thus, a practice that initially had served as an expedient measure also had become a permanent feature of both the colonial frontier economy and Americans' way of war.

III. The Coalescence of Extirpative War, Ranging, and Scalp Hunting into the First Way of War, 1710–1730

By 1710, extirpative war, ranging, and scalp hunting were well-established practices among Americans. A century of on-again off-again warfare in North America between Englishmen and first Indians and then Indians and Frenchmen had taught the colonists many lessons about war. The most significant of those was that when combined into a single way of war, extirpative war, ranging, and scalp hunting provided both an effective and a financially rewarding means to kill, conquer, and subjugate the Indian peoples of the Eastern seaboard.

Scalp- and slave-hunting rangers, motivated by the promise of personal financial gain, waged extirpative war against the Tuscaroras of North Carolina.[89] In September 1711, the Tuscaroras, angered by American squatters occupying their lands and slave raiders abducting their kinsmen, killed a handful of Indian traders as well as dozens of settlers and

---

87 *LOMBC*, October 1698: 198; March 1704: 48; October 1704: 83, 90; May 1709: 62.
88 Abstract of the Evidence in the Books of the Lords of Trade Relating to New York, n.d., *NYCD*, 6: 647.
89 For the role of the Indian slave trade in shaping the colonial Southeast, see Alan Gallay, *The Indian Slave Trade: The Rise of the English Empire in the American South, 1670–1717* (New Haven, CT: Yale University Press, 2002).

their slaves on the frontier. Although Virginia refused to send its militia to North Carolina's aid because it claimed that it previously had concluded a treaty of peace with the Tuscaroras, the House of Burgesses put a £20 bounty on Indian scalps to serve as an inducement for any scalp hunters who on their own initiative wanted to go Indian hunting. South Carolina proved more direct in providing aid.[90] Its Assembly authorized £4,000 for a punitive expedition under John Barnwell. As it prepared for the expeditions against the Tuscaroras – an Iroquoian nation with between 1,200 and 1,400 fighting men in 15 villages – South Carolina also enlisted the support of 800 Yamasee, Appalachee, Pedee, and Catawba "tributary savages" to complement its meager force of 50 rangers.[91] At first glance, that South Carolina would send only 50 rangers against 1,200-plus warriors seems striking. The Tuscarora War, however, was North Carolina's show, and South Carolina could offer only limited manpower support. More important, however, the colonists' goal was not to engage Tuscarora armies, but instead villages filled with women and children. South Carolina did not need large numbers of rangers, especially since Indians swelled its ranks. Events showed that the colonists who marched against the Tuscaroras did not lack for destructive potential.

The Carolinians pounced with "fury upon parts of the Tuscarora nation."[92] Barnwell's army methodically swept across the Tuscarora country, laid siege to villages, massacred Indians, burned fields, and then marched on to repeat the process. Barnwell wrote that the English ferocity shocked his Yamasee and Catawba allies, just as the New Englanders' ferocity had appalled the Narragansetts during the Pequot War. "It was Terror to our own heathen friend to behold us" reported Barnwell.[93]

Throughout the conflict, Barnwell's men made it a point to spare neither Tuscarora women nor children. Indeed, time spent killing noncombatants could even distract them from seizing the material goods of Indian villages. Upon seizing one village, for instance, Barnwell's Indian allies quickly set about plundering it while the colonists killed indiscriminately. There remained, it seems, differences between the colonists' and some Indians' conceptions of war. The colonists' native allies had entered the war for the booty and captives. The Catawbas particularly welcomed the war as an opportunity to hurt their traditional enemies and solidify their friendship

90   SAL, 4: 8; NC Records, 1: 836–837, 811–812.
91   Douglas W. Boyce, "Iroquoian Tribes of the Virginia–North Carolina Coastal Plain," HNAI, Vol. 15, Northeast, 288. John Barnwell, "Journal of John Barnwell," Virginia Magazine of History and Biography 5 (1897): 391–402. For the population of South Carolina, see Peter H. Wood, Black Majority: Negroes in Colonial South Carolina from 1670 through the Stono Rebellion (New York: W. W. Norton & Company, 1974), 152.
92   NC Records, 1: 954.
93   Barnwell, "Journal of John Barnwell," 394.

with American and British traders. They also were more than happy to cash in on the bounties Virginia and North Carolina offered for Tuscarora scalps.[94] Although not above plundering, the rangers had a more pressing task: extirpating the Tuscaroras. Although Barnwell bemoaned that his men missed some easy plunder, he nonetheless deemed the sacking of one village a success since the colonists killed and scalped 52 Indians, including 10 women. Not to be denied the long-term financial gain of their labors, however, the rangers also took some captives, whom they sold into slavery. While no one knows exactly how many Tuscaroras perished in the war – the number certainly was in the thousands – Americans forced at least 1,000 to 1,200, and perhaps as many as 1,800 to 2,000, of them into slavery.[95]

Enslaving and extirpating the Tuscaroras in fact soon surpassed any requirements for security in motivating the colonists. In March 1713, in one of the largest operations of the war, James Moore took his turn at leading the Carolinians. He chose to attack the Tuscarora village of No-ho-ro-co. The battle was a one-sided affair; more than 360 Indians perished trying to defend their homes, and Moore's army scalped 192 Indians and took another 392 prisoner – a veritable treasure trove of slaves. The surviving Tuscaroras could stand no more. Rather than suffer continued hammer blows by American scalp and slave hunters, 1,500 fled to New York to seek protection from their Iroquois cousins and became the sixth nation of the Iroquois League. Another 1,500 prostrated themselves as vassals to the Virginians.[96]

When the Yamasees turned to violence to break free from the growing English dominance, they found themselves sharing the Tuscaroras' fate. In a pattern Indians and colonists would repeat across the Southern frontier, the Yamasees initially allied themselves with the English. Expansion of colonial settlements, including the spread of the colonists' livestock, destroyed the habitat of deer, the Yamasees' most important trade commodity. With the deer populations depleted, many Yamasees fell into debt to Carolina traders. Ironically, many Yamasees traditionally had paid their debts by selling other Indians into slavery or by cashing in on scalp bounties. In what must have seemed no time to the Yamasees, however, the pool of enemies to sell into bondage or scalp dried up, while

---

94 James H. Merrell, *The Indians' New World: Catawbas and Their Neighbors from European Contact through the Era of Removal* (New York: W. W. Norton & Company, 1989), 54.

95 Peter H. Wood, "Indian Servitude in the Southeast," *HNAI*, Vol. 4, *History of Indian–White Relations*, 408, estimated the number of Indians forced into slavery as a result of the Tuscarora War at 400. I have used Alan Gallay's figure, found on page 298 of his more recently published *The Indian Slave Trade*.

96 *CVSP*, 1: 27. Dorothy Jones, "British Colonial Indian Treaties," *HNAI*, Volume 4, *History of Indian–White Relations*, 192; Boyce, "Iroquoian Tribes," 287.

debts to American traders increased. Many Carolina traders then took to seizing their Yamasee debtors and their kin as payment for debts. By April 1715, the Yamasees had had enough.

The war went well for the Yamasees until American rangers turned the tide. The Yamasees killed several British traders and convinced other tribes, including the Creeks and Catawbas, to take arms against the colonists. Throughout the spring and summer, Indians attacked frontier plantations across the South Carolina lowlands and drove most of the inhabitants to Charles Town (Charleston).[97] Fortunately for the settlers, in the wake of the Tuscarora War, South Carolina had created a full-time company of rangers to serve as the colony's first line of defense. In June 1715, that force, under Captain George Chicken, ambushed and killed 60 Yamasee warriors outside Charles Town.

With the capital safe, the South Carolinians looked to completely destroy, enslave, or drive the Yamasees from the colony. Reverend Gideon Johnson from the Society for the Propagation of the Gospel (SPG) witnessed the offensive. Scalp hunters, armed black slaves, and Iroquois proxies preyed upon Yamasees as if they were animals in the woods.[98] It was a powerful example of the first way of war in action. "Our Military Men," Reverend Johnson wrote, "are so bent upon Revenge and so desirous to enrich themselves, by making all the Indians Slaves that fall into their hands, but such as they kill (without making the least distinction between the guilty and innocent) that it is in vain to represent to them the Cruelty and Injustice of such a procedure."[99] The SPG minister's condemnation carried little weight. Over two campaigning seasons, first the Iroquois and then the Carolinians so thoroughly punished the Yamasees that all that remained for the survivors was to flee to Florida and live under Spanish protection at San Agustín.

97 Boyce, "Iroquoian Tribes," 285–286.
98 "In simple proportional terms," Peter Wood has written, "Negroes may never have played such a major role in any earlier or later American conflict as they did in the Yamasee War of 1715." See Wood, *Black Majority*, 127. Daniel Usner (*Indians, Settlers, and Slaves in a Frontier Exchange Economy: The Lower Mississippi Valley Before 1783* [Chapel Hill: University of North Carolina Press for IEAHC, 1990]) observes that in the Lower Mississippi Valley, French settlers likewise armed their slaves against the Choctaws and Chickasaws. For Indian participation in the 1715 campaign, see Merrell, *The Indians' New World*, 76–78. For a general account of the Yamasee War, see Verner W. Crane, *The Southern Frontier, 1670–1732* (Ann Arbor: University of Michigan Press, 1956). For the next 11 years, Yamasees launched sporadic raids against the American frontier in South Carolina, and not until 1728, after a South Carolina raid against the main Yamasee village in Florida did the Yamasee War officially end. See Douglas Edward Leach, "Colonial Indian Wars," *HNAI*, Vol. 4, *History of Indian–White Relations*, 140.
99 Gideon Johnson, December 19, 1715, in Edgar Legaré Pennington, "The South Carolina Indian War of 1715, As Seen by the Clergymen," *South Carolina Historical and Genealogical Magazine* 32 (1931): 261.

In Father Râle's War (also called Dummer's War, Lovewell's War, and Gray Lock's War) between the Abenakis and New Englanders, the first way of war dominated the military landscape.[100] Massachusetts and New Hampshire, as in Queen Anne's War, stood alone. New York remained aloof, and the home government in London did not intend to expend any resources for a local conflict on the New England frontier. The Iroquois, in spite of the offer of a £1,000 gift, refused to join the New Englanders in a war against the French-allied Abenaki. New England's only options, short of watching the Abenakis devastate the frontier, were to spend what few funds they could muster for static frontier defenses or capitalize on the colonists' antipathy for the Abenakis and mobilize rangers and scalp hunters for raids against Abenaki villages.

Massachusetts adopted both approaches. First, to counter Grey Lock's Abenaki raiders in western Massachusetts, the legislature funded construction of Fort Dummer on the Connecticut River. Although the fort never fell to the Indians, it proved of little value in either deterring or intercepting Grey Lock's raiders bent on reaching the settlements to the south. Massachusetts also turned to its rangers. In 1720, Massachusetts had placed a £100 bounty on Father Sébastien Râle's head on the grounds that he was most responsible for creating hostility among the Indians.[101] Once tensions between the colonists and the Abenakis heightened, the Assembly funded 300 rangers to find Râle and transport him to Boston for trial. When the ranger rolls did not fill as quickly as was hoped, the legislature provided added incentives of first £60 and then £100 rewards for Abenaki scalps.[102]

With the colony's defense almost exclusively in their hands, scalp-hunting rangers played a major part in the fighting that followed. The rangers decided to strike first, thinking that if they could capture Father

---

100 By the early 1720s, Jesuit Father Sébastien Râle had lived among the eastern Abenakis of Maine at his mission at Norridgewock on the Kennebec River for over 20 years. His influence among the Indians was such that he claimed that the Abenakis "would take up the hatchet whenever" he pleased. See Abstract of Certain Parts of a Despatch from Messrs. [Philippe de Rigaud, marquis] de Vaudreuil and [Charles, marquis de] Beauharnois; with Notes by the Minister, November 15, 1703, *NYCD*, 9: 755. Philippe de Rigaud, marquis de Vaudreuil, served as Governor-General of New France from 1703 and 1725. His son, Pierre de Rigaud de Vaudreuil (1698–1778), was the last Governor-General of New France.

101 For the details of Râle's anti-English activities, see Messers. de Vaudreuil and [Michel] Bégon [de la Picardière] to Louis XV, October 8, 1721, ibid., 9: 903. For Massachusetts's bounty on Râle, see *LOMBC*, July 1720: 14. In 1690, one French official in New France aptly remarked that the Americans regarded "all our Missionaries as their most bitter enemies, whom they will not tolerate amongst the Indians within their reach." See M. [Jacques René de Brisay, marquis] de Denonville to M. [Jean-Baptiste, marquis] de Seignelay, January 1690, *NYCD*, 9: 440.

102 *LOMBC*, August 1721, 112; July 1720: 14; November 1721: 126; May 1722: 204; August 1722: 258.

Râle they could nip the war in the bud. In the winter of 1721–1722, several parties of rangers set out to abduct Râle from his mission at Norridgewock. One party managed to reach the mission just behind an Abenaki sentry who warned Râle of the rangers' advance. The priest fled the mission with the church's chalice and crucifix in hand, hotly pursued by the rangers. Realizing that they had no chance of catching the Jesuit, the rangers returned to Norridgewock and plundered the church and the missionary's house. In a bit of braggadocio, they posted a note on the chapel door stating that they would return the next spring to relieve Father Râle of his scalp.[103]

The Abenakis and their Mi'kmaq, Maliseet, and Kahnawake (formerly called Caughnawaga) allies responded to the Norridgewock raid with attacks on the Massachusetts, Maine, New Hampshire, and Nova Scotia frontiers. The French saw an excellent opportunity to harass the English and quietly encouraged and supported their Indian allies.[104] It is unclear how important that support was to the Indians; they proved more than capable by themselves of hurting the English. Over the next two years Abenakis, Mi'kmaq, Maliseets, and Kahnawake-mission Iroquois slowly bled the English settlements on the frontier. Western Abenakis from the Jesuit mission at St. François (Odanak) sent their own war parties against western Massachusetts, as did the Kahnawakes. Philippe de Rigaud, marquis de Vaudreuil, Governor-General of New France, wrote the Council of the Marine that it seemed that the Indians were on the verge of sweeping the New England frontier of British settlements. Indeed, by the spring of 1724 the situation was so critical on the Maine frontier that William Dummer ordered its evacuation to fortified blockhouses. Although the inhabitants then were, from Boston's perspective, safe in their garrisons, Captain John Penhallow wrote to Dummer, "the Indians are Still about us... I expect we shall have 'em about us till we have Some reliefe, our weakness being now discovered."[105]

It was clear that the rangers had to do something to stem the tide of Indian raiders that was drowning the frontier. In late summer of 1724, Captains Johnson Harmon and Jeremiah Moulton therefore set out with four 50-man companies of rangers and 3 Indian guides in whaleboats to assassinate Father Râle and torch Norridgewock. Meanwhile, Râle's contempt for the New Englanders and their rangers continued to grow. "Did you ever see them come to attack you in the spring, summer, or

---

103   Messers. de Vaudreuil and Bégon to the Council of Marine, October 17, 1722, *NYCD*, 9: 910. Upon the failure of the first ranger company to capture Râle, Massachusetts increased the bounty on his head to £200. See *LOMBC*, November 1721: 126.

104   Louis XV to Messers. de Vaudreuil and Bégon, May 30, 1724, *NYCD*, 9: 936.

105   Penhallow to Dummer, April 29, 1724, *Baxter MSS*, 10: 197; Penhallow to Dummer, 18 May 1724, ibid., 10: 199–200.

in the fall," Râle asked another priest, "when they knew you were in your habitations?" "For if they knew there were but twelve men in your dwellings," Râle continued, "they dare not approach you with one hundred."[106] His disdain for the rangers' military prowess would cost him his life.

The raid on Norridgewock was well conceived and executed. The rangers managed to approach it undetected. Once near the mission, Moulton's company infiltrated the village while the others swept the surrounding fields. The rangers quickly dispatched Râle. Accounts of the priest's death conflict, but the most believable describe how upon hearing the English in the village he stepped from the door of his cabin, where a volley of musket fire killed him.[107] Luck, whether good or bad, usually trumps planning in war. Upon seeing Râle killed, the Abenakis abandoned the fight and fled headlong toward the Kennebec River. The rangers could not have planned so fortunate a turn of events. Moulton's company pursued the fleeing Indians and drove many into fusillades of fire from the other companies. Those Abenakis who reached the river had to run a gauntlet as rangers poured musket fire into crowded canoes of Indian men, women, and children. Harmon later lamented that the river's swift current washed over 50 Indian bodies downstream before the rangers could retrieve them for scalping. With the village then deserted of all but rangers, they occupied it for the night rather than risk returning to their lines in the darkness. Before they departed the next morning, they set the fields to flames and razed wigwams, storehouses, and cabins. One of their last acts was to profane the sacred vessels in the church and then burn the structure to the ground. Harmon returned to Falmouth with 27 scalps, including "the Fyars," the "squaw" of Abenaki leader Bombazee and three other Indian captives, and three English boys he had rescued. For his efforts, Dummer favored Harmon with a lieutenant colonel's commission. Samuel Penhallow, a contemporary chronicler of New England's early-eighteenth-century wars, described the attack on Norridgewock as "the greatest Victory we have obtained in the three or four last Wars."[108]

---

106 Father Rallé to Another Priest, August 1724, *CSPC, 1724–1725*, doc. 740–13.

107 M. de Vaudreuil to the Minister, November 28, 1724, *NYCD*, 9: 937. William Blake Trask, ed., "Letters of Colonel Thomas Westbrook and Others, Relative to Indian Affairs in Maine, 1722–1726," *NEHGR* 48 (1894): 187.

108 Anon., "Biographical Memoir of Father Rasles," *MHSC*, 2d ser., 8 (1826): 255. Col. T. Westbrook to Dummer, August 18, 1724, *Baxter MSS*, 10: 215–216. Trask, ed., "Letters of Colonel Thomas Westbrook and Others," 187. Samuel Penhallow, *History of the Indian Wars* (1726; reprint, Williamstown, MA: Corner House Publishers, 1973), 106.

Regarding the rangers' destruction of Norridgewock, Kenneth Roberts, in his novel *Northwest Passage*, described a similar scene when in 1759 Robert Rogers's Rangers drove Abenaki women and children into the river and poured fire on them as they tried to escape in canoes. The scenes described by Harmon and Roberts are in fact

The Abenaki survivors returned the next day to find their homes and fields smoldering, as well as Father Râle's corpse – minus its scalp. The men of the village had little choice but to lead 150 survivors to Canada, where they joined their Abenaki cousins and the Jesuit missionaries at St. François.[109]

The colonists hoped, naturally, that the destruction of Norridgewock would compel the Abenakis to accept peace on English terms. Instead, it further aggravated them.[110] The raid also encouraged more scalp hunters to enter the fray. Indeed, for the remainder of the war, with the exception of the brief campaign against the Penobscot Abenakis, scalp hunting was the centerpiece of New England's war effort. Captain John Lovewell soon emerged as the most famous scalp hunter not only of the war, but of the eighteenth century as well. His fortunes, both in monetary gain and fate, suggest the heights and depths that the first way of war had reached by the 1720s.

In November 1724, Lovewell petitioned the General Assembly of Massachusetts for a commission to take 40 or 50 frontiersmen on a scalp-hunting expedition into Maine. Lovewell and his fellow officers, Joshua Farnwell and Jonathan Robbins, wrote that they were "inclined to range and to keep out in the woods for several months together, in order to kill and destroy their enemy Indians, provided they can meet with Encouragement suitable." Lovewell was confident that he would find Indians sufficient in numbers to kill; for wages, Lovewell and his compatriots considered five shillings per day pay appropriate for one year of Indian hunting, and if they failed to kill any Indians, they agreed to accept no compensation from the colony. The Assembly authorized Lovewell and his men 2s.6d per day – half of what they asked – but granted them a £100 incentive for each male scalp they returned to Boston.[111]

Lovewell's first expedition met with almost immediate success. After filling the ranks of his company with experienced backwoodsmen, Lovewell led his scalp hunters into the wilds of Maine. On December 10, 1724, Lovewell's men came upon a wigwam where two Indians, a man and a young boy, were sleeping. Lovewell's men killed them, scalped them, and

so similar that one cannot help but suspect that Roberts based his narrative of the rangers' massacre of the St. François Abenaki in 1759 on Harmon's report of 1724. See Roberts, *Northwest Passage* (New York: Doubleday, Doran & Company, Inc., 1937).

109 M. de Vaudreuil to the Minister, November 28, 1724, *NYCD*, 9: 938.
110 Commissioners from Massachusetts Bay and New Hampshire to Canada, to the Commissioners of the Indian Affairs in Albany, 1725, *CSPC*, 1724–1724, doc. 740–30.
111 Lovewell's petition is quoted in Charles J. Fox, *History of the Old Township of Dunstable: Including Nashua, Nashville, Hollis, Hudson, Litchfield, and Merrimac, N.H.; Dunstable and Tyngsborough, Mass.* (Nashua, NH: Charles T. Gill, 1846), 111. *LOMBC*, November 1724: 484.

returned triumphantly to Boston, where they received £200, plus 2s.6d per day for their troubles.

Encouraged by his success, Lovewell enlisted 88 men for a second expedition. On February 9, 1725, the scalp hunters crossed the trail of 10 Indians near Lake Winnipesaukee. After tracking them for 11 days, they caught up with them just before sunset on the 20th. Lovewell waited until near midnight to spring his ambush. The Americans killed the Indians. Again, the men of Lovewell's company scalped their victims, took their possessions, and returned to Dover, where they sold the dead Indians' guns for £7 each and collected a fortune – £1,000 – from the public treasury.

Lovewell, like Dustan before him, became an instant celebrity. Few questioned whether his victims were hostile Indians or not. While we will never know if Lovewell killed innocent Indians, Thomas Symmes, the eighteenth-century chronicler of Lovewell's career, undoubtedly expressed the view of most colonists when he wrote, "some attempt against the Frontiers of New Hampshire [were] prevented; for these Indians were marching from Canada, well furnished with guns and plenty of ammunition."[112] It seemed that as long as the Indians were dead, no one would bother to inquire if they were warriors, boys and girls, or women.

In the spring of 1725, Lovewell embarked on his most famous and, as the Abenakis would have it, last scalp-hunting expedition. Lovewell planned to take his then pared-down 47-man company, many of whom were Boston townsmen unfamiliar with ranging, against the Abenaki village of Pequawket.[113] We can only speculate on why Lovewell's third company was so much smaller than his second command and consisted of so many townsmen. Perhaps the planting of the spring crop left only town dwellers available. Perhaps Lovewell wanted fewer experienced rangers in his company, since he would have to share a greater portion of the take with them as opposed to novices. Perhaps Lovewell thought 47 men were enough to take Pequawket, destroy its inhabitants, and collect their scalps.

Lovewell led his company to disaster. Near Saco Pond (now Lovewell's Pond), Maine, the scalp hunters came across what appeared to be a lone Indian. In their haste to fall upon what they thought was an easy victim, Lovewell's men threw caution to the wind, dropped their packs to the ground, and gave chase. It was a trap; nearly 100 Indians were waiting. Lovewell had made a mistake that Church, the Gorhams, Frost, and Harmon never made. In the quest for fame and fortune, Lovewell had

112 Thomas Symmes, "Lovewell Lamented, or a Sermon Occasion'd by the Fall of the Brave Captain John Lovewell" (1725; reprint, *Early American Imprints, 1639–1800*, ed. American Antiquarian Society [New Canaan, CT: Readex, 1981–1982]), microfiche 2705.

113 Ezra Scollay Stearns, "Lovewell's Men," *NEHGR* 63 (1909): 288.

ignored a basic rule of ranging: measured audacity. Lovewell fell at the Indians' first volley of fire, while his men, many of them panic-stricken, scrambled to find cover behind trees. Luckily for a handful of the scalp hunters, Lovewell, the previous day, had constructed a "fort" to the south and left nine men there with supplies. The overmatched and outnumbered survivors of the ambush rushed back to it. The Abenakis pursued them only a short distance before they returned to scalp and mutilate Lovewell's corpse. All told, only 12 of Lovewell's men, including Eleazer and David Melven, survived the ambush.[114]

Despite the drama that surrounds Lovewell's disaster, it remains a relatively little-known affair. Yet, we should not discount Father Râle's War as an obscure early-eighteenth-century conflict. Instead, we can see in it, as well as in the Tuscarora and Yamasee Wars, trends that helped shape the future of American military history. In them, Americans combined the lessons of a century's worth of experience with extirpative war, ranging, and scalp hunting into a single way of war. That first way of war, forged in the foundry of the seventeenth- and early-eighteenth-century's Indian wars, shaped American war making well into the nineteenth century. It is therefore with some irony that Thomas Jefferson, at the end of the colonial era's Indian conflicts, attributed the killing of innocent men, women, and children solely to "savage" Indians.

114   Eleazer Tyng to Dummer, May 12, 1725, *Baxter MSS*, 10: 268–269.

2

The First Way of War in the North American Wars of King George II, 1739–1755

In late 1752, Governor Peregrine Thomas Hopson dispatched to the Board of Trade a report in which he assessed the contributions that American rangers had made to Nova Scotia's defense. The Board wanted Hopson's opinion on the necessity and feasibility of keeping a company of rangers in that colony's defensive establishment. While Hopson failed to offer a precise recommendation on the exact number of them needed in Nova Scotia, he nonetheless provided a justification for keeping at least a minimal force of rangers on the colony's rolls. "I am not able to inform your Lordships that I have heard of any particular exploit worth remarking being done by the Rangers," Hopson wrote, "the nature of their service, being irregular, scarcely admits of it, but they have most assuredly been of great utility, such as protecting the out settlers, ranging the Country, and marching upon services the regulars would not be spared for."[1]

Hopson's assessment of the rangers' "great utility" points to the central and ubiquitous role that they played not only in Nova Scotia, but in each of the first three Wars of King George II – the War of Jenkins' Ear, King George's War, and Father Le Loutre's War.[2] British officials and

---

1 Hopson to Board of Trade, October 16, 1752, Thomas B. Akins, ed., *Selections from the Public Documents of the Province of Nova Scotia* (Halifax: Charles Annand, Publisher, 1869), 680, hereafter *NS Docs.*
2 No one has given the conflict of 1749–1755 in Nova Scotia a formal name. Since Father Jean-Louis Le Loutre was as responsible for the war in Nova Scotia in the early 1750s as Father Sébastien Râle was for the conflict that took his name, I therefore have chosen to refer to it as Father Le Loutre's War. The most modern account of Le Loutre's career is *DCB*, s.v. "Le Loutre, Jean-Louis." Lawrence Henry Gipson, in his *British Empire before the American Revolution*, Vol. 5, *Zones of International Friction: The Great Lakes Frontier, Canada, the West Indies, India 1748–1754* (New York: Alfred A. Knopf, 1942), 166–206, discussed the struggle between Americans and Britons with Acadians, Frenchmen, and Indians in Acadia without giving that struggle a name. Both John C. Webster and Norman Rogers discussed the career of Le Loutre in their respective *The Career of the Abbé Le Loutre in Nova Scotia, with a Translation of his Autobiography* (Shediac, NB: John C. Webster, 1933) and "The Abbé Le Loutre," *Canadian Historical Review* 11 (1930): 105–128. Le Loutre's autobiography can be found in "Une Autobiographie de L'Abbé Le Loutre," *Nova Francia* 6 (1931): 1–34. John Bartlet Brebner devoted chapter 7 of his *New England's Outpost: Acadia before the Conquest of Canada*

commanders in those conflicts, first out of military necessity and then out of preference, turned to American rangers. The rangers, in turn, used the first way of war as the first line of defense of the colonies and became the troops most capable of harassing, intimidating, and destroying enemy armies and noncombatants. In the War of Jenkins' Ear, rangers shielded the Georgia frontier from invasion by Spaniards and Indians and wreaked havoc upon large portions of Spanish Florida. During King George's War, they provided, albeit only with marginal effectiveness, the first line of defense for backcountry settlements along the New England and New York frontiers.[3] In Nova Scotia, during both King George's War and Father Le Loutre's War, the fate of the colony depended almost solely on the outcome of the clash between American rangers and the Acadians and their Mi'kmaq and Maliseet allies.

How those campaigns fit in the development of Americans' first way of war marks an important stage in the evolution of American military culture. While engaging in what the ranger captain John Gorham called "the most Hazardous and fatiguing Duty that is Required in this part of the World,"[4] American rangers won partial acceptance and legitimacy for their way of war from Britons in North America, as well as refined their tactics. Indeed, in the Wars of King George II, both colonists and Britons came to see the tactics of the rangers as both an acceptable and an effective means of campaigning.

I. The War of Jenkins' Ear, 1739–1743[5]

Through the late seventeenth and well into the first third of the eighteenth century, Carolina rangers employing the first way of war raided

(New York: Columbia University Press, 1927), 166–202, to the 1749–1755 conflict but did not give it a formal title. Francis Parkman covered the war in Nova Scotia in the fourth chapter of the first volume of *Montcalm and Wolfe*, 2 vols. (1884; reprint, New Library ed. [Boston: Little, Brown, and Company, 1905]).

3   In the late eighteenth century, Samuel Drake used a "Diary of Depredations," or a litany of devastation and death that French and Indian raiders wrought on American frontier communities, to describe the course of King George's War on the New England frontier. See Samuel G. Drake, *A Particular History of the Five Years French and Indian War in New England* (Albany, NY: Joel Munsell, 1870), 89. Modern scholarship, however, seems to have abandoned Drake's focus on the frontier aspects of the war to focus instead on the much better documented and more visible operations of the New England provincial troops, such as their success at Louisbourg or the stillborn Canada Expedition of 1746.

4   John Gorham to William Shirley, November 1749, John Gorham MSS, William L. Clements Library, Ann Arbor, MI.

5   The most detailed study of military affairs and the War of Jenkins' Ear on the Southern frontier is Larry E. Ivers, *British Drums on the Southern Frontier: The Military Colonization of Georgia, 1733–1749* (Chapel Hill: University of North Carolina Press, 1974). For

Spanish-allied Guale (Georgia) and Apalachee (Florida panhandle) Indians with devastating effectiveness.[6] In the 1680s and 1690s, Carolinians attacked the Spanish settlements in Guale, destroyed them, and compelled both the Spanish and their Indian allies to abandon the area. During Queen Anne's War, South Carolina's Governor James Moore led 50 scalp hunters and 1,000 Indian auxiliaries to "go a slave hunting" in Apalachee. After ravaging western Florida, Moore and his men returned to Carolina with over 4,000 Indian slaves.[7] A generation later, as their expertise in ranging and scalp hunting had improved, the colonists needed fewer Indians to support their forays into Florida. In 1727, in retaliation for Yamasee attacks on English traders traveling on the Carolina frontier, Colonel John Palmer led 100 rangers and 100 friendly Indians against Nombre de Dios, the Yamasees' main settlement outside San Agustín, to which they had fled in 1717 during the Yamasee War. Palmer's rangers and Indians approached Nombre de Dios undetected, killed 30 Yamasees, and drove the rest into Castillo de San Marcos – the Spaniards' fort at San Agustín. From inside the Castillo, the Yamasees watched the Americans sack and loot Nombre de Dios and then retreat with impunity to Carolina. Although his army could not take and hold San Agustín, South Carolinians saw Palmer's campaign as a great victory. "We have now Balanced accounts with them," one Carolinian noted after Palmer returned to Charleston, "and it's my opinion that they never will come near us more."[8]

American rangers played an even larger part in the defense of Georgia from the colony's first days of settlement. Brigadier General James Oglethorpe, Georgia's founder, knew that the fledgling British settlements offered easy targets to Spanish and Indian raiders.[9] Having received virtually no military support from Britain, Oglethorpe had little choice but

a study that focuses on the relationship between rangers, militia, and British regulars, see James M. Johnson, *Militiamen, Rangers, and Redcoats: The Military in Georgia, 1754–1776* (Macon, GA: Mercer University Press, 1992). Although Johnson's book focuses on the years after 1754 and shows how the militia became the dominant military entity in Georgia, his first and second chapters point to the important role that rangers had in the defense of early Georgia.

6   In the late sixteenth century, Franciscan friars labored to extend from San Agustín a string of Indian missions in Guale and Apalachee. For the Spanish and Franciscan efforts to settle and proselytize in Georgia, see David J. Weber, *The Spanish Frontier in North America* (New Haven, CT: Yale University Press, 1992), 6, 36–37, 67–68, 100–103, 117, 179–181, 349.

7   Quoted in J. Leitch Wright, Jr., *Anglo–Spanish Rivalry in North America* (Athens: University of Georgia Press, 1971), 64. For further details on Moore's 1702 San Agustín campaign, see Verner W. Crane, *The Southern Frontier, 1670–1732* (Ann Arbor: University of Michigan Press, 1956), 75–78. Weber, *Spanish Frontier*, 142–143.

8   Quoted in Crane, *Southern Frontier*, 250.

9   Although uninhabited by Spaniards, Guale technically remained a possession of Spain. See Harman Verelst to Earl of Wilmington, April 24, 1742, *CTBP*, 5: doc. 70.

to depend on colonists to protect Georgia's settlements. As one of his first acts upon arriving in Georgia as commander-in-chief of the colony, Oglethorpe therefore enlisted the services of Captain James McPhearson's company of South Carolina mounted rangers. McPhearson's Rangers offered Oglethorpe a highly mobile and responsive force with which to protect the out settlements. Posted in detachments along a string of blockhouses situated outside the first settlements, the rangers provided both early warning and reconnaissance functions and gave the settlers a cadre of trained soldiers around whom to rally in times of crisis.[10] For the first few years of settlement, the rangers were the only significant military force in the colony capable of responding to Indian or Spanish attacks.

Oglethorpe quickly came to appreciate the services the rangers provided. He tried to convert most of his small army of British regulars into rangers, understanding that in Georgia his troops had to learn to operate independently if they were to be of any use against mobile Indians and Spanish raiders. Shortly after the men of the Forty-second Regiment arrived from Scotland, Oglethorpe therefore commissioned Hugh Mackay, Jr., a Highlander and former British Army officer and settler agent for the Trustees of Georgia, to raise from the regulars a company of "Highland Rangers." Scottish Highlanders had a reputation as tough and often wild fighters. Such men, Oglethorpe hoped, would make the transition from European regular to North American ranger with relative ease.[11]

Oglethorpe's appointment of Mackay to lead the Highland Rangers was significant in that he chose an "American" to lead British regulars. Oglethorpe could have selected any one of the company officers of the Forty-second Regiment to command the rangers, yet he selected Mackay, an officer with military experience in both Europe and North America.

10   Sarah B. Gober Temple and Kenneth Coleman, *Georgia Journeys. Being an Account of the Lives of Georgia's Original Settlers and Many Other Early Settlers from the Founding of the Colony in 1732 until the Institution of Royal Government in 1754* (Athens: University of Georgia Press, 1961), 43.

11   Oglethorpe found soldiers for the 684-man-strong Forty-second Regiment of Foot by drafting 250 regulars from the Twenty-fifth Regiment of Foot stationed at Gibraltar and enlisting men from central and northern England, including many Scottish Highlanders. See Ivers, *British Drums*, 91, and James Michael Hill, *Celtic Warfare, 1595–1763* (Edinburgh: John Donald Publishers, Ltd., 1986), chap. 1. Hill has written, "Because the Celts emphasized the individual warrior, they were at their best in the field when operating in small, mobile armies" (p. 2). Of course, not all Irishmen were wildly independent soldiers; many served as regular infantry in the English armies. See Gervase Phillips, "Irish *Ceatharnaigh* in English Service, 1544–1550, and the Development of 'Gaelic Warfare'," *JSAHR* 78 (2000): 163–182. Anthony Parker has suggested that Highlanders were "both farmers and soldiers by training and tradition." From the start, the Trustees and Oglethorpe understood that Georgia would be both a plantation and a military outpost. See Parker, *Scottish Highlanders in Colonial Georgia: The Recruitment, Emigration, and Settlement of Darien, 1735–1748* (Athens: University of Georgia Press, 1997), 21.

Indeed, here was what normally would have been considered primarily a militia officer – although Mackay was a half-pay British officer – placed in command of British regulars. Oglethorpe understood that New World conditions necessitated a willingness to put aside any preconceived notions about the inherent superiority of regulars that their officers may have held. In the process, Oglethorpe became the first of several high-ranking British officers who, after serving in North America, realized that military success in the colonies would depend upon the British Army's ability to embrace the first way of war.

Between Oglethorpe and the Trustees for Georgia (the de facto ruling body of the colony), however, the General alone appreciated the colony's need for rangers. After the creation of the Highland Rangers, the parsimonious Trustees, even though Secretary of State for the Southern Department Thomas Pelham-Holles, duke of Newcastle, had advised them that war with Spain was imminent, refused to authorize funding to equip and pay for them. Oglethorpe responded with a flurry of letters and reports in which he predicted the dangerous state into which the colony's defense would fall without rangers. The regulars, he reminded the Trustees, "can defend the parts they are in, but they cannot march on foot over the waters without boats nor overtake horse or Indians on foot in the vast woods on the continent" – only the rangers could do that.[12] To the duke of Newcastle, he wrote that without rangers, he could not prevent Spanish cavalry from raiding and devastating Georgia, nor could he gain any intelligence or warning about enemy forces marching from Florida. He advised Harman Verelst (his personal agent in London) that he could not depend on Indians. Rum and smallpox carried by Carolina traders had alienated the Cherokees from the British side.[13] Oglethorpe traveled personally to the Cherokee towns in the hope of convincing them to assist the British if war broke out between Great Britain and Spain. In October 1739, just before the outbreak of hostilities, in exchange for 1,500 bushels of corn, Oglethorpe won from them a promise that they would take the field against the Spanish. At that time, however, he realized his Indian allies had their, not Great Britain's, best interests at heart and could change sides without notice. He also knew that all the while Spanish emissaries were doing their utmost to turn the Cherokees and other Indians against the British.[14]

12　Oglethorpe to Trustees for Georgia, November 16, 1739, *CSPC, 1739*, doc. 467.
13　Oglethorpe to Duke of Newcastle, October 8, 1739, ibid., doc. 409. Oglethorpe to Verelst, October 19, 1739, ibid., doc. 429.
14　Earl of Egmont's journal, October 5, 1739, *Colonial Records of the State of Georgia*, comp. Allen D. Chandler (1904–1916; reprint; 25 vols. [New York: AMS Press, 1970]), 5: 231; Thomas Causton to Trustees for Georgia, January 14, 1739, *CSPC, 1739*, doc. 17.

The answer, as Oglethorpe saw it, was to form two 30-man troops of American rangers and post them on the frontier, from where they could warn of, and slow, any Spanish advance into Georgia. Oglethorpe hoped that a third company of rangers patrolling Georgia's coastal waterways in specially designed shallow-draft "scout boats" would detect an amphibious Spanish or French invasion of the colony.[15]

Oglethorpe finally got the rangers he wanted after a Spanish force decapitated two soldiers on Amelia Island in November 1739. After the attack, Oglethorpe rushed a letter to the Trustees in which he claimed he must have the rangers immediately; "otherwise there will be no possibility of the people's going out to plant without being murdered as those Highlanders were." The Trustees consented and authorized Oglethorpe to act as he saw best. Oglethorpe immediately raised his companies for the frontier, as well as the rangers for the scout boat corps. Had it not been for rangers rushing to the field in November 1739, Oglethorpe later reported, the outlying settlements "must all have been destroyed."[16]

Before the Amelia Island raid by the Spanish, Oglethorpe had been concerned primarily with how the rangers fit into Georgia's defensive scheme; after November 1739, he looked for ways to use his rangers offensively. He quickly realized that they could be the linchpin of his design for the conquest of Florida. "I think the best way [to defeat the Spanish]," he wrote, "is to make use of our strength [in rangers] and beat them [the Spanish and Indians] out of the field and destroy their plantations and out settlements."[17] Such attacks, he reported, "would daunt them so heartily that we might take Augustine."[18]

In December 1739, Oglethorpe led the rangers on the first of his three invasions of Florida. He conceived the mission as little more than a raid to destroy Spanish plantations and intimidate the Indians and escaped slaves living in maroon communities in North Florida. As the rangers marched south, they accordingly sacked and looted villages in their path. As they burned and pillaged, Oglethorpe's Indian allies, with the General's encouragement, combed the countryside and scalped Spanish-allied Indians and runaway slaves from the British colonies. In a campaign that lasted for several weeks, the rangers "ravaged Florida" and seized Spain's northernmost outpost at San Francisco de Pupo.[19] Upon returning to his

15 Oglethorpe to Trustees for Georgia, October 5, 1739, "Letters from James Oglethorpe to the Trustees of the Colony and Others, from October 1735 to August 1744," *Georgia Historical Society Collections* 3, pt. 2 (1873): 82.
16 Oglethorpe to Trustees for Georgia, December 29, 1739, *CSPC, 1739*, doc. 536.
17 Oglethorpe to Trustees for Georgia, November 16, 1739, ibid., doc. 467.
18 Oglethorpe to Trustees for Georgia, December 29, 1739, ibid., doc. 536.
19 Oglethorpe to William Stephens, February 1, 1739/1740, "Letters from James Oglethorpe," 105. William Stephens was the secretary to the Trustees in Georgia. Anon., "A Ranger's Report of Travels with General Oglethorpe, 1739–1742," *Travels*

headquarters at Frederica, Oglethorpe informed the Trustees that he and his rangers would return to Spanish Florida in the spring and take San Agustín.[20]

The rangers proved invaluable in Oglethorpe's second and larger invasion of Florida. In the spring of 1740, Oglethorpe placed them in the lead of a 1,500-man army of Georgia and South Carolina militia and British regulars as it advanced toward San Agustín. The rangers performed admirably as the vanguard of the invasion force and, one ranger reported, "so harassed the Spaniards that they were afraid to appear without the walls of St. Augustine."[21] Indeed, the rangers' successes were the only ones of the campaign. In the ensuing siege of Castillo de San Marcos, Oglethorpe's dream of the conquest of Spanish Florida crumbled in the face of poor planning, inadequate supplies, lack of coordination between land and sea forces, and disease.[22]

During the lull between his offensive campaigns, Oglethorpe had little choice but to put the defense of Georgia in the rangers' hands. Because the War Office had earmarked virtually all military resources in North America and the West Indies for the campaign against Cartagena (in present-day Columbia), he realized that he could expect no reinforcements of British regulars or American provincials in either 1740 or 1741. Yet at the same time, he faced the threat of an invasion of Georgia by the Spanish-allied French garrison at Mobile and its 1,500 Choctaw allies. He also rightly suspected that the Spanish were preparing to launch an amphibious campaign designed to respond in kind to the rangers' two forays into Florida.[23]

After assessing the situation, Oglethorpe concluded that rangers were the only troops that could defend the outlying plantations and prevent the enemy's depredations. Since any overland invasion from Mobile would have to cross several major rivers, Oglethorpe hoped that "a large body of Rangers with the assistance of the Indians might stop them there." He added that other companies of rangers on the Georgia–Florida border

in the American Colonies, ed. Newton D. Mereness (New York: Macmillan Company, 1916), 225; Harman Verelst to Earl Wilmington, April 24, 1742, *Treasury Books and Papers* 5 (1742): doc. 70.

20 Oglethorpe to Trustees for Georgia, December 29, 1739, *CSPC, 1739*, doc. 536.
21 "A Ranger's Report," 228.
22 Trevor R. Reese, in "Britain's Military Support for Georgia in the War of 1739–1748," *GHQ* 43 (1959): 1–10, wrote that the Georgia–Florida theater of operations was a military sideshow for British planners. For Oglethorpe's siege, see Wright, *Anglo–Spanish Rivalry*, 92–93; William Stephens's Journal, July 18, 1740, *Colonial Records of Georgia*, 4: 622.
23 ? to Juan Franciso de Güemes y Horcasitas, October 31, 1741, C. DeWitt Wilcox, ed. and trans., "The Spanish Official Account of the Attack on the Colony of Georgia in America, and of Its Defeat on St. Simons Island by General James Oglethorpe," *Georgia Historical Society Collections* 8, pt. 3 (1913): 21–22.

would be "very useful in blocking up Saint Augustine" and intercepting and defeating Spanish and Indian raiders.[24]

The rangers in fact were instrumental in driving the Spanish army from Georgia in the summer of 1742 when the Spanish invasion finally materialized. Rangers were the first troops to detect Manuel de Montiano's 2,000-man invasion force off St. Simons Island, and once the Spanish army had landed in Georgia, they contained it on its beachhead until Oglethorpe could rush reinforcements of militia and regulars to the front. In two bloody engagements, ranger detachments took the lead in harrying the Spanish and inflicted most of the nearly 200 casualties they suffered as they tried to advance toward Frederica. Then, as the Spanish force sat dejectedly on the beach, rangers and Indians infiltrated the Spanish camp. One ranger bragged that he and several other rangers and Indians shot nine Spaniards inside their lines.[25] The Americans' sniping pushed the Spaniards' morale even lower, and with his inability to break out of the St. Simons Island beachhead, certainly contributed to Montiano's decision to retreat.

In the final major action of the war, in March 1743, American rangers again served Oglethorpe well. Oglethorpe had set out for Florida at the head of a party of Georgia rangers and Indians to plunder and pillage Spanish outposts. Wrongly called the "Second Siege" of San Agustín, Oglethorpe's 1743 invasion was a repeat of Palmer's 1727 operation – a spoiling raid. His intention was not to take San Agustín, but to inflict as much punishment as possible on the Spaniards and their Indian and runaway slave allies. In the face of the rangers' onslaught, "the usual terror took them and they retired within the walls of St. Augustine."[26] After looting what they could, Oglethorpe's rangers again burned the surrounding settlements and marched victoriously north.

Because of their exemplary service in the War of Jenkins' Ear, American rangers won from Oglethorpe and other high British officials a place in the royal military establishment. They recognized that regulars were of little use on the frontier with the Spanish, Cherokees, and Creeks. Only American rangers, or British troops trained to act like them, could secure Georgia's borders and perhaps expand the empire at the cost of the Indians and Spaniards. Thus, between 1743 and 1747, the British War Office and Parliament authorized two companies of American rangers

24 Verelst to the Treasury, August 5, 1742, *CTBP*, 5: doc. 149; Oglethorpe to Trustees for Georgia, June 29, 1741, "Letters from James Oglethorpe," 117.
25 "A Ranger's Report," 233. James Oglethorpe's Account of the Spanish Invasion of Georgia, July 30, 1742, "Letters from James Oglethorpe," 135; Ivers, *British Drums*, 157; "A Ranger's Report," 234–235.
26 Quoted in Wright, *Anglo–Spanish Rivalry*, 97.

and 115 men in the Highland Rangers for full-time service in Georgia.[27] In 1743, Oglethorpe returned to England in time to apply the lesson he had learned as the commander of rangers in America to suppressing the Jacobite rebellion of 1745.

II. King George's War, 1744–1748: New England and New York

In 1744, Governor William Shirley placed the responsibility for the defense of Massachusetts's frontier in the hands of American rangers. Shirley and the frontiersmen rightly suspected that if war erupted between France and Great Britain, waves of Canadian and Indian raiders would swoop down on the New England frontier. Knowing that the New England colonies had effectively employed rangers in previous wars, in March he raised ten 50-man companies of what he called "snowshoe men," or rangers. He described their mission to the duke of Newcastle as "to hold themselves ready at the shortest Warning to go in pursuit of any Party of Indians, who frequently in time of War make sudden Incursions, whilst there is a deep Snow upon the Ground, and retreat as suddenly into the Woods after having done what Mischief they can."[28] Shirley then ordered the snowshoe men to construct a line of blockhouses along the frontier as bases from which (he hoped) they could screen New England's out settlements. In June, with the campaigning season well underway, Shirley ordered Colonel John Stoddard, commander of Massachusetts's frontier forces, to move his rangers to positions from which they could intercept and destroy enemy raiders. In October, upon Shirley's recommendation, Massachusetts's General Assembly followed a then well-established tradition and offered a £100 bounty on Indian scalps.[29] However, with his

27 *CTBP*, 5: doc. 43-h; *Treasury Books and Papers 5* (1745): doc. 30; House of Commons Proceedings, January 16, 1745/1746, Leo Francis Stock, ed., *Proceedings and Debates of the British Parliaments Respecting North America, Volume 5, 1739–1754* (Washington, DC: Carnegie Institution, 1941), 227 (hereafter Stock, *Proceedings and Debates*); House of Commons Proceedings, March 10, 1748/1749, ibid., 300. Although King George II ordered the rangers disbanded in 1747 to reduce what seemed unnecessary costs in peacetime, Parliament continued to fund two companies of rangers as late as 1749. See Johnson, *Militiamen, Rangers, and Redcoats*, 12.
28 Shirley to Duke of Newcastle, March 23, 1743/1744, *The Correspondence of William Shirley*, ed. Charles Henry Lincoln, 2 vols. (New York: Macmillan Company, 1912), 1: 115.
29 Shirley to Lords of Trade, August 10, 1744, ibid., 1: 138. Shirley to Stoddard, June 2, 1744, ibid., 1: 127–128; Massachusetts General Court, *The Acts and Resolves, Public and Private, of the Province of the Massachusetts Bay*, 21 vols. (Boston: Massachusetts General Court, 1869–1922), 3: 218, hereafter *Acts and Resolves*.

thoughts turning increasingly to the Louisbourg campaign planned for the spring of 1745, the Iroquois League maintaining its long-held position of neutrality and thereby denying Shirley the substantial auxiliaries he needed, and nearly 200 miles of snowy wilderness separating the northernmost American positions from Canadian settlements, the Governor did not order a winter campaign.[30] He directed that the rangers remain in their garrisons and await the spring's French and Indian attacks on the frontier.

With the Americans on the defensive – Benjamin Doolittle noted that the colonists "never kept Men in the woods towards Crown-Point [Fort St. Frédéric] to discover their large Bodies coming down upon us, and give notice of an approaching Enemy"[31] – Abenakis from St. François fell upon settlements in New Hampshire and northern Massachusetts throughout the summer of 1745, killed dozens of settlers, and razed many undefended farms.[32] Among the homesteads the Abenakis attacked was one on the Great Meadow area belonging to James and Mary Rogers; their 14-year-old son, Robert, thereafter enlisted in Captain Daniel Ladd's ranger company as an Indian fighter.[33] Thus began the career for the man who would become North America's best-known ranger.

Yet Rogers's campaigns against the Abenakis lay far in the future, and the provincial troops' victory at Louisbourg had done little to stop the Indian raids on the frontier. In the summer and fall of 1745, therefore, the New England rangers and backcountry settlers watched from their blockhouses while French and Indian raiders destroyed large portions of the northern frontier. The rangers' task was much akin to trying to hold back the ocean with a broom. There were simply too many Frenchmen and Indians spread across a large area for the rangers to intercept them all. Two emblematic instances can stand as representative of a great many raids. In August, 700 Canadians and Indians marched undetected from

---

30   In late 1744 and early 1745, the Iroquois League remained committed to neutrality and the French determined to do nothing to antagonize them. See M. [Charles, marquis] de Beauharnois to Count [Jean-Frédéric Phélypeaux] de Maurepas, June 18, 1745, *NYCD*, 10: 2. It is no coincidence that in the summer of 1745 the New York Assembly also passed a law authorizing payment to both colonists and Indians for enemy scalps. See Lords of Trade Books, *NYCD*, 6: 647.

31   Benjamin Doolittle, "A Short Narrative of Mischief Done by the French and Indian Enemy on the Western Frontiers of the Province of Massachusetts-Bay" (1750; reprint, *Early American Imprints, 1639–1800* [New Canaan, CT: Readex, 1981–1982]), microfiche 6488: 21.

32   Colin G. Calloway, *The Western Abenakis of Vermont, 1600–1800: War, Migration, and the Survival of an Indian People* (Norman: University of Oklahoma Press, 1990), 149–150.

33   Lucius M. Boltwood, "Border Indian Massacres in Massachusetts, From 1703 to 1746," *NEHGR* 9 (1855): 163. John Cuneo, *Robert Rogers of the Rangers* (1952, reprint; New York: Richardson & Steirman, 1987), 7.

Crown Point and overwhelmed the company of Bay Colony militia stationed at Fort Massachusetts.[34] Three months later, another French force struck Saratoga. The Canadians and Indians, Robert Sanders reported, "appeared & did Beset all the houses there, Burnt & Destroyed all that Came before them Left only one Sawmill Standing which stood a Little out of their way it seems, took along with them such Booty as they thought fit, Kilt & took Captives 100 or 101 persons Black & white."[35]

After the bloodletting of 1745, settlers in the backcountry lived in fear that Indian or French raiders would strike them next. Frontier communities barraged crown officials in Albany, Boston, and Portsmouth with pleas for military assistance. Shirley and his coterie of politician-merchants in Boston responded with a plan for a large-scale and expensive two-pronged invasion of Canada from Albany and Louisbourg. That, of course, would do little or nothing to stop the raids in the near term, and many settlers simply fled their homes for the safety of the more settled areas, just as their grandparents and parents had done in earlier wars. Those with the fortitude to remain, Ebenezer Eastman reported from the Connecticut River settlements in March 1746, lived "in deadly fear that they shall be attacked" by a "Body of the enemy [that] is waiting an opportunity to do mischief!" If the Governor and Council of New Hampshire did not send troops to protect the settlers who stayed behind, Eastman warned, they too surely would "quit the Place."[36]

Shirley and Benning Wentworth, the Governor of New Hampshire, rushed ranger companies to the frontier to halt the exodus of backcountry settlers. The rangers, however, found themselves mired in a difficult and bloody war of attrition against an elusive enemy. Captain Daniel Ladd's company of rangers, for instance, spent nearly three months patrolling the New Hampshire wilderness. Only after five weeks in the woods did they encounter their first Indians, and only when 40 warriors ambushed eight rangers while on patrol. Daniel Gilman, the only survivor of the ambush, reported that as he came over the saddle of a hill, scores of Indians who had concealed themselves in the woods "rose up and shot a volley and run out into the path, making all sort of howling and yelling." Although the rangers tried to rally, the fight was over in an instant, and five rangers "were killed down dead on the spot" and two others taken captive. As Gilman ran the two miles back to the rangers' main

34 Abstract of Despatches received from Canada, *NYCD*, 10: 77.
35 Robert Sanders to William Johnson, November 28, 1745, *WJP*, 1: 43; Abstract of Despatches from Canada, *NYCD*, 10: 76. See also Military and Other Operations in Canada during the Years 1745–1746, ibid., 10: 38.
36 See Ebenezer Eastman to [New Hampshire] Council, March 12, 1746, Nathaniel Bouton, ed., *Documents and Records Relating to the Province of New Hampshire*, 23 vols. (Concord, NH: George E. Jenks, State Printer, 1867–1893), 5: 859.

camp, the Indians scalped the American dead and then melted into the woods.

The rest of Ladd's men had little stomach for pursuing the Indians. They took two hours to organize a relief party. Upon arriving at the site of the ambush, instead of following the Indians' trail, they chose to transport their dead back to camp. Then, after tracking for only a short distance the blood trail left by a wounded man, the rangers, fearing another ambush, lost their nerve and beat a hasty retreat for the blockhouse at present-day Rumford, Maine.[37] At the end of the campaigning season, Ladd's rangers, like many others on the frontier, had little to look back upon favorably. They had suffered seven causalities, inflicted only one on the enemy, and been driven from the field.

Nonetheless, in the minds of several British administrators, the best near-term hope for the frontier remained the rangers and scalp hunters. Newcastle, from his office in Great Britain and possessing probably little more than a rudimentary understanding of the distances and terrain that a ranger force would have to cover before it reached Canada, directed Shirley to use his rangers in the interim to "destroy the open country between Quebec and Montreal."[38] Shirley, although aware of the rangers' less than impressive record in the previous campaigning season, increased Massachusetts's bounty on Indian scalps to £250 in hopes of luring more capable and aggressive men into the backcountry service. In August, New York's Governor George Clinton, in hopes of enticing the Iroquois from their neutralist stance, authorized William Johnson to offer the Mohawks bounties on scalps if they would go "against the French & their Indians in Canada to harass and Alarm their Quarters in Parts and to take Prisoners for Intelligence."[39] Clinton earlier had reported to the Lords of Trade that upwards of 1,000 Iroquois seemed willing to raise the hatchet on the British side. Convinced that the British would supplant them with the Indians of the Ohio country as the primary recipients and distributors of trade goods, the Mohawks were more amenable to take up the hatchet for them. Johnson responded that he indeed could bring many Iroquois

37   Abner Clough, "Abner Clough's Journal," *New Hampshire Historical Society Collections* 4 (1834): 204–214. Robert Rogers joined Ladd's company after the ambush Gilman described. See Cuneo, *Robert Rogers*, 8.

38   Duke of Newcastle to Shirley, April 9, 1746, Douglas Brymner, ed., *Report on Canadian Archives, 1894: Calendar of Papers Relating to Nova Scotia* (Ottawa: S. E. Dawson for the Public Archives of Canada, 1895), 113, hereafter *RCA 1894*. Sara Stidstone Gronim, in "Geography and Persuasion: Maps in British Colonial New York," *WMQ* 58 (2001): 375, argues that the geography of New York was "assimilated slowly and erratically in Britain."

39   *Acts and Resolves*, 3: 342. George Clinton to William Johnson, August 28, 1746, *WJP*, 1: 60.

into Britain's camp, and that a promise of a mere £10 for each scalp was sufficient to get the Indians to go against the French.[40]

The rangers and Iroquois met with some successes in 1746. While most of the provincials returned home after the disbanding of Shirley's Canada expedition, others remained at Albany and used it as a base from which to raid northward in hopes of collecting the generous scalp rewards offered by the northern colonies.[41] Captain Eleazer Melven's company of rangers and allied Indians, for instance, ventured into Canada in search of Indian and French scalps. By early 1747 Johnson, perhaps exaggerating his influence among the Mohawks, wrote to Clinton that he had at his home "daily such Numbers of Indians about me for Scalping money" that he could not pay them all.[42]

Nevertheless, after the initial enthusiasm for scalp hunting passed, most of the rangers retreated to their blockhouses to wait out the winter, leaving the frontier for all practical purposes undefended. It was simply impossible to build an impermeable barrier of patrols along the frontier. Benjamin Doolittle, for instance, observed that it was "a rare thing" when an American obtained an Indian scalp.[43] Canadians and Indians, selecting only targets they felt reasonably certain of taking, continued to destroy isolated frontier settlements and to assault American forts and garrisons. The results were frightful for the settlers along the frontier. In January 1748, Roland-Michel Barrin, marquis de La Galissonnière, New France's Governor-General, reported that his Indians had "experienced their usual success in enemy territory" and brought him 150 American scalps and 112 prisoners.[44]

40 Clinton to Lords of Trade, July 24, 1747, *NYCD*, 6: 364; Johnson to Clinton, May 7, 1747, ibid., 6: 361. Ironically, after King George's War, the British crown cut its presents to the Iroquois. See Richard White, *The Middle Ground: Indians, Empires, and Republics in the Great Lakes Region, 1650–1815* (New York: Cambridge University Press, 1991), chap. 6, esp. 226.

41 Shirley's plan to take Canada unraveled in the fall of 1746. First, Lieutenant General James St. Clair's British regulars – troops that Whitehall had promised the provincials to support the invasion up the St. Lawrence – never arrived at Louisbourg. See John Rutherford to William Johnson, June 12, 1746, *WJP*, 1: 52. In the fall, the War Office and Shirley called off the campaign, disbanded the provincials, and presented Parliament with a bill for over £220,000 for an expedition that did not leave its muster points. House of Commons Proceedings, March 12, 1749/1750, Stock, *Proceedings and Debates*, 415–418.

42 Doolittle, "A Narrative," 21. Eleazer Melven, "Journal of Captain Eleazer Melven," *New Hampshire Historical Society Collections* 5 (1837): 207. Johnson to Clinton, May 31, 1747, *WJP*, 1: 96.

43 Doolittle, "A Narrative," 20.

44 In April, a Canadian–Indian war party attacked the 30 American rangers stationed at No. 4 (Charleston, NH). After a siege of several days, during which the Indians tried to immolate the rangers inside the walls of the fort, the Indians withdrew. See Jaazaniah Crosby, "Annals of Charlestown, in the County of Sullivan, New Hampshire," *New*

Only after British and French plenipotentiaries signed a preliminary treaty of peace at Aix-la-Chapelle did the French and Indian raids on the frontier, and with them an important evolutionary phase in the first way of war, end.[45] American rangers, acting in a defensive posture, for four years had tried to stop the enemy's depredations. But "we may observe," Doolittle wrote in 1750, "that in this War, as we increased *our* Number of Men in our *Forts* or *Scouts*, the Enemy have increased *their* Numbers; and the longer the War continued, the oftener they came, and the more bold they grew."[46] Perhaps the only tangible success that the American side experienced along the New England frontier was when the Mohawks and rangers raided Canada. If anything, the events between 1744 and 1748 on the New England and New York frontiers showed the futility of defensive applications of the first way of war. A valuable truth about ranger operations thus emerged from the experience of King George's War in Massachusetts and New York: the first way of war, to be effective, needed to be waged offensively. The course of King George's War and Father Le Loutre's War in Nova Scotia proved the veracity of that proposition and, in the process, solidified offensive ranger warfare as part of Americans' first military culture.

III. King George's War, 1744–1748: Nova Scotia

King George's War in Nova Scotia originated in the ambiguous and often acrimonious relations among Americans, Indians, and Acadians in Maritime Canada. Great Britain had won possession of Nova Scotia following Queen Anne's War. By 1744, however, Nova Scotia was a British colony in name only. The overwhelming majority of the colony's inhabitants remained pro-French Acadians or descendants of Acadian-Mi'kmaq and Acadian-Maliseet unions.[47] Together, they were virtually indistinguishable to the Americans and British. In 1745, for example, the Governor-General and Intendant of New France noted that the English

Hampshire Historical Society Collections 4 (1836): 111–113. Abstract of M. [Roland-Michel Barrin, marquis] de La Galissonière's Despatches, January 8, 1748, *NYCD*, 10: 132.

45 British and French representatives signed the preliminary treaty on April 30, 1748. See House of Commons Proceedings, November 29, 1748, Stock, *Proceedings and Debates*, 286.
46 Doolittle, "A Narrative," 22.
47 Great Britain claimed Nova Scotia based on the success of the conquest of Annapolis Royal in 1710. With the change in sovereignty came changes in names. Port Royal became Annapolis Royal, while a major portion of Acadia became Nova Scotia. For British and American attitudes toward the peoples of Acadia, see Geoffrey Plank, *An Unsettled Conquest: The British Campaign Against the Peoples of Acadia* (Philadelphia: University of Pennsylvania Press, 2001).

The Nova Scotia frontier, 1740–1765

garrison at Annapolis Royal amounted to only 300 men, while "All the rest of Acadia is inhabited exclusively by French people," including 2,500 men capable of bearing arms at Beaubassin, Minas, and Annapolis Royal. "As regards the dispositions of the inhabitants towards us," they wrote, "all, with the exception of a very few small portion, are desirous of returning under the French dominion."[48] The English settlements at Annapolis Royal and Canso were thus little more than islands of British influence surrounded by a sea of hostile Acadians, Mi'kmaq, and Maliseets.

In early 1744 it became clear that the British garrison was in no position to fight and win a war in Nova Scotia should the Acadians or Indians

---

48 Messers. [Charles, Marquis] de Beauharnois and [Gilles] Hocquart to Count de Maurepas, September 12, 1745, *NYCD*, 10: 4. After 1714, the British and American population in Nova Scotia remained small, while the Acadian and Mi'kmaq populations grew considerably. See Paul Mascarene to Duke of Newcastle, June 7, 1739, *RCA 1894*, 93.

revolt against English rule. Father Jean-Louis Le Loutre, Jesuit missionary to the Mi'kmaq, had threatened Nova Scotia's Lieutenant Governor
Paul Mascarene the previous October that the Mi'kmaq were ready to
raise the hatchet against the British. Although Mascarene responded to
Le Loutre's threat with a crash program to improve the dilapidated fortifications around Annapolis Royal, he still worried that his 400 regulars,
thinly spread from Annapolis Royal to Canso and Placentia, Newfound-
land, were the wrong troops to counter an Acadian rebellion. Mascarene's
fears were realized in May 1744. François du Pont Duvivier led a force
of mostly Mi'kmaq and Troupes de la Marine against Canso, put the
village to the torch, burned a British man-of-war tender stationed there,
and seized the British settlers and garrison and took them as prisoners
to Louisbourg.[49] Mascarene, meanwhile, was powerless to respond. The
Mi'kmaq would have destroyed any detachment of regulars that he sent
into the countryside.

Both Mascarene and Shirley realized that the British forces in Nova
Scotia were in dire need of rangers to "beat the bush" against the Indians
and Acadians. Shirley responded to the French excursion against Canso
with a request to the Massachusetts Assembly for funding to raise two
60-man companies of rangers to be stationed at Annapolis Royal since,
he wrote, "A Company of Rangers would be of great service."[50]

In the summer of 1744, John Gorham of Barnstable, Massachusetts –
great-grandson of John Gorham I of King Philip's War and grandson
of John Gorham II of Benjamin Church's rangers of King Philip's and
King William's Wars, and heir to a family tradition of participating in
New England's wars that was now seven decades old – began recruiting men for one of the Nova Scotia companies of rangers. For his first
company Gorham could find only 20 Americans. Shirley and Mascarene
had failed to offer the generous bounties that traditionally had drawn
scalp hunters into ranger service, and most New England frontiersmen
probably were enlisting in the companies for service on the Massachusetts frontier. Gorham thus turned to Indians to fill out the ranks of his

49 Minutes of Council on a Letter from Le Loutre, October 10, 1743, *RCA 1894*, 98. Mascarene served as Lieutenant Governor of Annapolis Royal and chief military and civilian
administrator of the colony. House of Commons Proceedings, March 13, 1743/1944,
Stock, *Proceedings and Debates*, 178. Canso merited a company because it was a
major outpost for New England fishermen who worked the waters off Nova Scotia. See
Daniel Vickers, *Farmers and Fishermen: Two Centuries of Work in Essex County, Massachusetts, 1630–1850* (Chapel Hill: University of North Carolina Press for IEAHC,
1994), 150. Mascarene to Bastide, June 4, 1744, *RCA 1894*, 100. For the most complete
recent study of Canso in this period, see Mark Power Robison, "Maritime Frontiers:
The Evolution of Empire in Nova Scotia, 1713–1758" (Ph.D. diss., University of Colorado at Boulder, 2000).
50 Shirley to the General Court of Massachusetts, May 31, 1744, *Correspondence of
Shirley*, 1: 122; Mascarene to Shirley, July 7, 1744, *RCA 1894*, 101.

company. Twenty-two Indians, whom Gorham called "Mohawks," enlisted. Gorham's Mohawks just as likely were Maine Indians. Americans often referred to all Indians as "Mohawks," the Iroquois League still professed its neutrality, and Gorham, from the Cape of Massachusetts, would have looked to Maine instead of the distant New York frontier for Indian allies. Moreover, one of Gorham's Indians, whom the Americans knew as "Captain Sam," deserted Gorham's company for the "Eastern" or Maine Indians. Whatever the case, following in the tradition of his grandfather, who had commanded a joint American–Indian company in King William's War, Gorham selected his subalterns and noncommissioned officers from his family and the American volunteers. In another gesture toward family tradition, Gorham appointed his 18-year-old son, John Jr., as the company's clerk.[51]

Gorham was an ideal choice to command the American rangers in Nova Scotia because he was intimately familiar with the Maritimes. By the 1730s and 1740s, the Cape and Barnstable area was the poorest part of Massachusetts, with most of the little available land taken. During those years, Gorham traveled extensively in the Maritimes as a merchant and land speculator. In 1737, as captain of the brigantine *Greenland*, he had plied the Bay of Fundy; in 1738, he had petitioned Mascarene's predecessor for a grant of land on Sable Island on which he proposed to settle Huguenot settlers from Boston. During his years as a trader, Gorham even traveled to the Acadian-controlled areas of the Minas Basin and Chignecto Isthmus.[52]

Gorham, in the best tradition of the first way of war, had economic self-interest in mind in forming Gorham's Rangers. During his prewar travels to Minas and Chignecto, he certainly saw the fertile lands, rich fields, and snug houses of the Acadians. It is little wonder that throughout King George's and Father Le Loutre's Wars, Gorham was the most vociferous proponent of seizing the Acadians' lands as punishment for their "rebellious" actions. In November 1748, he proposed to settle a township on the eastern coast of Nova Scotia. When that proposal fell by the

---

51 Muster Roll for Gorham's Rangers, n.d., Gorham MSS; John Gorham, "Col. John Gorham's 'Wast Book' Facsimiles," ed. Frank W. Sprague, *NEHGR* 52 (1898): 192. By 1749, after the threat to the New England frontier had been lifted, Gorham's Rangers were all Americans. See Names Officers & Men on Comd when took 3 French Men, January 1, 1749, Gorham MSS. An examination of Gorham's muster roll from 1744 and the muster roll from 1749 shows that not a single Indian private who served in 1744 remained with the company five years later, nor had any of them been promoted to a noncommissioned officer or junior officer. William Sherriff to Josiah Willard, May 7, 1750, *Baxter MSS*, 12: 60.

52 George T. Bates, "John Gorham, 1709–1751: An Outline of His Activities in Nova Scotia 1744–1751," *Nova Scotia Historical Society Collections* 30 (1954): 31–32.

wayside, Gorham, in 1749, suggested that Mascarene impose "large quit rents" to drive the Acadians off their lands "so as to encourage Its being settled with some of his Majesty's Protestant Subjects."[53] It is safe to assume that Gorham had to look no further than himself to find a proprietor for those settlements.

While Gorham raised his company, Great Britain's position in Nova Scotia deteriorated. The Mi'kmaq, led by Father Le Loutre and with the quiet support of the Acadians, seized control of the entire colony and left only Annapolis Royal under British control. Then, on July 1, 1744, 300 Mi'kmaq attacked Annapolis Royal itself. Although Mascarene ordered so-called loyal Acadian work parties to comb the countryside surrounding the fort for timber and supplies, not a single Acadian warned him of the advancing Mi'kmaq. One moment the British were repairing the walls of Annapolis Royal; the next, the Mi'kmaq had them surrounded. Mascarene managed to get most of his troops and settlers into the fort, only to find that he had on hand a mere 100 regulars to defend against a force three times its size. If it had not been for the fort's several artillery pieces, the Mi'kmaq surely would have overrun the garrison. Mascarene now faced the certainty that the Acadians and Mi'kmaq had him trapped inside his fort's walls; when two regulars ventured out, Indians quickly killed and scalped them in full view of soldiers who watched from the ramparts. But as Mascarene's luck would have it, the Mi'kmaq did not intend to besiege Annapolis Royal. Instead, they pillaged the town below the fort and then withdrew to the woods to await promised French cannon.[54]

The Mi'kmaq struck Annapolis Royal a second time two months later. In September, Duvivier led upwards of 600 Indians, Acadians, and Troupes de la Marine against the British. The French forces still lacked siege artillery, so Duvivier positioned his troops in the woods outside the town and fort. To pass the time as he waited for cannon to arrive from Louisbourg, the French commander allowed his Acadian and Mi'kmaq auxiliaries to pillage the town and scalp any Britons and Americans foolish enough to venture forth from the fort.

Gorham's Rangers sailed into Annapolis Royal harbor at that critical juncture and broke the siege. While Mascarene felt that the American

---

53 Petition of John Gorham on Behalf of Himself and Others, for a Township on the Eastern Coast of Nova Scotia, November 24, 1748, RCA 1894, 133 and Council minutes, January 4, 1748/1749, Charles Bruce Fergusson, ed., Minutes of His Majesty's Council at Annapolis Royal, 1736–1749 (Halifax: NSARM, 1967), hereafter Annapolis Royal Council Minutes. Gorham to Mascarene, 1749, Gorham MSS.

54 Mascarene to Shirley, December 1744, NS Docs., 140–141. Mascarene to Lords of Trade, July 7, 1744, RCA 1894, 101.

force remained too weak "to cope with such a number of adversaries," Gorham thought otherwise, and ordered his men to secure the lower town and drive the Mi'kmaq and Acadians from the countryside.[55] After several brisk skirmishes, the rangers reoccupied the town and fortified its largest house as a forward base of operations. With the rangers in the field, the entire complexion of the battle changed. In the face of the rangers' attacks on his Mi'kmaq allies, which quickly eroded their interest in standing by the French, plus a lack of cannon and other supplies, Duvivier determined that the best course of action was to withdraw to Minas and Chignecto.[56]

Gorham's Rangers then set about consolidating the British hold on the countryside around Annapolis Royal, and intimidating the Acadians into submission. The Acadians, Gorham believed, had shown their true colors when the French and Indians had attacked Annapolis Royal. After securing the lower town, the rangers thus took to the woods to root out French sympathizers and collaborators. They announced that they would treat any Indian they found as an enemy, and soon proved it by bringing back the scalps of an entire Indian family – adults and children – that they claimed they had found skulking in the woods. While it is doubtful that a Mi'kmaq war party would have taken women and children on the warpath, Mascarene nonetheless praised Gorham and his men for their outstanding service in killing the "enemy."[57] For the Acadians, many of whom were of mixed Acadian and Indian blood, the rangers' aggressiveness suggested that they too could find themselves on the wrong end of a scalping knife.

Gorham, however, was not content to focus his rangers' activities and operations on Annapolis Royal alone. An aggressive and audacious officer, he wanted to take the war directly to the Mi'kmaq and Acadians in their sanctuaries of Minas and Chignecto. Gorham suspected that his troops could strike fear into the hearts of the enemy; he "was very well Inclined to do anything that Might tend to the distressing the Indian Enemy."[58] Gorham certainly believed that with his rangers he could even the odds of the war.

In December 1744, Gorham therefore presented Mascarene with a detailed plan to punish the Mi'kmaq and Acadians. Gorham's design was

---

55　Mascarene to Lords of Trade, September 20, 1744, John C. Webster, ed., *Thomas Pichon: "The Spy of Beauséjour." An Account of His Career in Europe and America, with Many Original Documents Translated by Alice Webster* (Halifax: NSARM, 1937), 132, hereafter *Pichon Papers*.
56　Bates, "John Gorham," 29–30.
57　Ibid., 30.
58　Copy of Minutes of Council, December 6, 1744, NSARM MSS, vol. 11, doc. 16.

to march stealthily to Minas and Chignecto in a winter campaign, kill Acadians and Mi'kmaq, and loot and pillage all that the rangers could carry. Gorham stated that he would treat all in Minas and Chignecto as enemies. When he requested from Mascarene permission to draft Acadians as "guides" – hostages – Gorham's intentions were clear. He then offered a one-eighth share of the booty that he and his rangers would seize to the captain of a sloop if he agreed to ferry a detachment of the rangers up the Bay of Fundy. It seems that Gorham wanted to catch the Acadians between a hammer and an anvil. One party of rangers would march overland and drive the enemy into another group advancing by sea.[59] Before Gorham could realize his ambition of punishing the Acadians and Mi'kmaq of Minas and Chignecto, however, British officials called him to other duty. Gorham put aside his plan for the conquest of Minas, with every intention of executing it as soon as he returned to Nova Scotia.

Starting in early 1745, the impending Louisbourg campaign sidetracked Gorham's attention and substantial energies from Nova Scotia. Gorham had traveled to New England in January to recruit more rangers for the Minas–Chignecto expedition. His and his rangers' reputations had preceded him. Shirley and William Pepperrell, then in the early stages of organizing the provincial army to go against Louisbourg, wanted Gorham and his rangers to join their army. To encourage the ranger captain to abandon ranging for provincial service, Shirley commissioned Gorham a lieutenant colonel in the 7th Massachusetts Regiment, the same regiment Gorham's father commanded.[60]

Gorham and his rangers, then absorbed into the 7th Massachusetts, contributed significantly to the conquest of Louisbourg. He commanded the whaleboats that ferried the New England troops from their transport ships to their landing zones and directed the landing of the provincial army. Gorham stepped forward when Pepperrell needed a volunteer to lead a dangerous night attack on the Island Battery protecting Louisbourg. On May 23, 1745, Gorham's provincials, with the assistance of Lieutenant Colonel Arthur Noble's men, attacked the battery. Although the French repulsed them with heavy losses, Gorham's behavior was exemplary. When Commodore Peter Warren and Pepperrell – joint commanders of the Louisbourg force – convened a court-martial to fix blame on a scapegoat for the defeat at the Island Battery, they found that Gorham had performed bravely in the attack. After Louisbourg fell in June, Gorham remained with the New England troops, only to see hundreds succumb to infectious diseases. Upon his father's death in one of the many plagues that wracked the army, Pepperrell promoted Gorham

59 Council minutes, December 8, 1744, *Annapolis Royal Council Minutes.*
60 Bates, "John Gorham," 35.

to colonel and commander of the 7th Massachusetts.[61] Even so, Gorham looked to return as the leader of the rangers to Nova Scotia, where greater personal gain beckoned.

Gorham sailed to Annapolis Royal in April 1746 to find that the state of the colony's defenses had significantly deteriorated in his absence. Several companies of New England militia had replaced the rangers at Annapolis Royal and had done little to secure the colony. They rarely ventured outside the security of the lower town and spent the Nova Scotia winter days killing time and consuming valuable provisions. Meanwhile, the Mi'kmaq and Acadians again turned to harassing and raiding British out settlements.[62]

Gorham remained convinced that the most effective way to prevent the Acadian and Mi'kmaq excursions was to execute his rangers' raid on Minas and Chignecto. With Gorham and company back in Nova Scotia, Mascarene dismissed the militia and turned over conduct of the war to Gorham.

Mascarene, at the same time that he gave Gorham command of the American forces in Nova Scotia, planned to offer the Acadians both the carrot and the stick.[63] He hoped that many of the Acadians would submit to the rangers without a fight and therefore authorized Gorham to administer to as many Acadians as were willing to accept it the oath of allegiance to King George II. Those who took the oath would receive amnesty. At the same time, he instructed Gorham to build several blockhouses in Minas and Chignecto as forward operating bases for future ranger operations. The Acadians saw the blockhouses, and not the offer of amnesty, as the true intentions of the British. They viewed Gorham's Rangers for what they were: invaders determined to occupy Acadian homes and lands. Many of the Acadians feared, Gorham later reported, that the letter of amnesty that the rangers carried was "only to make them [the Acadians] easy until we can get them in our power to Remove them."[64]

In May 1746, Gorham's Rangers set out for his long-anticipated mission to Minas and Chignecto. Intelligence reports estimated that upwards of 500 Acadians of military age, well supplied with cattle and corn, awaited

61   By January 1746, 500 of the New England troops had died and another 1,000 were sick. See Warren and Pepperrell to Secretary of State, January 18, 1746, *RCA 1894*, 110. John Gorham, "Col. John Gorham's 'Wast Book' and the Gorham Family," *New York Genealogical and Biographical Record* 28 (1897): 198.
62   Mascarene to Secretary of State, December 9, 1745, *RCA 1894*, 109.
63   Shirley to Duke of Newcastle, May 22, 1746, NSARM MSS, vol. 13, doc. 22.
64   Shirley to Duke of Newcastle, August 15, 1746, *Correspondence of Shirley*, 1: 336. Copy of a Letter from Lieut. Colonel Gorham to Governor Shirley, November 15, 1746, NSARM MSS, vol. 13, doc. 34.

them.[65] The Acadians, however, chose not to counter the rangers in one large battle but instead turned to raids to harass and wear down the invaders. After several clashes in which his rangers bested Acadian parties, the enemy, Gorham wrote to Shirley, deserted their homes and "Lodge in the Woods at Nights for fear" of facing the Americans. Gorham responded by burning Acadian villages and farms.[66] In the ensuing campaign, Gorham's Rangers quickly won a reputation as being "far more terrible than European soldiers."[67]

In the fall of 1746, Gorham's Rangers again proved their great utility to the British cause and nearly set the stage for a major British victory. The rangers disguised themselves as Frenchmen and captured an Acadian farmer as he worked his fields. Gorham learned from the prisoner that storms had wrecked at sea a French armada (under Jean Baptiste-Louis-Frédéric, duc d'Anville) bound for Annapolis and Boston. The prisoner also related that most of the French and Indian troops on the Nova Scotia peninsula had retreated across the Isthmus of Chignecto, except for a force (consisting of 700 men commanded by Jean-Baptiste-Nicholas Roche, chevalier de Ramezay) that had marched to take Annapolis Royal from the rear. Gorham determined that Ramezay's column was exposed and vulnerable. He therefore moved to cut off its retreat and harass it outside Annapolis Royal. His rangers, he boasted, would "so Annoy & Surprise this Army as to oblige them to make as precipitate and Lucky Retreat as Monsieur Du Vivier [sic: Duvivier] did before in the Like Case."[68] Ramezay's army, however, withdrew overland to Minas and Beaubassin before the rangers could intercept it and whittle away its strength with harassing attacks.

By late January 1747, the rangers were back in Annapolis Royal after having spent the better part of late December and early January serving as scouts for the 460 Massachusetts provincials assigned to garrison the blockhouses in Minas. Mascarene had ordered Lieutenant Colonel Arthur Noble, the officer with whom Gorham had led the attack on the Island Battery at Louisbourg, to take his newly arrived troops to Minas, where they would spend the winter among the not-so-friendly Acadians in the village of Grand Pré.[69] Mascarene had detailed Gorham's Rangers to teach the provincials the basics of waging war in Nova Scotia. After

65 Council minutes, November 8, 1745, *Annapolis Royal Council Minutes*.
66 Gorham to Shirley, October 4, 1746, Gorham MSS.
67 William Bollan to the Duke of Newcastle, August 17, 1747, *Baxter MSS*, 11: 387–388.
68 Gorham to Shirley, October 4, 1746, Gorham MSS.
69 The Acadians of Grand Pré had petitioned the French government in Québec for "a detachment at the said place to protect them from the incursions of the English, which detachment they will supply with everything they can for its support." See Military and Other Operations in Canada during the Years 1745–1746, *NYCD*, 10: 66.

spending several weeks with the Bay Colony's soldiers and familiarizing them with their new surroundings, the rangers marched back to Annapolis Royal.

Had the rangers remained at Grand Pré, they might have averted the disaster that befell Noble's party on the last day of January 1747. An army of nearly 300 Canadians and Indians under Captain Nicholas-Antoine Coulon de Villiers and Chevalier Louis de La Corne managed to march undiscovered against Grand Pré. After a 12-hour battle in a howling snowstorm that left Noble and 130 of his men dead and 34 wounded, the provincials surrendered. Upon receiving word of the defeat at Grand Pré, Mascarene immediately rushed Gorham and his rangers to Minas. Unable to catch the French army as it retreated across Chignecto, the rangers escorted the defeated survivors of Noble's party safely back to Annapolis Royal.[70]

After Noble's defeat at Grand Pré, British leaders in both Nova Scotia and Boston abandoned all hopes of defending Nova Scotia with provincial troops. They agreed that they faced a war that required substantial numbers of rangers. Shirley even proposed to raise 2,000 of them for service in Nova Scotia. However, suspecting that there was resistance in Great Britain to paying for such a large force, especially after he had presented Parliament with the bill for the failed Canada Expedition, Shirley dispatched Gorham to the duke of Newcastle to lobby for the ranger companies.[71] "I think the great service which Lieutenant-Colonel Gorham's Company of Rangers has been to the garrison at Annapolis Royal," Shirley wrote in Gorham's letter of introduction, "is a demonstration of the usefulness of such a corps."[72]

Gorham's trip to London signaled an occasion when the highest levels of the British government legitimated the first way of war. John and Elizabeth Gorham arrived in England in the late spring of 1747, after which the ranger captain made a lasting impression on Newcastle and the King's advisors. The Secretary of State was so taken with Gorham

---

70 Journal of Occurrences in Canada, 1746, 1747, *NYCD*, 10: 92. The French account of the battle of Grand Pré states that Coulon's detachment set out on snowshoes for Minas on January 23 and arrived there on February 10. Those dates are old style, thus placing the French forces at Grand Pré on January 31, 1747. The French officers did not treat the American survivors of the battle badly. Although Mi'kmaq comprised a significant proportion of Coulon's forces, the French prevented them from scalping their prisoners or the wounded. See Capitulation of the Garrison at Grand Pré, Nova Scotia, *NYCD* 10: 78, and William Blake Trask, ed. "Battle of Minas," *NEHGR* 9 (1855): 105–112. Mascarene to the Commander and All the Other Officers of the Part Returning from Minas, February 7, 1746, NSARM MSS, vol. 13, doc. 38.
71 Bates, "John Gorham," 42. The War Office did not grant Shirley's request. Gorham to ?, March 1746/1747, Gorham MSS.
72 Shirley to Duke of Newcastle, February 27, 1747, quoted in Bates, "John Gorham," 42.

that he arranged an audience for him with King George II at St. James's Palace. After his audience with the King, John Russell, duke of Bedford, wrote that Gorham and his rangers were "more than ever absolutely necessary for the immediate preservation of the Province of Nova Scotia."[73] Newcastle then informed Gorham that the King had commissioned him a captain in the regular British Army in recognition of his outstanding service.[74]

Gorham's commission in the British Army is significant on several levels. He was the first of three prominent American rangers – himself, his brother Joseph, and Robert Rogers – to earn such commissions in the British Army. The crown commissioned other Americans (usually high-ranking crown officials like governors or lieutenant governors) as officers in the British Army, while many others, George Washington included, strove unsuccessfully for British rank. King William, for example, made William Phips a major general for the 1690 Canada expedition. Phips's commission, however, had less to do with his military prowess than with his connections and position within the imperial bureaucracy.[75] Gorham, on the other hand, won his captaincy because of his military acumen. More important, the King commissioned Gorham because of the name he had made for himself as a ranger. While the King may have given Gorham a commission to better wage war on the cheap, he also acknowledged Americans' first way of war as vital to British military success in Nova Scotia and in effect sanctioned it as a legitimate form of war making.

Gorham, with his new commission in his pocket, returned to Nova Scotia in late 1747 to find that peace was breaking out everywhere. Mascarene had put offensive operations in the colony on hold in the ranger captain's absence, forcing Gorham to start again from near scratch and spend the winter of 1747–1748 collecting reinforcements and provisions for a spring campaign against Minas and Chignecto. The Peace of Aix-la-Chapelle, however, precluded Gorham's further operations. Upon news of a preliminary peace, Mascarene extended an olive branch to the Acadians.[76] He sent Joseph Gorham, John's younger brother, to Minas to

73 Duke of Bedford to the Duke of Newcastle, September 11, 1747, *Baxter MSS*, 11: 389.
74 Bates, "John Gorham," 44; "Col. John Gorham's 'Wast Book' and the Gorham Family," 198.
75 Leonard W. Labaree, "The Royal Governors of New England," *Publications of the Colonial Society of Massachusetts, Volume 32, Transactions 1933–37* (Boston: Colonial Society of Massachusetts, 1937), 120–131.
76 Word of the peace would have reached Annapolis Royal relatively quickly. Following Queen Anne's War, Great Britain had created a regular packet service that carried mail and government communications between Great Britain and the North American

pay the Acadians for the provisions they had supplied Noble's troops, even though they had failed to come to the aid of Noble's men when they fought for their lives against Coulon and La Corne. The politic Mascarene was prepared to forgive past behavior. John Gorham was not. While he agreed to grant leave to some of his rangers so that they could see their families in New England, he simultaneously sent recruiting parties to Massachusetts with the promise of a £15 advance in pay to anyone willing to enlist for what he expected would be the next war that soon would wrack the colony.[77]

At the end of King George's War, Gorham could take pride in his rangers' service. His troops had been the key to protecting Britain's interest in Nova Scotia. As the war progressed, they had become the only effective American or British troops in the colony. By 1748, they thoroughly dominated British military affairs in Nova Scotia. In the struggle that followed, Father Le Loutre's War, they would play an even larger role in winning Britain's final victory in Nova Scotia.

IV. Father Le Loutre's War, 1749–1755

Between 1749 and 1755, Nova Scotia was the scene of an Acadian–Indian insurgency against British rule. Father Le Loutre's War originated in the failure of the Treaty of Aix-la-Chapelle to settle the central question that shaped Americans' and Britons' relations with the Acadians. Although France had given Acadia to Great Britain two generations before, neither side established the degree to which the Roman Catholic Acadians and the progeny of Acadian–Indian unions would maintain their status as neutrals in the Anglo–Franco rivalry. Clearly, many Americans and Britons – among them Gorham and Shirley – wanted to colonize Nova Scotia. In that respect, both the Acadians and Mi'kmaq stood as a roadblock to Anglo–British colonizers' aspirations. For the many combatants of King George's War, especially the vehemently anti-British Jesuit priest Le Loutre and his mixed Indian–Acadian flock, the Treaty of Aix-la-Chapelle signaled not a lasting peace but merely a temporary cease-fire.[78] Within a year of the British Parliament's ratification of the treaty, American rangers,

---

colonies. See Ian Steele, *The English Atlantic, 1675–1740: An Exploration of Communication and Community* (New York: Oxford University Press, 1986).

77 Mascarene to Duke of Bedford, September 8, 1748, *NS Docs.*, 164. Gorham to Capt Bourn, December 13, 1748, Gorham MSS.

78 Le Loutre was not a man to accept peace with the English. His epitaph reads "Si les Anglais te mordent, mords-les!" ["If the English are killing you, kill them!"]. See Rogers, "Abbé Le Loutre," 128.

Acadians, and Indians embarked on what became a two-phase contest for the final control of Nova Scotia.

American rangers were at the center of the events leading up to the start of Father Le Loutre's War. In September 1748, Mascarene had ordered Gorham's Rangers to the French missions in present-day New Brunswick to inform the Acadians and Maliseets that they must send deputies to Annapolis Royal to explain their behavior during the late war. The Acadians agreed to dispatch representatives to parley with the British, but the Maliseets adopted a more belligerent stance. On one occasion, after the rangers and Maliseets exchanged harsh words, some Maliseets fired on the Americans and killed two of Gorham's men. Gorham responded by kidnapping two Indians and burning a Maliseet village. Coupled with an earlier instance in which Gorham had expelled a Roman Catholic priest from Minas and burned the homes of two Acadians judged to have "appeared too openly in the Enemies interest," Gorham's actions convinced French and British officials that war was imminent.[79] As the campaigning season ended, both sides watched to see what the other would do. Governors Shirley and Mascarene exchanged terse letters with the Governor-General of New France, marquis de La Galissonnière, condemning the other side's "hostile" actions. La Galissonnière singled out Gorham as particularly responsible for the depths to which relations in the colony had fallen. "The acts and threats of Mr. Gorham," La Galissonnière warned, had nearly pushed the French and British into war.[80]

Not until the return of Father Jean-Louis Le Loutre to Nova Scotia in the summer of 1749, however, did the much expected conflict begin.[81] Le Loutre arrived in Chignecto to find his Mi'kmaq flock "*dans la consternation générale.*"[82] That summer, 1,400 British settlers under Colonel Edward Cornwallis had established the settlement and naval base at Halifax on Chebucto Bay. Le Loutre, with the encouragement of the French Ministry of Marine and leaders in Québec, moved to exacerbate the tensions between the English and Mi'kmaq and weaken the Britons'

---

79 William Shirley to Marquis La Galissonnière, May 9, 1749, *Baxter MSS*, 11: 465; Mascarene to Duke of Bedford, September 8, 1748, *NS Docs.*, 164.

80 Count de La Galissonnière to Mascarene, January 15, 1749, *Baxter MSS*, 11: 362–364; Mascarene to de La Galissonnière, April 25, 1749, ibid., 365–367; Shirley to de La Galissonnière, May 9, 1749, *Correspondence of William Shirley*, 1: 481.

81 In 1747, a British warship captured Le Loutre as he attempted to return to France to win monetary support for his mission. He won his freedom in a prisoner exchange after three months of captivity. He spent most of 1748 lobbying influential friends in France for support of the mission and returned to Acadia in 1749 to bring about the restoration of Acadia to France. See Gipson, *Zones of International Friction*, 187.

82 L'Abbé Le Loutre au Minister, July 29, 1749, Placide Gaudet, ed., *Report Concerning Canadian Archives for the Year 1905: Acadian Genealogy and Notes* (Ottawa: S. E. Dawson for the Public Archives of Canada, 1906), appx. N, 283, hereafter *RCCA 1905*; L'Abbé Le Loutre au Minister, October 4, 1749, ibid., appx. N, 296.

increasingly strong hold on eastern Nova Scotia. "As we cannot openly oppose the English venture," Le Loutre wrote,

> I think that we cannot do better than to incite the Indians to continue warring on the English; my plan is to persuade the Indians to send word to the English that they will not permit new settlements to be made in Acadia. . . . I shall do my best to make it look to the English as if this plan comes from the Indians and that I have no part in it.[83]

Then "the missionary did not cease," Le Loutre wrote of himself in his autobiography, "while at the same time urging them [the Mi'kmaq] to uphold their rights and their claims to their lands, their hunting areas and their fishing, of which the English wished to gain control."[84] Governor Cornwallis, with only a small force at Halifax, suspected that the French would try to spark a war between the Mi'kmaq and the British and therefore instructed his military officers – Gorham especially – "to avoid quarrel with the Indians if possible."[85]

Cornwallis's efforts to preserve the fragile peace were to no avail. Starting in August, bands of Mi'kmaq and Maliseets, at Le Loutre's urging, raided English outposts across Nova Scotia. They took 20 English prisoners at Canso, attacked 2 English sloops in Chignecto Bay, and killed 4 settlers. In October, Cornwallis advised the Secretary of State that the French and Indians had "begun their usual game – their Missionary to the Indians De Loutre [*sic*: Le Loutre], the same that led them before Annapolis Royal [in 1744], has once more persuaded them to begin hostilities." Cornwallis, however, refused to declare the Acadians in rebellion. As he understood it, the problem resided in the influence of the "good for nothing scoundrel" Le Loutre among the Mi'kmaq. As such, he followed the pattern that had been well established in the British North American colonies and issued a proclamation that declared the Mi'kmaq "bandits" and offered 10 guineas for each Indian taken or killed. Upon the public issuance of Cornwallis's bounty, "all the savages," wrote Le Loutre, "raised the hatchet."[86]

Facing a full-scale Indian war, Cornwallis turned to the American rangers. He realized that "some effectual method should be taken to pursue them [the Indians] to their haunts and show them that after such

---

83 Quoted in *DCB*, s.v. "Le Loutre, Jean Louis."
84 Webster, *Career of Abbé Le Loutre*, 40.
85 Cornwallis to Lords of Trade, September 11, 1749, *NS Docs.*, 583.
86 Cornwallis to Lords Commissioners for Trade and Plantations, October 17, 1749, ibid., 591; Cornwallis to Duke of Bedford, October 17, 1749, NSARM MSS, vol. 40, doc. 9. The crown fixed the value of a guinea at £1.1s (sterling) in 1717. "Autobiographie de Le Loutre," 16.

actions they should not be secure within the Province." The rangers proved the best troops for that mission. Cornwallis immediately called for 100 New England rangers to "join with Gorham's during the Winter and go over the whole province" searching for Indians to kill and capture. At the same time, he authorized Captain William Clapham to raise a 50-man company of rangers for the defense of Halifax.[87]

As the Nova Scotia Council's advisor on military affairs, Gorham hoped to translate Cornwallis's enmity for the Mi'kmaq into a war against the Acadians.[88] "Securing & Settling this province," Gorham wrote, "can not be done but by Force of Arms." Since "these Inhabitants [Acadians] by Influence of the French Neighboring Government all Refuse to take the Oath of allegiance," they too should feel the sting of war. It was time, the ranger captain suggested, that the British focus their attention not on the Mi'kmaq, but on the Acadians.[89]

In the spring of 1750, Cornwallis adopted Gorham's recommendations and unleashed the rangers directly against the Acadians. In December 1749, Cornwallis had acknowledged in a private letter to Robert Napier that "the Acadians [were] certainly more Friends to the French than us."[90] The next month he determined to punish the friends of the French and ordered Captain Silvanus Cobb, a former company commander in Gorham's regiment at Louisbourg, to take his sloop and a party of rangers to Chignecto to apprehend Le Loutre. Along with seizing the priest, Cobb was to capture several Acadian women and children "to remain as Hostages of their better behavior."[91]

Cornwallis then sent Gorham's Rangers and Captain Francis Bartelo's newly raised company to Minas and Chignecto, where they were to terrorize and intimidate Acadians.[92] In a repeat of the rangers' 1746 campaign, as Gorham's men marched overland from Chebucto toward Beaubassin, Bartelo's corps sailed up the Bay of Fundy on Cobb's sloop. Along the

---

87 Cornwallis to Duke of Bedford, October 17, 1749, NSARM MSS, vol. 40, doc. 9.
88 By 1749, Gorham sat on the Nova Scotia Council. See Thomas B. Akins, "The First Council," *Nova Scotia Historical Society Collections* 2 (1881): 26.
89 Gorham to Shirley, November, 1749, Gorham MSS.
90 Cornwallis to Napier, December 6, 1749, Stanley Pargellis, ed., *Military Affairs in North America, 1748–1765: Selected Documents from the Cumberland Papers in Windsor Castle* (New York: D. Appleton-Century Company, 1936), 8.
91 *DCB*, s.v. "Cobb, Silvanus." Cornwallis to Cobb, January 13, 1749/1950, *Pichon Papers*, 178–179. Cobb aborted his mission because he advertised his intentions in the Boston papers and word of the impending attack reached Le Loutre.
92 Little is known of Francis Bartelo's career before he served as a ranger in Nova Scotia. The documents rarely mention him. In "Readers' Questions," *JSAHR* 32 (1954): 45, however, one reader claimed that Bartelo was the same Captain Bartelo "who commanded the Duke's [Cumberland's] Free Companies in Flanders" [1745?] during the War of Austrian Succession (1740–1748). Perhaps Bartelo learned part of his craft in Europe fighting French *Grassin*.

way, both forces arrested Acadians and pillaged their property. It was Cornwallis's intention to "make an example of these lads" and convince the Acadians that they must abandon the French interest. Cornwallis hoped that if the English continued "for some time to harass and hunt them by Sea and Land they will either abandon the Peninsula or come in upon any terms we please."[93]

Le Loutre turned to a Fabian strategy. All along the Bay of Fundy, Cornwallis complained, the Acadians "if they did not think their Strength sufficient to dispute our landing they would at first retire to the Woods with a resolution of committing every mischief that they were capable of."[94] Le Loutre, meanwhile, complained that he did not have the proper force to confront the Americans. "Why do we not imitate the English," Le Loutre asked, "who have free companies, rangers, who are at liberty to do all the mischief they can, and may be disavowed if circumstance made it necessary? It is true that it would cost the King a trifle, but great advantages would also be derived therefrom."[95]

When his Mi'kmaq failed to stop the rangers, Le Loutre adopted a scorched-earth policy to deny the Americans the benefits of occupying Minas and Chignecto. Le Loutre had first resorted to this tactic the previous fall to harass the rangers as they patrolled Minas.[96] In the spring of 1750, he returned to it with frightening efficiency. He not only ordered the evacuation to Chignecto of all the Acadian families of Minas, but also threatened that he would put to death any Acadians who returned to their homes. When several Acadians refused to comply with the missionary's instructions, Le Loutre turned his Mi'kmaq followers on them. Then, after the British succeeded in September 1750 in building Fort Lawrence on Chignecto, Le Loutre ordered all the Acadian settlements in Beaubassin burned to the ground and drove the Acadians further into New Brunswick and to Baie Verte.[97] Minas and large parts of Chignecto thus became a no-man's land where only American rangers and Mi'kmaq dared tread.

For most of 1750, it seemed that Le Loutre's strategy was slowly paying dividends. In April, the rangers failed to secure the approaches to Chignecto, allowing a party of Acadians and French troops to drive

---

93 Cornwallis to Gorham, March 12, 1749/1750, *Pichon Papers*, 181. Cornwallis to Lords of Trade, March 19, 1749/1750, NSARM MSS vol. 35, doc. 1.
94 Enclosure in a Letter of Cornwallis to Lords of Trade, July 10, 1750, *RCCA 1905*, appx. N, 320.
95 *Pichon Papers*, 65.
96 Gorham's Journal, September 9–16, 1749, Gorham MSS.
97 Cornwallis to Duke of Bedford, March 19, 1749/1750, *Pichon Papers*, 183; Cornwallis to Charles Lawrence, April 15, 1750, *The Journal of Joshua Winslow*, ed. John C. Webster (St. John: Publications of the New Brunswick Museum, 1936), 31. Le Loutre also asked for but did not receive permission to excommunicate those Acadians who expressed sympathy or support for the British cause. See *DCB*, "Le Loutre, Jean-Louis."

Colonel Charles Lawrence's detachment of regulars from the isthmus.[98] Lawrence succeeded in building the fort that took his name six months later, only to find his regulars – like Mascarene's at Annapolis Royal half a decade earlier – trapped inside by Indians and Acadians. Acadian and Indian parties then defeated Bartelo's and Gorham's Rangers in two bloody skirmishes. In September, they ambushed Bartelo and 60 of his men. The Acadians and Indians killed seven of the rangers, wounded Bartelo, and took captive several rangers, whom they tortured and killed. The Acadians then repulsed Gorham and 30 of his rangers in a raid on an Acadian–Indian settlement. Emboldened by their victories, Le Loutre detailed several bands of his Mi'kmaq to spend the winter ravaging the countryside and searching for English scalps outside Halifax.[99]

Yet just when events seemed to be reaching a crisis point for the British, the first phase of Father Le Loutre's War suddenly ended. The costs of continuing the war had reached exorbitant levels and forced a peace. In 1750, Parliament had expended slightly less than £174,000 – significantly more than the £39,000 it had estimated – for the maintenance of Nova Scotia. Maintaining the rangers alone accounted for almost 7 percent of the colony's budget.[100] For a colony of only 5,000 settlers, such costs were unacceptable. Both Cornwallis and his successor, Peregrine Hopson, understood that Parliament would hold them responsible for any excesses in expenditures. On the French side, meanwhile, the costs of continuing Le Loutre's war likewise were becoming intolerable to the Ministry of Marine. Le Loutre reported in the spring of 1751 that the Acadian refugees whom he forcibly had evacuated to Baie Verte were out of provisions, and many of them had complained that they wanted to return to their former homes. Le Loutre, in a stopgap measure, transferred many of the trade goods intended for the Mi'kmaq to the Acadians. Upon their loss of presents, the Mi'kmaq refused to take to the field against the rangers.[101]

The de facto cease-fire of 1751 gave the key antagonists of the war – Le Loutre and Gorham – much needed opportunities to attend to their personal affairs. In August 1751, Gorham sailed for Great Britain to settle the debts he had incurred when he first raised the rangers in 1744. Although

---

98 "Autobiographie de Le Loutre," 17.
99 Journal de ce qui s'est passé à Chinectou et autre parties des frontières de l'Acadie depuis le 15 septembre 1750 jusqu'au 28 juillet 1751, *RCCA 1905*, appx. N, 325. "Autobiographie de Le Loutre," 19.
100 House of Commons Proceedings, February 27, 1750/1751, Stock, *Proceedings and Debates*, 451–452; House of Commons Proceedings, March 7, 1749–1750, ibid., 410–411.
101 *DCB*, s.v. "Le Loutre." Philip Bock has noted that smallpox epidemics, alcoholism, and warfare all contributed to significant reductions in the Mi'kmaq populations. See Bock, "Micmac," *HNAI*, Vol. 15, *Northeast*, 117. Peace thus would have served the interests of the Mi'kmaq as well as those of the French and British.

the crown welcomed the services of Gorham's Rangers, Parliament remained less than generous in paying them or supplying them with even edible rations.[102] Gorham would never return to Nova Scotia; he died of smallpox in England in December 1751. Le Loutre, meanwhile, traveled to Québec to lobby for more supplies for the Acadians and Mi'kmaq. After his requests were ignored, he sailed for France to lobby personally for their support.[103]

With Le Loutre and Gorham both out of the colony, Nova Scotia entered a period of tranquility for almost four years. Leaders on both sides refused to allow tension to escalate into war. In October 1752, for example, Mi'kmaq abducted several New England fishermen and took them as captives to Louisbourg; the French commander of the fortress immediately returned them to Hopson's custody in Halifax. Before the transfer of power from Cornwallis to Hopson, Cornwallis ordered the reduction of the rangers to one company.[104] Cornwallis, who had complained that Gorham was a wild and uncontrollable ruffian, thought peace stood a chance as long as he could restrain the rangers from their excesses.

In 1754, however, a clash of arms between Great Britain's colonists and the French in the Ohio Valley shattered Nova Scotia's brief calm. Le Loutre had returned to Chignecto the previous spring and had tried with no success to break the state of peace that existed between the British and Mi'kmaq. However, when news of George Washington's battle with French and Indian forces reached Nova Scotia, Le Loutre had all he needed to push the Mi'kmaq into war. Upon the missionary's promise to pay for scalps, the Mi'kmaq again agreed to take up arms for the French.[105] To prove their loyalty, they traveled to Québec and presented the Governor-General of New France with 30 English scalps. Meanwhile, Le Loutre did his best to raise the Acadians against the British. "Moses [Le Loutre]," the British spy Thomas Pichon reported from inside Fort Beauséjour on Chignecto, "preached a most vehement sermon" against the British. Two weeks later, Moses advised the Acadians that they soon must expect war with the British.[106]

By the summer of 1755, fighting had broken out in Nova Scotia, starting the brief but climactic second phase of Father Le Loutre's War. One of Great Britain's main military objectives at the start of the Seven Years'

102 Gorham to Erasmus James Philipps, January 17, 1746/1747, Gorham MSS.
103 Gorham's widow, Elizabeth, wrote in June 1752 that her "dearly beloved husband in his loyal service to the King, has expended his entire fortune." Quoted in John Gorham, "Col. John Gorham's 'Wast Book'," ed. Sprague, 187. *DCB*, s.v. "Le Loutre," 457.
104 Hopson to Lords of Trade, October 16, 1752, *NS Docs.*, 680.
105 *DCB*, s.v. "Le Loutre, Jean Louis."
106 Pichon to Lt. Col. George Scott, September 17, 1754, *Pichon Papers*, 39; Pichon to Scott, October 14, 1754, ibid., 44; Pichon to Scott, November 2, 1754, ibid., 53.

War, from London's perspective, was to remove French "encroachments" on British colonial frontiers, and in the case of Nova Scotia, that meant the reduction of Fort Beauséjour – Fort Lawrence's opposite number on the Chignecto Isthmus. The Americans and Britons in Nova Scotia, however, directed their activities in 1755 against the Acadians, not France's imperial position in the Maritimes. Following the capitulation of Fort Beauséjour, Americans and Britons in North America moved to settle the "Acadian problem."[107]

Although historians continue to debate who, either Shirley or Charles Lawrence, was most responsible for the deportation of the Acadians, the Acadian expulsion cannot be separated from mid-eighteenth-century Americans' conceptualization of war.[108] Despite eventual opposition to the policy of expulsion voiced after the fact by some British officials and Americans, American soldiers were in fact Britain's willing executioners in the Acadian proscription. Colonel John Winslow, commander of one of the battalions of American troops, noted, "Although it is a Disagreeable Part of Duty we are Put Upon, I am Sensible it is a Necessary One."[109] Captain Abijah Willard, one of the provincial officers assigned the task of gathering the Acadians for deportation, recorded the methods and details of the four-month campaign against Acadian civilians. On August

---

107   For the differing perspective on the need to attack either Fort Beauséjour or the Acadians, see LO 477 and Extract of Letter from Govr. Lawrence to Govr. Shirley, November 5, 1754, NS Docs., 376–377. The French began construction on Fort Beauséjour in 1751. See Cornwallis to Duke of Bedford, June 24, 1751, NSARM MSS, vol. 40, doc. 32. In June 1755, British Colonel Robert Monkton led 2,000 New England provincials and 270 British regulars against Fort Beauséjour. The French garrison within the fort surrendered on June 16 to Monkton and John Winslow. Le Loutre escaped from the fort. A British man-of-war apprehended him later in the war when he tried to flee to France.

108   In his writings, Lawrence tried to exculpate himself. "It was determined," Lawrence wrote in a classic use of the passive voice, "to bring the inhabitants to compliance or rid the Province of such perfidious subjects." See Lawrence to Lords of Trade, July 18, 1755, RCA 1894, 206. Naomi E. S. Griffiths, in *The Contexts of Acadian History, 1686–1784: The 1988 Winthrop Packard Bell Lectures in Maritime Studies* (Montréal and Kingston: McGill-Queen's University Press for the Center for Canadian Studies, 1992), 63, provided an earlier synthesis regarding Lawrence's guilt and argued, "Charles Lawrence, Lieutenant-Governor of Nova Scotia in 1755, [was] the person who must bear the major responsibility for the policy" of expelling the Acadians. Brebner, in *New England's Outpost*, 190, similarly stated that Lawrence "conceived and ordered the expulsion of the Acadian population." Carl A. Brasseaux, *The Founding of New Acadia: The Beginnings of Acadian Life in Louisiana, 1765–1803* (Baton Rouge: Louisiana State University Press, 1987), places the blame on Shirley. One should note, however, that as early as 1749 John Gorham had proposed a plan by which the British and Americans could drive the Acadians from Nova Scotia. Plank shows that almost from the start of British "possession" of Nova Scotia, administrators in both Britain and Nova Scotia proposed expulsion of the Acadians. See Plank, *An Unsettled Conquest*, 91.

109   Plank, *An Unsettled Conquest*, 158–159. Winslow to Lawrence, August 30, 1755, RCCA 1905, appx. B, 17.

15, 1755, for example, Willard and his company arrived at Tatmegoush. After confiscating the Acadians' arms, Willard's men went from house to house, arrested all the Acadian males, and transported them to Fort Cumberland (Fort Beauséjour). Twelve days later, Willard saw Major Joseph Frye take 200 men to Shepody with orders to "take, burn and Destroy all the French in that part of the world." On September 17, Willard's company marched from Fort Cumberland and set fire to 190 Acadian buildings; in November, on another raid, his men burned 157 more. On November 20, as the harsh Nova Scotia winter rapidly approached, Willard's company fanned out across the countryside surrounding Fort Cumberland to kill the Acadians' livestock. Except for the animals they seized for their own stores, the Americans left the carcasses of nearly 100 head of cattle "to Rott upon the Ground."[110]

The Acadians were the single largest population of Europeans forcibly dispersed in American history. As an episode in the history of the North Atlantic world, it ranks second in magnitude only to the expulsion of the Huguenots after the revocation of the Edict of Nantes in 1685. Winslow's troops, in a matter of only weeks, forcibly removed nearly 4,000 noncombatants from Nova Scotia, of whom at least half perished in the Acadian Diaspora.[111] Another 8,000 fled to the woods and across the isthmus of Chignecto to avoid deportation.

The deportation of the Acadians by Winslow's men marked the culmination of Americans' war of conquest in Nova Scotia. As such, it, more than any other event up to that time, shows the extent to which the first way of war had permeated the thinking of both British and American officers who served in North America. For well over a decade, they had fought a war aimed at enemy noncombatants and civilians. The Acadian proscription thus grew in an environment that was ripe with the killing, intimidation, and plundering of noncombatants. In the process, Americans and Britons of all ranks, from the privates in Willard's company to Governors William Shirley and Charles Lawrence, accepted noncombatants as just and proper targets of violence.

The British acceptance of Americans' military culture and their skill in offensive operations would achieve further legitimization and refinement after 1755. Before examining that important period in the development of American military history, however, it is important to add one further

---

110 "Journal of Abijah Willard, 1755," ed. John C. Webster (Shediac, NB: John C. Webster's private reprinting of the *Collections of the New Brunswick Historical Society* 13, 1930): 39–69.
111 Lawrence to Lords of Trade, October 18, 1755, *RCA 1894*, 207. For an accounting of the numbers involved in the Acadian proscription, see Adams G. Archibald, "The Expulsion of the Acadians," *Nova Scotia Historical Society Collections* 5 (1886–1887): 11–95.

element of context and discuss contemporary European practices of *petite guerre*, the European form of warfare most analogous to the first way of war. Only thus is it possible fully to grasp the notions and assumptions British regulars brought with them when they came to North America to fight the Seven Years' War and the significance of their eventual embrace of the first way of war.

3

Continental and British Petite Guerre, circa 1750

On May 11, 1745, over 50,000 British, Hanoverian, Austrian, and Dutch soldiers suffered defeat at the hands of 56,000 Frenchmen and their allies at Fontenoy, one of the classic battles of the eighteenth century. Fontenoy symbolizes the mid-eighteenth-century European conceptualization of regular war, the highly stylized enterprise in which soldiers marched in perfect order and straight lines to exchange volleys of musket fire within a stone's throw of one another. From the decorum of Lord Charles Hay's apocryphal challenge to the French line – "*Messieurs les Gardes Françaises, tirez le premiers!*" [Gentlemen of the French Guard, fire first!] – to the ordered advance of the British infantry against the French lines, British soldiers looked to Fontenoy as a model of bravery and behavior that they should strive to emulate.[1]

Decorum and order, however, made up only part of mid-eighteenth-century Europeans' martial culture. The mid-eighteenth century was also the age of unchivalrous and chaotic irregular warfare, what the French called *petite guerre*. For most eighteenth-century Western European soldiers, Britons particularly, *petite guerre* was the antithesis of regular warfare. Their view of regular war revolved around images of battles like Fontenoy, battles between professional soldiers using parade ground tactics; *petite guerre*, they knew, focused on raids against enemy detachments, ambushes of isolated outposts, devastation of enemy fields, villages, and towns, and, in many cases, the rape and murder of innocent women and children. For the eighteenth-century regular officer, *petite guerre* was not a form of war, but rather a manifestation of criminality. Even Thomas Auguste le Roy de Grandmaison, one of the eighteenth century's most vociferous advocates of irregular

---

1 John W. Fortescue, *A History of the British Army, Vol. 2, First Part – To the Close of the Seven Years' War* (London: Macmillan and Co., Limited, 1910), 114. "Names of the general and other officers, and number of private men, killed, wounded, and missing," *Gentleman's Magazine* 15 (1745): 249.

war, described it as a kind of war usually practiced by "Barbarous Nations."[2]

Notwithstanding Fontenoy's status as the premier example of open-field engagement, the countryside surrounding the battlefield was the scene of some of the most extensive *petite guerre* operations in the mid-eighteenth century. Sir John Fortescue, the premier historian of the British Army, noted that the villages and fields that surrounded Fontenoy were "crammed with mercenary irregular troops – Pandours, Grassins, and the like."[3] Contemporaries of the battle knew that irregulars on both sides played pivotal roles in the battle's outcome. Grandmaison, for example, detailed how on the day before the battle, a detachment of French *Grassin* drove an advance-party of Austrian *huszars* from Fontenoy and thus allowed the regulars commanded by French Marshal Hermann Maurice, comte de Saxe, the crucial hours they needed to entrench. Perhaps if the *huszars* had held Fontenoy for only a few hours longer, the British would not have lost nearly 7,500 men in their ordered but self-destructive frontal assault against the French line. Another French commentator anonymously wrote that Saxe's irregulars "did wonders all these days," as they cut the allies' supply and communication lines.[4] Saxe, Grandmaison wrote, not only learned of the movements of the British Army from his *Grassin*, but he used them throughout the battle to harass the British, Austrians, and Dutch.[5]

If *petite guerre*, as Grandmaison and others believed, played such an important role in the battle of Fontenoy, where then did the practice of irregular war fit in the eighteenth-century European way of war? The answer is clear: by the middle decades of the eighteenth century, *petite guerre* had come to occupy a central place in the thinking of Western European strategists and the practices of Western European soldiers. In fact, by 1755, the year that saw British soldiers arrive in significant numbers in North America for the first time, every major Western European army had its own tradition of *petite guerre*.

It is, however, the differences among those traditions that partially explain why the British Army failed at waging *petite guerre* with Britons in North America. At the risk of overgeneralization, two varieties of *petite guerre* evolved in the first half of the eighteenth century: a Continental tradition and a British tradition. Approaches differed within Continental armies, but all possessed a common element of concern for finding the

2   Thomas Auguste le Roy de Grandmaison, *La Petite Guerre, ou traité du service des troupes legeres en campagne* (n.p., 1756), 7. Note that there are one- and two-volume versions of *La Petite Guerre*. I have used the one-volume edition.
3   Fortescue, *British Army*, 110.
4   *Gentleman's Magazine* 15 (1745): 314.
5   Grandmaison, *La Petite Guerre*, 407.

proper role of irregulars within a military context dominated by regular armies. The result was not only the creation of *petite guerre* corps, but also what modern theorists would call "doctrines of irregular war." In the British Army, on the other hand, *petite guerre* never attained the acceptance that it did in the armies of the Continental powers. Ironically, the British Army, in the colonization of Ireland and the suppression of Jacobitism in Scotland, forged an effective, albeit brutal, tradition of *petite guerre*. Unlike the Continental powers, however, British officers never embraced their tradition of *petite guerre* as a legitimate or effective way of war except as applied against rebellious populations. Thus, no institutionalized or sanctioned doctrine of *petite guerre* existed in the mid-eighteenth-century British Army.[6] As Major General Edward Braddock's march in 1755 on Fort Duquesne in western Pennsylvania showed, British officers' narrow understanding of *petite guerre* could lead to disastrous results on the battlefields of North America, where irregular war was supreme.

I. The Rejection of Unlimited War in Western Europe

The prohibition against waging war on noncombatants and civilians emerged as a central tenet of civilized warfare in the early eighteenth century. This marked a great change, for Western Europeans had waged war against noncombatants for hundreds of years. Tacitus, for instance, wrote that the Roman legions under Germanicus crossed the Rhine River in Germany and "ravaged and burnt the country for fifty miles around. No pity was shown to age or sex."[7] Near the end of the fourth century, Flavius Vegetius Renatus devoted a section of his *Epitoma Rei Militaris*, which would later become one of the most widely read military treatises in Europe during the Middle Ages and the Early Modern Era, to the ways that a commander could deal with enemy noncombatants. He contended that starving or terrorizing civilians could lead to easy victory.[8] During the

---

6 Peter Russell has argued that the British Army gained its familiarity with irregular war in Flanders, Central Europe, and Scotland. Those experiences, he postulated, became the seedbed from which grew its doctrine in the Seven Years' War in North America. See Russell, "Redcoats in the Wilderness: British Officers and Irregular Warfare in Europe and America, 1740 to 1760," *WMQ* 35 (1978): 629–652. The success of British regulars at "little war" in North America, as Chapter 4 argues, came mainly from Britons incorporating American rangers into their army.

7 Tacitus, *The Annals of Imperial Rome*, trans. Michael Grant, rev. ed. (New York: Penguin Books, 1989), 61–62.

8 Flavius Vegetius Renatus, *Epitoma Rei Militaris*, ed. and trans. Leo F. Stelten (New York: Peter Lang, 1990), 213.

Crusades, Christian "rules of war" evolved further to sanction the killing of women and children, provided that they were pagans or Muslims.

By the end of the Wars of Religion, however, the propriety of targeting noncombatants had come under scrutiny within Western European military culture. The Reformation had shattered the old prohibitions on war among Christians that the medieval church tried to enforce, leading to the mass slaughter of noncombatants. The devastation of the Wars of Religion shocked Europeans. During the Thirty Years' War (1618–1648) in Germany alone, over 8 million people died or became war refugees.[9]

The horrors inflicted on innocent men, women, and children compelled the Dutch jurist Hugo Grotius to develop principles – rules of war – that he hoped would control violence and avert bloodshed on the scale that was occurring in Germany and the Low Countries. One of Grotius's foundational principles was his contention that noncombatants were never legitimate targets for armies. Although he acknowledged that what he called "Force and Terror" were "the proper agents of war," and that a state or monarch could legally "attack in every place where the enemy may be killed," he also argued that under no circumstances should women and children be killed. Revenge, Grotius told his readers, was not a reason for retaliation, nor should a state ever use minor acts of brutality committed by an enemy to justify laying waste to the enemy's countryside or civilians. Moderation in "despoiling" the enemy's homeland, Grotius wrote, was the most militarily as well as morally effective way to wage war. Since the purpose of war, as he explained, was to end hostilities as soon as possible on favorable terms, moderation and limitation of violence made sense. Proportionality was advantageous to both sides. In forgoing the temptation to extirpate one's enemies by massacring their civilians, one did not make intractable enemies. If both sides knew that defeat in war did not necessarily mean complete annihilation, wars could end more quickly and thus spare all parties involved the financial and human costs of prolonged conflicts.[10]

After 1648 and the Treaty of Westphalia, when the Reformation and Counter Reformation no longer fueled the passions of war and the emergent nation-state system began to assert its dominance in the politico-military affairs of Western Europe, European war entered its limited phase. Following the War of Spanish Succession (1701–1713), the direct effects of wars on Western Europe's civilian population were minimal. The

9 For a discussion of the devastation wrought by soldiers in the Thirty Years' War, see John Childs, *Armies and Warfare in Europe, 1648–1789* (New York: Holmes and Meier Publishers, 1982), chap. 1.

10 Hugo Grotius, *The Rights of War and Peace, Including the Law of Nature and of Nations*, trans. A. C. Cambell (Washington, DC: M. Walter Dunne, Publisher, 1901), 294, 324–330, 364–365.

first decade of the eighteenth century signaled a new period in European war in which states assigned "frontier provinces" – Bohemia and Alsace, for example – a military role, but the "interior" of the new nation-states withdrew from military activities except for increased taxes and the occasional levies of troops. Preservation of the international balance of power became the raison d'être of the nation-states' armies. The officers who made up those armies understood themselves to be gentlemen whose role was not to wage unlimited wars against civilians, but to protect and defend the interests of the monarchs they served. As conservative entities, the Continental monarchies of the eighteenth century had no interest in radically affecting the status quo and thus would not use their armies against another monarch's civilian populace.[11]

On a more practical level, the European officer corps believed that it needed to control its rank and file if it hoped to maintain its military effectiveness. Much has been written, based primarily on the aristocratic officer class's perspective, about how eighteenth-century armies were little more than mobile prisons manned by the poorest and most destitute members of European society. Officers and noncommissioned officers, to keep the "meaner sorts" in line both on campaign and in garrison, brutalized their men with corporal punishments.[12] Discipline, wrote Raimundo Montecuccoli, was the "soul of all armies; and unless it is established, and supported with unshaken resolution, they [soldiers] are no better than so many contemptible heaps of rabble, which are more dangerous to the very state that maintains them, than even its declared enemies."[13]

Marauding soldiers could meet peasants who did not take kindly to the pillaging of their homes and upset even the most brilliant captain's plan for victory. Saxe complained that during the War of Austrian Succession (1740–1748), for instance, the French Army failed to make one march in Bohemia "without considerable Loss of Soldiers, either taken or slain by the Enemy or Peasants, when they straggled out for Pillage."[14] There was within the Western European officer corps a sentiment that once their men pillaged, much like a housedog that gets the taste of blood, they were ruined.

Controlling pillaging, and thus desertion – the greatest threat to all eighteenth-century armies – became one of the main responsibilities of the

11 André Corvisier, *Armies and Societies in Europe, 1494–1789*, trans. Abigail T. Siddal (Bloomington: Indiana University Press, 1979), 15.
12 Officers and noncommissioned officers watched individual soldiers closely in battle with the intention of encouraging "their men to make flight of the enemy, and to despise danger." See Thomas Simes, *The Military Guide for Young Officers Containing a System of the Art of War* (London: J. Millan, 1781), 95.
13 Montecuccoli quoted in Samuel Bever, *The Cadet, A Military Treatise* (London: W. Johnston, 1762), 1.
14 Saxe, quoted in ibid., 29.

Western European officer and noncommissioned officer corps, and in turn shaped their attitudes toward civil–military relations. For example, Frederick the Great's *Regulations*, the model handbook for Western European officers, forbade "all irregularities" against civilians. "All acts of violence, on whomsoever they are committed by Soldiers," the *Regulations* read, "shall be punished with the gantlope [gauntlet]; as soon, therefore, as a complaint of this kind is made against any Soldier, he must be confined, examined, tried by a court-martial and sentenced to run the gantlope." The draconian system of military discipline (not military justice) under which Prussian soldiers lived further convinced them that civilians were off limits. "Every Soldier is not only to avoid treating his landlord," the *Regulations* continued, "or any other person not belonging to the house, with abuse, but, on the contrary, to behave to him even with respect and civility."[15] Violations of those directions resulted in running the gauntlet or another form of corporal punishment.

Of course, there is always a discount between theory and practice. Although legal theorists like Grotius and commanders like Montecuccoli, Saxe, and Frederick may have called for lessening of the violence directed against women and children, there was no mechanism in place other than beatings to ensure that soldiers would abide by the rules. Yet, perhaps because of the writings and efforts of Grotius and eighteenth-century officers and noncommissioned officers, eighteenth-century Western European soldiers generally acted with greater restraint toward noncombatants than their predecessors had in the Wars of Religion. In time, the relatively benign treatment of noncombatants became the norm for Western European armies, even for Western European practitioners of *petite guerre*, who functioned not as independent forces but as auxiliaries under the control of regular generals. Captain Johann von Ewald, one of the foremost Western European irregulars of the eighteenth century, whose *Treatise on Partisan Warfare* became the German classic of irregular war, believed that "above all one can not deal harshly enough with those villains who mercilessly torment the peasants who are innocent of the war."[16] We need to remember that Carl von Clausewitz, Europe's greatest theoretician of war, detested violence inflicted upon noncombatants as immoral, improper, and counterproductive militarily. Clausewitz did not develop his abhorrence for *petite guerre* in a vacuum. Rather, it was the product of his personal experience and disgust at seeing the behavior of the Cossacks after the Battle of Borodino in 1812, as well as at least a century and a

15 William Faucitt, trans. *Regulations for the Prussian Infantry. Translated from the German Original* (1756; reprint, New York: Greenwood Press, 1968), 350, 363.
16 Johann von Ewald, *Treatise on Partisan Warfare*, trans. Robert A. Selig and David Curtis Skaggs (New York: Greenwood Press, 1991), 69.

half of development of a Western European martial culture that looked upon the killing of noncombatants with opprobrium.

II. Continental *Petite Guerre*

The marchlands of Eastern and Central Europe that separated the Austrian, Russian, and Ottoman Empires were home to traditions of irregular war dating back centuries. In the Hungarian–Turkish borderlands, for instance, Hungarian, Croat, and Serb nobles often resorted to terrorism to maintain their independence from the Austrian and Ottoman Empires. In the process, Eastern Europe became "the classical region of guerrilla warfare, [and] peasant risings were perhaps even more common, partly perhaps for topographical reasons, partly because clashes between social strata were intensified by overlaying religious and ethnic tension."[17]

To the north, on the wide-open plains of Poland between the Austrian and Russian Empires, Polish soldiers developed a tradition of *petite guerre* that confounded Western soldiers. Even a commander as astute and skilled as Saxe found confronting the Polish irregulars perplexing. Saxe knew that the Poles "made war in such a vague and irregular manner, that, if an enemy makes a point of pursuing them, he will thereby be presently rendered incapable of opposing their continual inroads." Like the rangers and Indians of North America after 1675, the Poles, Saxe continued, would march unseen, "thirty, and sometimes forty miles a day in large bodies," fall upon isolated outposts and destroy them, and then escape unharmed into the countryside like phantoms.[18]

For the Central and Eastern European irregulars, civilians, not opposing armies, were the objects of armies in times of war. The Austrian Prince Johann Joseph Khevenhüller-Metsch, for instance, noted that the war in the eastern half of the Austrian Empire focused on criminal behavior more than soldiering. The focus of the typical *huszar, dragon*, or *pandur*, Khevenhüller-Metsch wrote, was "setting fire to houses, pillaging churches, cutting off ears and eyes, murdering citizens and raping women."[19] The Eastern European partisans often seemed to the regulars who confronted them more specters than soldiers. "Before they [Magyar *huszars*] begin an attack," George Smith observed, "they lay themselves so flat on the necks of their horses, that it is hardly possible to discover their force; but being within pistol-shot of the enemy, they raise themselves with

17 "The classic": Lewis Gann, *Guerrillas in History* (Palo Alto, CA: Stanford University Press, 1971), 9.
18 Maurice Count de Saxe, *Reveries, or, Memoirs Concerning the Art of War* (Edinburgh: Alexander Donalson, 1776), 134, 137.
19 Khevenhüller-Metsch quoted in Ewald, *Partisan Warfare*, 13.

such surprising quickness, and fall on with such vivacity, that it is very difficult for troops to preserve their order. When a retreat is necessary, their horses have so much fire, and are so indefatigable, their equipage so light, and themselves such excellent horsemen, that no cavalry can pretend to follow them."[20]

Eighteenth-century Western Europeans, when they first encountered the variety of war that Khevenhüller-Metsch and Smith described, did not know how to respond. However, first the Austrians and then the French found ways to make Eastern-style *petite guerre* part of their regular military structures. In fact, the French led the way among the Continental powers in forging a protocol for *petite guerre* – a protocol that put irregular war in their military establishment and legitimated it.

In the first third of the eighteenth century, the Austrian Hapsburgs found that they could not control the eastern reaches of their empire without the support of the *huszars, dragons,* and *pandurs* who dominated the military situation there. The Hapsburgs needed a way to harness the military energies of the eastern irregulars and, like the North American colonial assemblies, responded by privatizing war. The Hapsburgs encouraged their subject Slav and Magyar noblemen to raise personal armies, whom the Austrians then organized as the *Grenz* (border troops). The Hapsburgs in Vienna granted the eastern nobles free rein in much of the day-to-day governance of their lands on the condition that they maintain military allegiance to the central government in Vienna and, when called upon, march against the Hapsburgs' enemies. To encourage the rank-and-file *Grenz*, commanders, with the tacit approval of their Hapsburg senior commanders, granted them the right to pillage and take booty normally prohibited to regulars. In time, war by the *Grenz* became a way for the Austrians to wage war cheaply, just as scalp hunting offered the New England provinces a relatively inexpensive way to strike at the Abenakis. As on the American frontier, *Grenz* service became a way of life on the eastern frontier of the Austrian Empire. By the time of the Seven Years' War, Empress Maria Theresa had incorporated nearly 40,000 *Grenz* soldiers in her regular army of over 200,000 men.[21]

The second third of the eighteenth century, especially in the wake of the French Army's difficulty in dealing with the Austrian *Grenz* in Bohemia during the War of Austrian Succession, saw an explosion of French interest in *petite guerre*. That led directly to the development of a doctrine incorporating it in formal practice.[22] That doctrine developed in three

20 George Smith, *An Universal Military Dictionary: A Copious Explanation of the Technical Terms &c* (1779; reprint, Ottawa: Museum Restoration Service, 1969), 59.
21 Childs, *Armies and Warfare in Europe*, 42.
22 John Ellis, *A Short History of Guerrilla Warfare* (New York: St. Martin's Press, 1976), 204–205. Ellis writes that the *Grenz* campaigns in Bohemia, along with the American

stages. The first, initiated by Saxe, legitimated *petite guerre* and molded it to French conceptions of regular war. In the early 1750s, the second stage in the development of the French *petite guerre* began. First, Armand François de La Croix's *Traité de la Petite Guerre pour les Compagnies Franches* was the first widely read work in French primarily devoted to *petite guerre.*[23] Then, Grandmaison's *La Petite Guerre* postulated the need for an irregular corps in the French Army. Captain Louis de Jeney's *Le Partisan* started the third phase. His book was the first tactics manual that detailed how one actually conducted irregular operations.

Saxe's posthumously published memoirs, the *Reveries*, although designed primarily as a text for regular war, legitimated elements of *petite guerre* in French military circles. In the *Reveries*, Saxe presented the means by which a European regular army could adopt parts of eastern-style irregular war to its military structure. Saxe's conceptualizations of the *guerre des postes* and the formation of a light infantry arm, both tools for *petite guerre*, set the course of the French Army's irregular doctrine and influenced British, Prussian, and Austrian understandings as well.

Saxe contended that the most effective way to combat irregulars was to force them to fight regulars on regulars' terms. With that in mind, Saxe developed his idea for the *guerre des postes* (war of the posts). The proper way to fight partisans, Saxe wrote, was "to avoid pursuing them, and to secure those posts which are properly situated, from whence one may be able, by parties of infantry, to subject the whole country about to contribution."[24]

The *guerre des postes* was well suited to anti-irregular operations in eighteenth-century Europe. Although they often spoke of "partisans" – English, French, and German soldiers all used the term to describe irregulars – the eighteenth-century meaning of the word was bereft of political connotations.[25] Eighteenth-century partisans generally did not fight for political and ideological reasons, as today's partisans do; controlling an enemy's hinterlands or winning the hearts and minds of an eighteenth-century peasantry was not necessary to secure victory in the ancien régime. In an age when armies needed not to subdue enemy populations, but only enemy governments and monarchs, the *guerre des postes* offered a potential solution to the constant harassment of enemy partisans.[26]

campaign against the British in South Carolina in 1780–1781, are the "notable guerrilla wars" of the eighteenth century.

23 Armand François de La Croix, *Traité de la Petite Guerre pour les Compagnies Franches* (Paris: A. Boudet, 1752).
24 Saxe, *Reveries*, 137–138.
25 Robert Aspery, *War in the Shadows: The Guerrilla in History*, 2d ed. (New York: William Morrow and Company, Inc., 1994), 48–49.
26 Loren B. Thompson argues that the most common form of war in the modern world is low-intensity conflict, which he defines as terrorism and counterterrorism, insurgency

The second technique of *petite guerre* that Saxe championed centered on his creation of light infantry companies for service in the French regular establishment.[27] Saxe proposed to attach one company of 70 "light-armed foot" to each regiment. (The building block of the eighteenth-century infantry was a company of approximately 30 privates, eight noncommissioned officers, one captain, one lieutenant, and one drummer. Ten or more companies would make up a battalion. Within the French Army in the Seven Years' War, two battalions of 16 line companies and one light infantry or grenadier company made up a regiment.) The light companies, Saxe noted, were to become expert marksmen and focus on training and conditioning for the rigors of *petite guerre*. Saxe suggested that the light-armed foot should consist of the youngest, most fit men in the army and the officers chosen from the regiments based not on seniority but on merit. "A body of infantry composed according to this plan," Saxe believed, "and thoroughly inured to labour, can march anywhere with the cavalry, and, I am confident, will be capable of doing very considerable service."[28]

Saxe suggested that lightly accoutered infantrymen could work equally well in irregular and regular operations. They could patrol the country surrounding his *postes*, defend regular troops on the march against enemy partisan attacks, and serve as an effective tool to defeat other regular armies.[29] The mobile light infantry could cover the front, rear, and flanks of French columns and, with rifled weapons that could hit targets 300 paces away, protect them from marauding bands of *huszars* and *dragons*.[30] Similarly, in battles between regular forces, the light troops could use their skills as marksmen to kill the opposing side's officers. With the leadership of the other army thus devastated, its rank and file would panic and open itself to defeat.[31]

Every major Western European army adopted a variation of light-armed foot to protect its convoys and detachments from enemy partisans. The

and counterinsurgency, and other special operations. A common characteristic of all modern low-intensity conflicts is their highly politicized nature, which "tend[s] to blur the traditional distinction between soldier and civilian and between front-lines and rear areas." See Thompson, ed., *Low-Intensity Conflict: The Pattern of Warfare in the Modern World* (New York: D. C. Heath and Company, 1989), ix.

27 For the organization of a typical mid-eighteenth-century European army, see Lee Kennett, *The French Armies in the Seven Years' War: A Study in Military Organization and Administration* (Durham, NC: Duke University Press, 1967). In the provincial armies in North America, most regiments were single-battalion regiments.

28 Saxe, *Reveries*, 41.

29 Ibid., 40–41.

30 Volleys were the only effective way that regulars with smooth-bore muskets could deliver shock-inducing fire on eighteenth- and early-nineteenth-century battlefields. See B. P. Hughes, *Fire Power: Weapons Effectiveness on the Battlefield, 1630–1850* (New York: Charles Scribner's Sons, 1974), 10–11.

31 Saxe, *Reveries*, 50.

British Army, for instance, in 1741 and 1742 attached light infantry companies to each of its regiments. Thirty years later, it institutionalized a light company for each battalion.[32] In the War of Austrian Succession and the Seven Years' War, Frederick the Great formed the Königlich Pruessisches Feld Jäger Corps and the Feld Jäger Corps zu Fuß – both corps of light infantrymen – to act as irregulars. Frederick found that his much-vaunted regulars were more than a match for Maria Theresa's but could do little against her *Grenz*. Frederick's officers levied their *Jägers* from Central European hunters and game wardens who were skilled in the use of rifles. In time, the Prussian *Jägers* became more than light troops; they also served as military police. By the era of the American Revolution, *Jäger* corps were home to the elite infantry of Europe and the training ground for the top officers in the Prussian Army. Ewald, for instance, noted that the *Jäger* Corps was the ideal place for a young officer to learn the art of war. *Jäger* officers, he wrote, "do on a small scale what a general does on a large scale."[33]

By the end of the Seven Years' War, most of the minor German principalities had followed Frederick's example and created their own *Jäger* companies. The most famous were, of course, the Hessian *Jägers*, of whom two companies, one commanded by Ewald, fought for the British in North America in the War of Independence. In 1758, the Hapsburgs raised a *Jäger* corps of ethnic Germans. Also by the same year, the French distributed *chasseurs à pied* – their version of *Jägers* – throughout their Army. In that year, for example, the French Army of the Lower Rhine included one company of *chasseurs à pied* within each 16-company line battalion.

The naming practices of the German and French irregulars point to the growing legitimacy of *petite guerre* within the Continental culture of war making. In Hungarian, *huszar* means "freebooter," while "Cossack," derived from *quzaq*, means "adventurer" or "freebooter." But when the French and Prussians created their corps of irregulars in the early and mid-eighteenth century, they followed the example of the Serbs. In Old Serb, *pandur* means "constable" or "guardian of the public peace." *Chausseur* is the French word for "hunter," and *Jäger* is loosely translated as "game warden." The Continental powers chose not to call their irregulars either *voleur* or *Dieb* ("thief"). The British Army, on the other hand, referred,

---

32 For the European side of the development of British light infantry see Charles Messenger, *For Love of Regiment: A History of the British Infantry, Volume One, 1660–1914* (London: Leo Cooper, 1994), 57–86. Peter Paret notes that the Prussian General Staff reforms of the Napoleonic era that resulted in the incorporation of light infantry and partisan troops originated not in colonial America, but in the eighteenth-century military experience in Central Europe. See Paret, "Colonial Experience and Military Reform at the End of the Eighteenth Century," *Bulletin of the Institute of Historical Research* 37 (1964): 49–59.

33 Ewald, *Partisan Warfare*, 68.

perhaps through ignorance, to its irregulars with derogatory terms. For example, while horse-mounted French irregulars took the name "free companies," British horse-mounted irregulars became known as "dragoons," an Anglicization of the Turkish *dragon*, "scum."

The development of the French tradition of *petite guerre* entered a second phase in the 1750s. In 1752, Armand de La Croix published his memoirs recounting his service as a French irregular; this became the first widely read work on *petite guerre*.[34] Before the *Traité*, the only work devoted explicitly to *petite guerre* was Jean Charles de Folard's *De la Guerre des Partisans*. However, Folard never published his work; he only circulated it in manuscript form to friends and select officers.[35] Thus, Folard has gone down in European military history not as the originator of a doctrine of irregular war, but instead as one of the first proponents of column-based tactical units.[36] La Croix's work, on the other hand, won an instant following. Indeed, only three years after its publication in French, a German-language version became available and would remain the classic work on *petite guerre* in that language until Ewald's *Treatise of Partisan Warfare* was published.

The *Traité* prepared the ground for Grandmaison's seminal *La Petite Guerre*, published in 1756. *La Petite Guerre* was Grandmaison's attempt to bring irregular war to the forefront of the mid-eighteenth-century French Army's collective consciousness by calling for the creation of a large, full-time irregular corps in the French regular establishment. Before Grandmaison, commanders formed irregular units, like the Compagnies Franches, on an ad hoc basis as the need for them arose. Grandmaison, however, argued that the War of Austrian Succession had shown that a "new age" of European war had begun, an age in which irregulars would play a pivotal role.

Grandmaison had fought the *Grenz* in Bavaria and Bohemia and believed that the most important lesson that the French Army could learn from that conflict was the value of irregulars to a regular army. Grandmaison argued that the War of Austrian Succession proved the utility of "light & irregular troops" in modern war. The *Grenz*, he wrote, ceaselessly harassed French convoys, hospitals, baggage trains, foragers, detachments, and marauded across the countryside in "*grand nombre*." Grandmaison argued that although "neither seeing nor fighting" the main French Army, the *Grenz* managed to bring ruin to it.[37]

---

34 Ibid., note 11, 138.
35 Ibid., note 12, 41. Neither La Croix, Grandmaison, nor Jeney listed Folard as inspiring their writings.
36 Hans Delbrück, *The Dawn of Modern Warfare: History of the Art of War, Volume IV*, trans Walter J. Renfroe, Jr. (Lincoln: University of Nebraska Press, 1985), 399.
37 Grandmaison, *La Petite Guerre*, 4–5.

L A

PETITE GUERRE,

Duler ajedu Major

TRAITE DU SERVICE

DES TROUPES LEGERES

EN CAMPAGNE.

Par M. DE GRANDMAISON, *Capitaine, avec Commiſſion de Lieutenant-Colonel de Cavalerie au Corps des Volontaires de Flandre.*

PREMIERE PARTIE.

M. DCC. LVI.

Title page of Grandmaison's *La Petite Guerre*

Grandmaison believed that the French Army had taken appropriate steps to combat the problem of the *Grenz* during the war. In 1744, for example, it heeded the advice of officers like him and created the regiments Grassin, La Morlière, and Volontaires-Bretons, all units modeled on the *Grenz*. The next year it placed the Compagnie Franche in the regular establishment as the Legion Royal. "In Flanders, after the formation of the Regiments *Grassin* & *La Morlière*," Grandmaison wrote, "we enjoyed in our camps the same tranquility as the Austrians in Bohemia and Bavaria."[38]

Grandmaison, after the war, wanted the French Army to create several irregular battalions, and, if necessary, hire what he called "German" – Central European – mercenaries to man them. With such a force, Grandmaison wrote, the French Army could harass its enemies night and day, cover its own convoys and foragers, secure its marches, ensure the security of its posts, guard its supplies, gather intelligence, and keep order in camp. As Grandmaison envisioned it, for an irregular corps "there are often occasion where the General can employ them as the *avant-garde* and the rear guard, to attack the small posts that he finds on his march, to reconnoiter the movements of the enemy, to guard a forest or a defile during a battle." Indeed, he continued, irregular troops were the best troops possible to guard the rear and flanks of the army; to traverse woods, mountains, marshes, and canals that the enemy had to cross; and to establish ambushes at strategic points.[39]

The development of the French doctrine of *petite guerre* entered its third stage in 1759 with the publication of Jeney's *Le Partisan*. Whereas Grandmaison had presented an argument showing the need for irregulars, Jeney composed the first European manual on the mechanics of *petite guerre* operations. We can see *Le Partisan* as a precursor to a "special forces" tradition of highly trained and elite troops that operated primarily behind enemy lines not as freebooters, but in close coordination with a regular army.

Jeney stressed that partisans must be the best soldiers from the regular army; their officers had to exemplify professional knowledge of war and leadership skills. The ideal partisan officer must possess *coup d'œil* (an intuitive grasp of military matters including strategy, tactics, and leadership), an "intrepid heart against all appearances of danger," self-assurance, robust and indefatigable health, and the confidence of his men.[40] When brought together, the best soldiers and best officers could

---

38   Ibid., 5–6.
39   Ibid., 12, 8–9, 397, 399.
40   Louis Jeney, *Le Partisan; ou, l'art de faire la petiteguerre avec succès selon le génie de nos jours* (La Haye, France: H. Constapel, 1759), 6–7.

then accomplish the demanding tasks of *petite guerre*. For their bravery and skill, Jeney promised, they would attain the highest place of honor and glory in the army.[41]

Jeney insisted that the most self-disciplined men comprise the partisan corps because irregulars had to operate without close supervision. The main objective of irregulars previously had been to protect the regular army by harassing the enemy's regulars. Jeney, on the other hand, argued that French irregulars should operate apart from the main army to infiltrate enemy lines, ambush outposts, disrupt convoys, raid garrisons, gather intelligence, and put into "use all the proper ruses to surprise them or disturb" the enemy supply and communication networks.[42] Self-discipline engendered through esprit de corps, meanwhile, could prevent the French partisan from engaging into Cossack-like looting and atrocities.

Jeney therefore developed a detailed protocol for operating behind enemy lines. Since partisans would operate in hostile territory, they needed to blend into the countryside. Jeney, for instance, suggested that partisans be fluent in foreign languages to aid in gathering intelligence.[43] He described how one conducted "secret marches." He discussed in detail the procedures for establishing ambushes behind enemy lines. He instructed partisan officers to divide their corps into two parties, one to attack the enemy from behind while the other held it in place. Jeney advised that an ambush must be executed from a position that would allow the partisans an avenue of retreat should they encounter a superior force. Jeney even devoted a section of *Le Partisan* to the eighteenth-century version of field-condition medicine. Since the partisans would operate behind enemy lines, and no troops were "more exposed to the intemperance of air, to the fatigues of a campaign & to the dangers of war," partisan officers would have to treat their soldiers' wounds and illnesses without the aid of a regimental surgeon. Thus Jeney suggested treatments for the typical eighteenth-century ailments, including indigestion, sore throats, eye and ear injuries, ulcers, pleurisy, and fevers.[44]

Jeney's *Le Partisan* was the last European-produced treatise on *petite guerre* for nearly 20 years. As such, it was the apogee in the mid-eighteenth-century's development of a Continental way of irregular war. Indeed, by the middle of the eighteenth century, Western European soldiers

---

41 Ibid., 8.
42 Ibid., 2–3.
43 Not until 1776, when Lewis Lochée, superintendent of the quasi-official military college at Woolwich, published his *An Essay on Military Education* (London: T. Cadell, 1776), did the British Army specifically suggest that officers speak languages in addition to English. See ibid., 48–49.
44 Jeney, *Le Partisan*, 35, 115, 150.

had created a tradition of *petite guerre* rooted in both experience and doctrine, from the *Grenz* through the *Grassin* to the *Jägers*, and in the doctrines of Saxe, La Croix, Grandmaison, and Jeney. By the Seven Years' War, *petite guerre* was well on its way to becoming an accepted and legitimate part of the Continental conceptualizations of war. Within the British Army, no similar development occurred.

III. The British Army and *Petite Guerre*

The English conquest of Ireland in the sixteenth and seventeenth centuries proceeded without the kinds of restraints that characterized military activities between nation-states in the eighteenth century. The English quite consciously used unlimited warfare to subdue the "heathen" and "savage" Irish. At the center of the English military solution to the "problem of Ireland" was a dependence on the feedfight, terrorism, and indiscriminate killing of noncombatants.[45] In the second half of the seventeenth century, Englishmen in Ireland in fact embraced an unlimited paradigm of campaigning that was more in line with fighting in North America than with evolving Continental patterns of limited war.[46]

Three factors shaped the English military experience in Ireland. First, Englishmen perceived Ireland as a land for exploitation: a place capable of enriching England only if they could turn the troublesome Irish into a tractable peasantry. Second, the divisions within Irish society between Protestants and Catholics fortified the military conflict and, in turn, led it to take on the emotional fervor of the Wars of Religion.[47] Third, England faced no regular military establishment in Ireland. The Irish peasantry never had an army large or skilled enough to challenge the colonizers in a regular-style battle, and Irish soldiers, at any rate, preferred to fight as partisans.[48] Irishmen and Irishwomen used the tools of irregular war – arson, murder, and terrorism – to oppose British occupation of their

---

45 William Edward Hartpole Lecky, *A History of Ireland in the Eighteenth Century*, 5 vols. (1892; reprint, New York: AMS Press, 1969), 1: 3–6, wrote that Elizabethan Englishmen routinely killed Irish noncombatants and destroyed "all means of human subsistence."

46 For the similarities between the English conceptions of the Irish and Indians, see Nicholas P. Canny, "The Ideology of English Colonization: From Ireland to America," *WMQ* 30 (1973): 575–598, and James Muldoon, "The Indian as Irishman," Essex Institute *Historical Collections* 111 (1975): 267–289.

47 Hugh Kearney, *The British Isles: A History of Four Nations* (New York: Cambridge University Press, 1995), 162.

48 For the Irish way of war, see David Beers Quinn, *The Elizabethans and the Irish* (Ithaca, NY: Cornell University Press, 1966), 41–43.

homeland. Those factors combined to make Ireland, in English circles, a place where conventional norms of military behavior did not apply.[49]

The English adapted to the military situation in Ireland through three nontraditional approaches to war – a *guerre des postes*, feedfights, and forced transportation. As a first response, the English garrisoned strategic seaports and provincial capitals and used their army to "hold down" the "natives" within the Pale of Settlement. Of course, that approach, like all uses of the *guerre des postes*, abdicated most of the control of the Irish countryside to potentially anti-English elements. In times of rebellion, the *guerre des postes* offered little protection to either isolated garrisons or Anglo-Irish settlers. At the start of the Rebellion of 1641–1642, for instance, Viscount Montgomery of the Ards wrote that the Irish rebels, unopposed by regular troops, would easily seize towns and garrisons and make "spoil of the rest of the country."[50]

During times of rebellion, the English abandoned the *guerre des postes* for the feedfight. In the winters of 1641 and 1642, the English garrison in Dublin executed a feedfight against every Irish town within a dozen miles of the town. The raids of 1641–1642 were no exception to the rule of wanton destruction aimed at reducing an entire population to submission – or starvation – and dependence on their conquerors. George Cook's account of his 1652 feedfight against Irish rebels presents a further stark view of the English operations in Ireland. "In searching the woods and bogs," Cook reported, "we found great stores of corn, which we burnt, also all the houses and cabins we could find: in all which we found great plenty of corn. We continued burning and destroying for four days: in which time we wanted no provision for horse or man, finding housing enough to lie in; though we burnt our quarters every morning, and continued burning all day after."[51]

The most successful and largest-scale irregular practice that the English inflicted on the Irish was the expropriation of Irish lands and forced transportation of Irishmen and Irishwomen to the West Indies and North America. One way to force the Irish to accept English domination of Ireland, the English thought, was to deny Catholic proprietors their landed property. When resistance rose, plans were set afoot for the distribution

49   Nicholas Canny, in "The Marginal Kingdom: Ireland as a Problem in the First British Empire," *Strangers within the Realm: Cultural Margins of the First British Empire*, eds. Bernard Bailyn and Philip D. Morgan (Chapel Hill: University of North Carolina Press for IEAHC, 1991), 61, has made the similar argument that Ireland was a place where accepted norms of behavior generally did not apply.
50   Viscount Montgomery of the Ards to the King, October 24, 1641, *CSPI*, 2: 341.
51   Stephen Saunders Webb, *The Governors-General: The English Army and the Definition of the Empire, 1569–1681* (Chapel Hill: University of North Carolina Press for IEAHC, 1979), 40–41.

of this property among English soldiers and officials who had served in Ireland, or to English and Scottish favorites.[52] In 1645, for instance, the English Parliament ordered that the estates of all "Papists and Delinquents discovered in Ireland" be seized and used to pay for the establishment of more troops in the colony.[53] The Irish, with their land occupied by Englishmen, Scots, and pro-English Irish, had few options. By the start of the eighteenth century, "it would be difficult indeed to conceive of a national condition less favorable than that of Ireland to a man of energy and ambition." English Protestants stigmatized Catholics, excluded them from every position of trust and influence, and barred them from virtually every means of acquiring wealth. Irish Protestants, meanwhile, were "almost compelled to emigrate, for industrial and commercial enterprise had been deliberately crushed." The result was a steady tide of Irish emigration to the New World.[54]

The English experience in Scotland mirrored its experience in Ireland. Like Ireland, the English viewed the Scottish Highlands as marchland, a place where traditional rules of civilized behavior did not apply to Englishmen fighting against "wild and barbarous" Highlanders, so long as they permitted greater control of the Highlands. Complicating British attempts to bring Scotland into the English orbit was the resistance of much of the Highland nobility to English rule, the opposition of Scottish Roman Catholics to Anglican dominance of their homeland, and the fact that neither the English nor the Scots could agree on who "owned" the border between England and Scotland. Indeed, between 1040 and 1745, every English monarch but three suffered a Scottish invasion or invaded Scotland.[55] To the mix was added Jacobite sentiment following the overthrow of James Stuart as King James II of England. Indeed, for most of the first half of the eighteenth century, Jacobitism was a major threat to the stability of the Hanoverian monarchs of England.[56]

The first major outbreak of militant Jacobitism in the eighteenth century occurred in 1715 in the wake of the War of Spanish Succession and the accession of King George I to the British throne. Ironically, much of the

---

52 See Canny, "The Marginal Kingdom," 38.
53 Further Orders of the Committee of Both Houses for Irish Affairs, September 27, 1645, *CSPI*, 2: 416.
54 "It would be difficult": Lecky, *History of Ireland*, 1: 244–248.
55 "The Highlands," Eric Richards notes, "represented the most resistant and challenging marchland in Britain, a province so backward that it was often compared with America as a proper zone for colonization." See Richards, "Scotland and the Uses of the Atlantic Empire," *Strangers within the Realm*, 81. David Hackett Fischer, *Albion's Seed: Four British Folkways in America* (New York: Oxford University Press, 1989), 623.
56 See Lord Lovat to Stanhope, January 28, 1717, Great Britain, Public Records Office, *State Papers, Domestic Series, George I (S.P. 35), Typescript Calendar* (London: Swift Printers, 1977–1980), 8.

English debate on civil–military affairs from the English Civil War through the Glorious Revolution had centered on how monarchs would use standing armies to destroy their subjects' liberties. Indeed, a major cause of the Glorious Revolution was the fear that the Catholic King James II would enlarge and use the standing army to deny Englishmen their rights. When his place on the throne was endangered, however, King George I cared little for the ideological sentiment that opposed the use of the British Army against British subjects. Upon hearing that the Pretender might land in Scotland, George I placed a bounty of £100,000 on his head.[57] Similarly, George instructed the Army to arrest all suspected Jacobites. Much of the indigenous Scottish leadership wisely fled to France.

Unlike the poorly organized rising of 1715, the Jacobite Rebellion of 1745 posed a serious threat to the stability and security of the Hanoverians. In the summer of 1745 Prince Charles Edward Stuart (the Young Pretender), grandson of James Stuart, landed in Scotland at the head of a small French army. One of King George II's first responses was to place a £30,000 bounty on Bonnie Prince Charlie's head and dispatch a regular army under the command of Sir John Cope to meet him in battle. As Cope dallied and spent time requisitioning supplies for an army much larger than the one he commanded, thousands of Highlanders flocked to the Young Pretender's banner. Robert Craigie, Lord Advocate of Scotland, complained that while the British Army sat by and did nothing, the Highlanders moved about the countryside "arming and increasing their numbers, and send their emissaries over all the Highlands to stir up a general insurrection by threats and promises."[58]

By mid-August, it was clear that the Jacobites had gained control of the land surrounding the two main garrisons of the British in the Highlands, Forts William and Augustus. The Highlanders controlled the road between the forts and had cut all communication between them. The British commander in Fort William had little choice but to send out a party to reopen the road. On August 16, he ordered two companies of the Royal Scots to march from Fort William to Fort Augustus in a show of force. A short way into their march, an unknown number of Highlanders ambushed and killed a dozen of them and took the rest prisoner.[59]

The defeat of the Royal Scots gave the Jacobite cause the upper hand and led more neutrals to join the rebellion. The day before the rebels ambushed the Royal Scots, the earl of Findlater wrote to Craigie that

---

57 Proclamation for the Pretender, September 15, 1714, ibid., 1.
58 Marquis of Tweeddale to the Lord Advocate [Robert Craigie], August 1, 1745, *Memoirs of the Pretenders and their Adherents*, ed. John Heneage Jesse (London: George Ball and Sons, 1890), 459. The Lord Justice's Clerk to the Marquis of Tweeddale, August 20, 1745, ibid., 483.
59 Ibid.; Fortescue, *British Army*, 126.

if "a few regiments" of regulars were sent north from England into the Highlands, "it would be in their power to quell the insurrection before it can be brought to any great length."[60] After the defeat of the Royal Scots, however, the marquis Tweeddale understood that regulars were of little use in the Highlands. The Highlanders, like the natives of North America, would "retire" in the face of a regular attack into "the country where there might be any difficulty to get at them with regular troops."[61]

The military situation in Scotland quickly reached a crisis point for the Hanoverians. By September, it appeared that the Young Pretender's army would march directly on London. Cope therefore sent his army north to meet the Jacobites in battle. The ensuing battle of Prestonpans was a disaster for the British Army. Cope's raw and undisciplined regulars panicked at the first sight of the claymore-wielding, screaming Highlander irregulars. As Cope aligned his men to fight a traditional eighteenth-century set-piece battle, the Highlanders rushed "upon the enemy sword in hand, as soon as they saw them, without order and without discipline."[62] In the ensuing 10-minute melee, the Highlanders killed 400 of Cope's Redcoats and took 1,000 prisoners. "Never," wrote Sir John Fortescue, "was a victory so complete."[63]

Yet even after the defeat of the Royal Scots and Cope's army at Prestonpans, most Englishmen were slow to grasp the nature of the war they faced. Expressing the hostility of most British professional soldiers toward *petite guerre*, Lord John Ligonier wrote peevishly from Flanders that eight regiments of regulars could "putt out this infernal flame [Jacobism] at ones" and crush the "Beggarly banditry."[64] Another Englishmen suggested that the Scots irregulars were not serious military opponents; rather than "waste" the regular army on the Scots, they should be hunted and exterminated like vermin. "Do not," he wrote, "let us lavish the expense of preparation necessary to be made against an *Alexander* in opposition to a ragged hungry rabble of Yahoos of *Scotch Highlanders*; let us not hunt a rat with the charge, pomp, and terror of apparatus with which he would meet a lion on the plain."[65] What that commentator failed to realize, of course, was that it was the "Yahoos" who were doing most of the "hunting" of the regular British Army in the Highlands.

---

60 Earl of Findlater to Lord Advocate, August 15, 1745, Jesse, *Memoirs of the Pretenders*, 474.
61 Marquis of Tweeddale to Lord Advocate, August 24, 1745, ibid., 489.
62 Chevalier de Johnston, *A Memoir of the 'Forty-Five*, ed. Brian Rawson (London: Folio Society, 1958), 33.
63 Fortescue, *British Army*, 131.
64 Ligonier quoted in Rex Whitworth, *Field Marshal Lord Ligonier: A Story of the British Army, 1702–1770* (Oxford: Clarendon Press, 1958), 108.
65 Anon., "A Popish Pretender to be cutt, and the Growth of Popery to be prevented," *Gentleman's Magazine* 15 (1745): 547.

James Oglethorpe, fresh from his service in Georgia, could see that the regulars were the wrong type of troops to fight an enemy like the Scottish Highlanders in rough and wild terrain. As soon as he arrived in Scotland in the winter of 1745–1746, he changed the way that the British Army confronted the Jacobite rebels. One of his first acts was to confine the regulars to their garrisons and distribute arms among the Scottish population still loyal to Britain. Upon the outbreak of the rebellion, Duncan Forbes of Culloden had raised 20 "independent companies" of pro-British Scots. Oglethorpe instructed that those "irregulars [the independent companies] were to be detached in small patrols, supported by parties of the regulars, with orders to attack any patrols of the rebels they might fall in with."[66]

Oglethorpe's use of loyal Scottish irregulars for *petite guerre* solved the major problem that had faced the British Army in the previous months, namely, its inability to march through the Highlands. The Scottish irregulars "were more suitably attired and of greater utility than those of the line, who were unused to a mountainous and difficult country where even the language was not understood. . . . They could traverse peat bog and mountain with ease, where the cumbersomely clad and accoutered soldiers of the line, whether horse or foot, would flounder helplessly or be unable to proceed or only with difficulty."[67]

With his irregulars providing intelligence and forcing the Jacobites onto the defensive, British regulars could concentrate on consolidating their hold on the areas that they occupied and rooting out Jacobitism. The regulars' preferred method quickly became intimidating the family members of suspected Jacobites. In Edinburgh, for example, British officers warned the town's inhabitants that "they would be punished with military execution if they aided the rebels."[68]

When William Augustus, duke of Cumberland, finally arrived in Scotland in the spring of 1746, Oglethorpe's loyal Scots had gone far toward reestablishing control in the Scottish countryside. Then, ignoring the recommendation of his French military advisors, Bonnie Prince Charlie chose to accept battle with Cumberland at Culloden on April 16, 1746. The Young Pretender insisted on placing his Highlander irregulars in a linear formation, from which he expected them to stand and exchange volleys with Cumberland's regulars, many of whom were veterans of Fontenoy. The outcome of the battle was never in doubt. In a reversal of Prestonpans,

---

66 I. H. Mackay Scobie, "The Highland Independent Companies of 1745–1747," *JSAHR* 20 (1941): 17. Anon., "Motions of the Rebels," *Gentleman's Magazine* 15 (1745): 624.
67 Scobie, "Highland Independent Companies," 31–32.
68 Anon., "Retreat of the Rebels," *Gentleman's Magazine*, 15 (1746): 26; anon., "Behaviour of the Rebels at Derby," ibid., 709; anon., "Extract of a Letter from a Gentleman at Derby, Dec. 13," ibid., 16 (1746), 90; Donald Cameron and Alexander McDonnell to Mr. Steward, March 20, 1746, ibid., 173–174.

the veterans of Fontenoy killed 1,000 of the Pretender's troops and took 500 captive.

With the Pretender's main army defeated, the British Army focused its attention on ending the rebellion and punishing those responsible for it. Cumberland unleashed his regulars and loyal Scots partisans on Highlander rebels and noncombatants alike. For three months, the "Butcher of Culloden" proscribed the leaders of the rebellion, executed or transported them to North America, and garrisoned the Scottish countryside with soldiers whose primary mission was to intimidate the local populace into submission. In the eighteenth-century version of show trials, the English and their Scottish allies summarily tried, convicted, and imprisoned or executed many of the Highland leaders.[69] The Scottish irregulars proved particularly valuable "both in guarding the passes and cooperating with the troops of the line in searching both mainland and isles for the fugitive Jacobites."[70] Fortescue, 150 years after the fact, defended the British terror campaign in the Highlands as the way "a victorious campaign against mountaineers must always end, in the hunting of fugitives, the burning of villages, and the destruction of crops."[71]

The suppression of the '45 was the high point of Cumberland's military career and the most successful "counterinsurgency" of the eighteenth century. After Culloden and the terror campaign against the rebellious Scots, Jacobitism never again threatened the political stability of Great Britain. The British Army, with the use of irregular means, had resolved the most pressing internal problem facing the British state and the Hanoverian monarchy. Yet when the British Army looked back on its victory over Jacobitism, it saw it as a victory of regulars over irregulars, not the successful application of a mix of regular and irregular tactics.

In January 1746, at a time when British forces had conceded the Scottish countryside to bands of "Yahoos," there appeared in *Gentleman's*

---

69   Robert C. Jarvis, ed., *Collected Papers on the Jacobite Risings*, 2 vols. (New York: Manchester University Press, 1972), 2: 283.

70   Scobie, "Highland Independent Companies," 31. Part of the success of the anti-Jacobite campaign after 1746 was the incorporation of even greater segments of the Lowland Scots into British society and their assignment to positions of power and influence within the British colonial system. Still, Parliament felt compelled in July 1746 to root out all potential sources of Jacobitism and ordered the "restraining the use of the Highland dress" and the disarming of the Highland clans. See House of Commons Proceedings, July 4, 1746, Leo Francis Stock, ed., *Proceedings and Debates of the British Parliaments Respecting North America, Volume 5, 1739–1754* (Washington, DC: Carnegie Institution, 1941), 239.

71   Fortescue, *British Army*, 146. The British victory at Culloden occasioned great celebrations and numerous contemporary artistic depictions of the '45. However, in the contemporary visual images (paintings, engravings, and sketches) of the '45, nothing, understandably, was printed of the terror campaign. See Peter Harrinton, "Images of Culloden," *JSAHR* 63 (1985): 208–219.

Magazine a brief anonymous "Essay on Regular and Irregular Forces."[72] The "Essay" is significant in that, as a thoroughgoing diatribe against irregular soldiers and irregular methods, it exemplified the British attitude toward *petite guerre* at midcentury.

The author of the "Essay" believed that well-disciplined regulars always would prevail over irregulars. He argued that the methods of the Scottish Highlanders, and their victory over Cope's regulars, were not the result of the superiority of the irregular way of war, but rather were caused by the ineptitude of Cope and his soldiers. In fact, the author explained, every defeat of a regular army at the hands of an irregular force resulted from three basic reasons: disparity in numbers (even the best of troops could be overrun by overwhelming numbers); misconduct of officers (manifested in "surprise, temerity, [or] cowardice"); and poor training, which made regulars confronted by the "difference of weapons" between irregulars and themselves, and disoriented by the "confusion" of battle, prone to panic. Regulars who maintained proper order had nothing to fear from partisans. To suggest that they adopt irregular tactics, he argued, was to invite disaster. "It is particularly to be observed," he wrote, "that regular men can never fight well when reduced to the form of a mob, no more than a mob can fight like regular men."[73]

The author of the "Essay" misunderstood the nature of eighteenth-century *petite guerre*, both in Europe and in North America. Indians and French Troupes de la Marine in North America, and *Grassin* and Highlanders in Europe, never intended to stand and fight British regulars in a battle in which the British would have a numerical advantage. Moreover, irregulars always used surprise to strike at their enemies. Amid that confusion, regular officers would, irregulars hoped, make mistakes. Eighteenth-century irregulars used surprise to close quickly on the enemy and to defeat it before the enemy could react. However imperfect his grasp of irregular war, the author of the "Essay" could hardly have provided a more perfect summary of the conventional professional officer's point of view on *petite guerre*.

With the regular victory at Culloden and the explanation in the "Essay" for the defeat at Prestonpans in hand, the British Army chose to ignore *petite guerre*. Not until 1775 did British Anglophones have a manual for *petite guerre*. But Roger Stevenson's *Military Instructions for Officers Detached in the Field: Containing, a Scheme for Forming a Corps of a Partisan* was published and printed in America and was only partially devoted to *petite guerre*. In 1777, Grandmaison's *La Petite Guerre* was

---

72 Anon., "Essay on Regular and Irregular Forces," *Gentleman's Magazine* 16 (1746): 30–32.
73 Ibid., 31.

finally translated and published in English. Even then, the title of the English translation led readers to believe that the book was not about *petite guerre*, but about cavalry operations.[74] Indeed, it took until 1896 and the publication of Colonel Charles E. Calwell's *Small Wars* for the British Army to have a formalized doctrine of *petite guerre* written by one of its own.[75] Thus, any mid-eighteenth-century British officer who wished to read about little war had no choice but to consult foreign works in foreign languages. Even if the translations had been true to the originals, only an exceptional few junior officers in the British Army would have read them. Since patronage was the basis of promotion in the eighteenth-century British Army, "Once started in the service a young officer had few incentives to study or interest himself in the theory of war."[76] Senior officers, meanwhile, focused their professional study on regular war. George Smith's 1779 recommended reading list of the "chief instruments of acquiring knowledge" of the military science is instructive. His list of books in English centered on drill, discipline, field fortifications, and the exploits of the Great Captains – Maurice of Orange, Gustavus Adolphus, and the duke of Marlborough, to name three. Smith's list of foreign works contained neither Saxe, La Croix, Grandmaison, nor Jeney. In their place, he recommended francophone books on the fortification system of Vauban and Marlborough's campaigns.[77] Without a base of doctrine to grow, the British Army devoted almost no time to training its men or junior officers in *petite guerre*.[78] Without hands-on experience of fighting in

---

74 Roger Stevenson, *Military Instructions for Officers in the Field: Containing, a Scheme for Forming a Corps of a Partisan* (1775; reprint, *Early American Imprints, 1639–1800* [New Canaan, CT: Readex, 1981–1982]), microfiche 14475. Grandmaison, *A Treatise on the Military Service, of Light Horse, and Light Infantry, in the Field, and in Fortified Places* (Philadelphia: Robert Bell, 1777). The translator took significant liberties with the original title of *La Petite Guerre, ou traité du service des troupes legeres en campagne* [*Little War, or a Treatise on the Service of Light Troops in the Field*].

75 Charles E. Calwell, *Small Wars: Their Principles and Practice* (London: HMSO, 1896).

76 "Once started": James W. Hayes, "The Social and Professional Background of the Officers of the British Army, 1714–1763" (M.A. thesis, University of London, 1956). The British Army did not abolish the purchase system until November 1, 1871. The tradition of giving a commission to the individual who raised a regiment lasted until 1858. See H. Biddulph, "The Era of Army Purchase," *JSAHR* 12 (1933): 229.

77 Ira Gruber has argued that most of the professional British soldiers who fought in North America during the Revolution were intellectual heirs to two lines of strategic thought – the primary classical one, based on works like Caesar's *Commentaries*, and the more modern one, based on the European model of dynastic war. See Gruber, "Classical Influences on British Strategy in the American War of Independence," *Classical Traditions in Early America*, ed. John W. Eadie (Ann Arbor, MI: Center for Coordination of Ancient and Modern Studies, 1976), 175–190. Smith, *An Universal Military Dictionary*, 32–34.

78 J. A. Houlding, *Fit for Service: The Training of the British Army, 1715–1795* (Oxford: Clarendon Press, 1981), 95.

North America, as James Oglethorpe had, it is likely that a British officer would have understood very little of the practice – or dangers – of *petite guerre*.

It was in North America that British soldiers would pay dearly for their officers' ignorance of the basics of *petite guerre*. British officers, including the commander of the Fort Duquesne expedition, Major General Edward Braddock, believed that their North American enemies were no different from the "bandit" *pandurs* or *huszars* of Eastern Europe. As he prepared to march into the North American wilderness, Braddock only halfheartedly tried to raise four companies of "Foot Rangers" and one squadron of "horse rangers" to "secure" his march against Fort Duquesne.[79] Braddock then "slighted & neglected" the handful of American rangers who volunteered and treated his potential Indian allies even worse. When Benjamin Franklin suggested to Braddock that he might need more rangers and Indians than he had requested, Braddock, Franklin wrote years after the fact and perhaps to justify the superiority of all things American over British, "Smiled at my Ignorance, & replied 'These Savages may indeed be a formidable Enemy to your raw American Militia; but, upon the King's regular & disciplined Troops, Sir, it is impossible they should make any Impression.'"[80]

The "savages," however, made a profound impression on the King's regulars when they met them in battle on the Monongahela River on July 9, 1755. As Braddock and his 1,469 men approached Fort Duquesne, they collided with a joint French–Indian army of nearly 900 Indians, Canadian militia, and Troupes de la Marine that was moving east to engage them.[81] The advance party under Lieutenant Colonel Thomas Gage fired on the French and Indians at far range, killed their commander, and created momentary confusion among the French; but the Indians quickly spread down both sides of the British line. Gage regrouped his troops but could find no French line to attack. The advance party then "gave way, and fell back upon the van, which very much disconcerted the Men, and that added to a manner of fighting that they were quite unacquainted with, struck such a Panic" in the regulars.[82] The British officers tried to rally their men by shouting orders fit for a battle like Fontenoy. But, Lieutenant Colonel Thomas Dunbar later noted, the British "fought an invisible Enemy . . . both Officers and Soldiers they did not

---

79 Edward Braddock to Thomas Robinson, May 29, 1755, CO 5: 46.
80 Benjamin Franklin, *The Autobiography of Benjamin Franklin*, ed. Louis P. Masur (Boston: St. Martin's Press, 1993), 135.
81 Journal of the Operations of the Army from 22 July to 30 September 1755, *NYCD* 10: 337.
82 Major Robert Orme to Robert Dinwiddie, July 18, 1755, CO 5: 46.

see One of the Enemy the whole day."[83] Even the Britons' artillery pieces, which they had so laboriously lugged across the mountains, were of no use. "The Indians," recalled one British officer, "whether ordered or not I cannot say kept an incessant fire on the Guns & killed the Men very fast. These Indians from their irregular method of fighting by running from one place to another obliged us to wheel from right to left, to desert the Guns and then hastily return & cover them."[84] Then, as the British tried to retreat from the field, "The Enemy," the officer continued,

> pursued us butchering as they came as far as the other side of the River; during our crossing, they Shot many in the Water both Men & Women, & died the stream with their blood, scalping & cutting them in a most barbarous manner. On the other side of the river most of us halted to resolve on what to do; but the Men being so terrified desired to go on, nay indeed they would; melancholy situation! expecting every moment to have our retreat cut off (which half a dozen men would easily have done) & a certainly of meeting no Provisions for 60 miles. I must observe that our retreat was so hasty that we were obliged to leave the whole Train; Ammunition, Provision, and baggage to the plundering of the Indians.[85]

In the end, Braddock's aide de camp, Captain George Washington, noted that the Britons became "struck with a deadly *Panic*," while the "poor Virginians behaved like men, and died like Soldiers."[86] All told, the French and Indians either killed or wounded 977 regulars, including 60 of 86 officers.

Segments of the British Army's post-battle investigation on the conduct of its troops at the battle on the Monongahela read as if Gage and Dunbar, the two officers who conducted the investigation, took them directly from the "Essay on Regular and Irregular Forces." Gage and Dunbar explained away the defeat of the British regulars at the hands of the French and Indians by claiming that the enemy outnumbered Braddock's army and that the misconduct of the enlisted men contributed to a military disaster.[87] However, on July 9 the British force was nearly half again as large

---

83   Dunbar to Robert Napier, July 24, 1755, *Military Affairs in North America, 1748–1765: Selected Documents from the Cumberland Papers in Windsor Castle*, ed. Stanley Pargellis (New York: D. Appleton-Century Company, 1936), 106.

84   "The Journal of a British Officer," *Braddock's Defeat: The Journal of Captain Robert Cholmley's Batman; The Journal of a British Officer; Halkett's Orderly Book*, ed. Charles Hamilton (Norman: University of Oklahoma Press, 1959), 50.

85   Ibid., 52.

86   George Washington to Robert Dinwiddie, July 18, 1755, CO 5: 46.

87   Historians have debated for years why the British lost on the Monongahela. For a review of the various arguments, see Robert L. Yaple, "Braddock's Defeat: The Theories and

as their enemy was. Likewise, the British troops panicked because their officers proved incapable of leading them effectively in a chaotic wilderness battle; they stood their ground for nearly three hours and retreated only after their officers failed to lead them, as the Americans' officers had done, out of the trap in which they found themselves.[88]

In an age when the Army tied promotion closely to political connections, however, Gage and Dunbar refused to fix responsibility for the defeat on Braddock or British "doctrine." Yet Braddock's unwillingness to incorporate more Americans and Indians into his army certainly deserved much of the blame for the defeat. Franklin perhaps summed up Braddock best when he described him as "a brave Man, and might probably have made a Figure as a good Officer in some European War. But he had too much self-confidence, too high an Opinion of the Validity of Regular Troops, and too mean a One of both Americans and Indians."[89] Of course, the French understood exactly why the British lost the battle on July 9, 1755. There was a simple explanation: "none of their (the French) Officers were in the least Surprised at it [Braddock's defeat], as it was a Maxim with them never to Expose Regulars in the Woods without a sufficient Number of Indians and irregulars for any Attack that might be Expected."[90]

Braddock's defeat on the Monongahela clearly indicates the disregard of even the most rudimentary tactics and techniques of *petite guerre* in mid-eighteenth-century British military culture. Unlike Continental soldiers, whose rich tradition of irregular warfare was rooted in both experience and doctrine, British soldiers tended to dismiss irregular tactics out of hand. The British Army had fought little wars of conquest in Ireland and Scotland, but carried away the wrong lessons from both, particularly from the '45. Eighteenth-century British soldiers mistakenly believed that regulars would always defeat irregulars, and thus *petite guerre* remained

---

a Reconsideration," *JSAHR* 46 (1968): 194–201. Yaple has argued that two factors were primarily responsible for Braddock's defeat. Gage panicked and failed to do his duty properly as commander of the van, and Braddock had "bad luck" because the French and Indians ambushed him in the place where he, in Yaple's terms, "was most susceptible to being trapped." Yaple wrote, "there were woods in Europe, after all, and Braddock was no amateur" (p. 201). Given North American conditions, and the fact that the French and Indians managed to ambush Braddock in the place where "he was most susceptible to being trapped" suggests that Braddock's methods were in fact inappropriate.

88 Inquiry into Behavior of Troops at Monongahela, November 21, 1755, CO 5: 46.
89 Franklin, *Autobiography*, 135.
90 William Shirley to Thomas Robinson, November 5, 1755, CO 5: 46. In 1756, for example, the French Army outside Quebéc had nearly 700 Indian and Canadian auxiliaries led by regular officers whom the French called "Officers attachés aux Savages." The Indians allies served as the avant garde of the French Army. See Ordre de Bataille sur Trois Colonnes M. le B. de Dieskau General, 1756, CO 5: 46.

fit not for soldiers, but "savages and robbers."[91] Thus, whereas *petite guerre* entered the regular martial culture of the Continental powers, it never attained a mark of legitimacy within British military circles. Indeed, the British Army possessed a collective temerity in its disdain for irregular war. But as the author of the "Essay on Regular and Irregular Forces" knew, and as Edward Braddock learned, regulars' temerity was perhaps the irregulars' greatest asset.

91 Quoted in Jeremy Black, *A Military Revolution? Military Change and European Society 1550–1800* (Atlantic Highlands, NJ: Humanities Press International, Inc., 1991), 60.

4

The First Way of War in the Seven Years' War, 1754–1763

At Crown Point, on September 13, 1759, Major Robert Rogers received orders from Major General Jeffery Amherst to lead a force of hand-picked American rangers, British volunteers, and Stockbridge Indian scouts against the Abenaki village at St. François in the St. Lawrence Valley, 150 miles to the north. "Remember the barbarities that have been committed by the enemy's Indian scoundrels on every occasion where they had an opportunity of showing their infamous cruelties on the King's subjects, which they have done without mercy," Amherst reminded Rogers. "Take your revenge," he continued, "but don't forget that though those villains have dastardly and promiscuously murdered the women and children of all ages, it is my orders that no women or children are killed or hurt."[1]

Rogers ignored Amherst's prohibition on the killing of noncombatants. After a grueling march of 22 days, Rogers and 142 raiders arrived outside St. François.[2] When he reconnoitered the village, Rogers discovered hundreds of scalp-festooned poles flying from lodges and the Abenakis celebrating the successes of a recent scalp-hunting foray on the American frontier.[3] Rogers determined that vengeance would be the rangers'. He returned to his trail-weary troops, granted them a few hours to rest, and then deployed them for a predawn attack on the village. "At half an hour before sun-rise," he recalled, "I surprised the town when they [the Abenakis] were all fast asleep." As the rangers emerged out of the darkness,

> the enemy had not time to recover themselves, or take arms for their own defense, till they were chiefly destroyed, except some

---

1 Amherst to Rogers, September 13, 1759, Robert Rogers, *Journals of Major Robert Rogers* (London: J. Millan, 1765), 145.
2 For a description of the route Rogers and his men traveled to and from St. François, see Albert Gravel, "Les Origines du Mot Coaticook et L'Expédition Rogers en 1759," *Le Canada Français* 12 (1925): 531.
3 Rogers, *Journals*, 154.

115

few of them who took to the water. About forty of my people pursued them, who destroyed such as attempted to make their escape that way, and sunk both them and their boats. A little after sunrise I set fire to all their houses, except three, in which there was corn, that I reserved for the use of the party.

The fire consumed many of the Indians who had concealed themselves in the cellars and lofts of their houses. About seven o'clock in the morning the affair was completely over, in which time we had killed at least two hundred Indians, and taken twenty of their women and children prisoners, fifteen of whom I let go their own way, and five I brought with me, viz. two Indian boys, and three Indian girls. I likewise retook five English captives, which I also took under my care.[4]

Rogers's St. François raid, and Amherst's order to him to execute it, suggest the place that the first way of war had come to occupy in both American and British military cultures by the late 1750s. The rangers' campaign against the noncombatants of St. François was the logical extension of the American tradition of war making that had developed over the previous 150 years. Amherst's willingness to employ rangers, British troops, and Indian allies in such a capacity, meanwhile, points to the British Army's acceptance of American-style war making as effective, necessary, and legitimate. Although Amherst forbade Rogers to kill or harm women and children, his instructions were at best pro forma and at worst disingenuous. He must have known that Rogers and his rangers would kill innocents; Rogers had said as much when he first proposed raiding Canada three years earlier.[5] More important, Americans' past record of fighting Indians – one that Amherst knew well – showed that they rarely offered vanquished enemies quarter, whether combatant or noncombatant. By sending Rogers at the head of a party of American rangers, British

4 Ibid., 147. There is some debate about how many Abenakis Rogers's force killed. Other sources dispute Rogers's claim of 200; enumerations vary between 30 and 250. See Ian Steele, *Warpaths: Invasions of North America* (New York: Oxford University Press, 1994), 228, and Francis Jennings, *Empire of Fortune: Crowns, Colonies, and Tribes in the Seven Years War in America* (New York: W. W. Norton & Company, 1988), note 42, 200. Even if the rangers killed only a couple of dozen Abenakis, the raid was still an important victory for the Americans and Britons. Rogers temporarily destroyed St. François and forced the survivors to flee to the Kahnawake mission at St. Regis. See Colin G. Calloway, *The Western Abenaki of Vermont, 1600–1800: War, Migration, and Survival of an Indian People* (Norman: University of Oklahoma Press, 1991), 179. William Johnson reported in 1763 that since Rogers's raid, the Abenakis had "lived scattered." See Enumeration of Indians within the Northern Department, November 18, 1763, *NYCD*, 7: 582.
5 Rogers to John Campbell, fourth earl of Loudoun, August 11, 1756, LO 1467.

regulars, and friendly Indians against St. François, Amherst in effect sanctioned the first way of war.

The British Army came to terms with Americans' first way of war in the Seven Years' War and the Indian Wars of the early 1760s (the Cherokee War of 1759–1761 and Pontiac's War of 1763), conflicts in which rangers played an important, and in some instances dominant, role.[6] Those wars were significant points in the development of Americans' military heritage because they signaled the British Army's acceptance and legitimization of American war making. The process of acceptance and legitimization passed through four stages between 1755 and 1763. Britons entered the struggle against France in North America in 1755 and quickly learned that they would have to depend on substantial assistance from rangers (in the absence of Indian allies) to win the war. By mid-1756, Britons began a second stage in which they turned to American rangers. Yet many Britons distrusted the rangers and held them in contempt as little more than expensive and undisciplined murderers. The British Army in late 1757 and early 1758 entered a third stage in which it experimented with replacing American rangers with Britons. That experiment failed, and by 1759, British commanders had abandoned the notion that British regulars could replace American rangers. In the final campaigns of the Seven Years' War,

6 Analyses of those struggles generally have focused on the war's grand sieges and battles, like those outside Fort William Henry in 1757, Fort Ticonderoga in 1758, Québec in 1759 and 1760, and the siege of Detroit in 1763. The sieges, in effect, overshadow other aspects of the war. Steele's *Warpaths*, chaps. 9–12, is the exception. He places those struggles in the context of the arrival of European regular war to North America. The best study of the Seven Years' War is Fred Anderson's *Crucible of War: The Seven Years' War and the Fate of Empire in British North America, 1754–1766* (New York: Alfred A. Knopf, 2000). Most studies that focus on the rangers concentrate primarily on the life and career of Robert Rogers. For brief biographies of Rogers and descriptions of the major events of his career, see *DCB*, s.v. "Rogers, Robert" and *Colonial Wars of North America, 1512–1763*, s.v. "Rogers, Robert." The 1950s and 1960s saw the publication of two major studies on the rangers. John Cuneo's *Robert Rogers of the Rangers* (1952; reprint, New York: Richardson & Steirman, 1987) is the best book-length account of the rangers' activities, although it verges on American military hagiography. Burt Garfield Loescher offered his three-volume *The History of Rogers' Rangers* (San Francisco: Burt Garfield Loescher, 1946–1969). Other students of Rogers's Rangers have used local or state historical publications to focus on individual events in Rogers's career or ranger operations. For example, see Richard John Curry, "Rogers' Battle on Snowshoes," *New-England Galaxy* 15 (1974): 26–33, and Mary Cochrane Rogers, *Rogers' Rock, Lake George, March 13, 1758: A Battle Fought on Snow Shoes* (Derry, NH: Mary Rogers, 1917). For the St. François raid, see Gravel, "Les Origines." Victor H. Paltsits's "Journal of Robert Rogers, the Ranger, on His Expedition for Receiving the Capitulation of the Western French Posts," *New York Public Library Bulletin* 37 (1935): 261–276, focuses on Rogers's activities in accepting the surrender of the western French forces after the Seven Years' War, as does Milo M. Qaife's "Robert Rogers," *Burton Historical Collections Leaflet* 7 (1928): 1–16. For Rogers's postwar service as British commander at Fort Michilimackinac, see Josephine Mayer, "Major Robert Rogers, Trader," *New York History* 15 (1934): 388–397; and William L. Clements, "Rogers's Michilimackinac Journal," *American Antiquarian Society Proceedings*, New Series, 28 (1919): 224–273.

both Amherst and Major General James Wolfe turned to Americans and friendly Indians to strike terror in Indian and Canadian noncombatants. In the fourth and last stage, during the Cherokee War and Pontiac's War, British commanders depended almost exclusively on the first way of war, then waged by both American rangers and British regulars, that focused on defeating their enemies by destroying noncombatant populations. By the end of 1763, Britons therefore not only had accepted American-style war making as a morally acceptable way of making war, but they also gave it a central position in their own military culture.

I. Britons Realize the Need for American Rangers, 1755–1756

Senior British Army commanders entered the Seven Years' War in North America believing that regulars would be more than a match for the Indian "savages" of North America and the troops of New France. They, of course, were wrong. Braddock's defeat was a disaster that resulted in the expulsion of British regulars from the Virginia and Pennsylvania back-country for three years. After their shellacking, British officers and their men were in no mental state to march back into the wilderness and try their hand at fighting the French and Indians. They simply abandoned the frontier.[7]

Yet even after Braddock's defeat, it took time for some Americans and Britons to realize that victory in North America would depend on more than the presence of British regulars. Expressing an opinion reminiscent of that stated a decade earlier in the "Essay on Regular and Irregular Forces," an anonymous author wrote from Boston, "nothing will ever be done here without veteran [regular] troops."[8] "I can not help flattering myself, that, when once you have recruited your regular Force in that Part of the world," the duke of Cumberland encouraged John Campbell, the fourth earl of Loudoun and newly appointed commander in chief of the North American army, "you will be an over-match for our Enemy's."[9] Well into 1756, the British high command outside North America gave little thought to how campaigning in North America might differ from that in Europe.[10]

---

7   Steele argues that even after the disaster on the Monongahela, the British still could have pushed on to Fort Duquesne "with a good chance of success." See Steele, *Warpaths*, 190.
8   Extract of a Letter from Boston, December 6, 1755, LO 690.
9   Cumberland to Loudoun, October 22–December 23, 1756, LO 2065.
10   In April 1756, for instance, Cumberland sent to North America his instructions for the "Exercises for the American Forces." Those exercises contained no mention of the

Nontraditional approaches, however, indeed were in order. Two separate but interrelated issues – wilderness logistics and the enemy's mastery of *petite guerre* – shocked British commanders into embracing other solutions. Perhaps the greatest obstacle for British arms to overcome was that regular troops simply could not operate effectively in the "vast inhospitable desert, unsafe and treacherous" wilds of North America. In such a place, William Smith astutely noted, "victories are not decisive, but defeats are ruinous."[11] Until late 1758, that "desert" presented British commanders with what seemed an insurmountable obstacle.[12] Commentators noted that wilderness operations – and "it is impossible to convey to the reader," one of them wrote, "without he has been in America, a just idea of . . . [a] country . . . perhaps never . . . trodden by human feet, if we except the savage" – sapped the strength of both men and the vast number of animals needed to move supplies over the miserable tracks that connected the backcountry forts.[13] As if matters were not sufficiently complicated for British commanders, their French and Indian enemies took great advantage of the remote and isolated location of British military objectives. One prophetic author in late 1754 described the "Difficulty on the part of the English of bringing any proper Force" to attack the French positions. Because of their distance from British centers of power, the "French in and about the Forts already built, with their Indian Auxiliaries, may be able to defend them at least against four times their Number."[14] In Europe, commanders usually assumed that besieging forces twice the size of defending

need to prepare British troops to operate in the woods of North America. Cumberland instead modeled his guidance on the Prussian system of regular drill. See Exercises for the American Forces, April 18, 1756, LO 1060.

11 William Smith, *An Historical Account of the Expedition Against the Ohio Indians in the Year MDCCLXIV* (Philadelphia: n.p., 1765), ix.

12 Daniel Beattie has argued that the main enemy of the British Army in the first three years of the Seven Years' War was neither the French Army nor its Indian allies, but instead the North American wilderness. Beattie has contended that the catalyst for British victory after 1758 was that the British Army finally could project and support its forces in the wilderness. See Beattie, "The Adaptation of the British Army to Wilderness Warfare, 1755–1763," in *Adapting to Conditions: War and Society in the Eighteenth Century*, ed. Maarten Ultee (Tuscaloosa: University of Alabama Press, 1986), 56–83. King Parker has written that in spite of the failure of Loudoun to win a single significant military victory, he made an important contribution to the British conquest of Canada through his reorganization of the military transport and supply system in the colonies. Loudoun's other significant contribution was his encouragement and backing for the formation of American ranger units. See Parker, "Anglo–American Wilderness Campaigning 1754–1764: Logistical and Tactical Developments" (Ph.D. diss., Columbia University, 1970).

13 David Ramsay, *Military Memoirs of Great Britain, A History of the War, 1755–1763* (Edinburgh: n.p., 1779), 169.

14 Considerations Relating to Measures to Be Taken with Regard to Affairs in North America, November 1754, *Military Affairs in North America, 1748–1765: Selected Documents from the Cumberland Papers in Windsor Castle*, ed. Stanley Pargellis (New York: D. Appleton-Century Company, 1936), 37.

garrisons were adequate. Indeed, only in 1758, with the success that accompanied Brigadier General John Forbes's and Colonel Henry Bouquet's capture of Fort Duquesne and Lieutenant Colonel John Bradstreet's capture of Fort Frontenac, did British regulars, augmented with Americans and led by British officers who fully embraced *petite guerre*, prove that they could fight offensively in a wilderness campaign.

Worse even than the distances to and the remoteness of the French positions was the fact that the British faced foes well prepared to obstruct their advances into the backcountry. French leaders could select from three distinct military forces within New France, each well schooled in *petite guerre*: Indians; the Canadian militia; and the colonial regulars, or the Troupes de la Marine. Indians were masters at skulking. The Canadian militia was, Cumberland noted, "God knows, many Degrees above" the American militia in military prowess. While the militia of New France, like their American opponents, often frustrated their French officers, the Troupes de la Marine comprised the best-trained and most battle-hardened European force on the continent.[15]

Since the seventeenth century, the leaders of French Canada had embraced *petite guerre* and had taken care to train the Troupes de la Marine in its techniques. Decades of fighting against and alongside Indians had served the Troupes de la Marine well. Technically regulars, the Troupes de la Marine thought and fought more like American rangers. They organized themselves in independent companies rather than regiments. Moreover, their officers, primarily Canadians, hailed from a society imbued with a military ethos and, more important, obtained their commissions not by purchase, but on merit or when a vacancy occurred in the officer corps.[16] Benjamin Doolittle observed how they would "not give Men Commission, until they have been out in the War and done some Spoil on their Enemies."[17] "Against them the American provincial troops and militia were no match," William Eccles wrote. He added, "Great mobility,

15 Cumberland to Loudoun, October 22–December 23, 1756, LO 2065. Martin L. Nicolai, "A Different Kind of Courage: The French Military and the Canadian Irregular Soldier During the Seven Years' War," *Canadian Historical Review* 70 (1989): 53–75.
16 Eccles wrote that as in mid-eighteenth-century Prussia, the primary industry of New France was war. See Eccles, "The Social, Economic, and Political Significance of the Military Establishment in New France," *Canadian Historical Review* 52 (1971): 1. In 1760, for instance, Canada's European population was 76,172. From that population, the government was able to muster 16,412 militia in 170 companies. Five years earlier, at the start of the war, 54 companies of Troupes de la Marine were stationed in New France, with another 24 companies at Louisbourg and 36 more in Louisiana. See Stephen Brumwell, *Redcoats: The British Soldier and War in the Americas, 1755–1763* (New York: Cambridge University Press, 2002), 25, n. 48.
17 Benjamin Doolittle, "A Short Narrative of Mischief Done by the French and Indian Enemy on the Western Frontiers of the Province of Massachusetts-Bay" (1750; reprint,

deadly marksmanship, skillful use of surprise and forest cover, high morale and, like the Royal Navy, a tradition of victory, gave the colonial regulars their superiority."[18] It is little wonder then that both Americans and Britons viewed the Troupes de la Marine as almost supermen. "The New England Men, by all Accounts," noted Loudoun, "[were] frightened out of their Senses, at the name of a French Man."[19] It thus must have been with some foreboding that Loudoun estimated that there were at least 4,000 of them waiting to ambush and possibly destroy his army when he marched it into Canada.[20]

It is important to note, however, that French commanders never made full use of their Troupes de la Marine. Indeed, France lost its North American empire only after Louis-Joseph, marquis de Montcalm-Gozon de Saint-Veran, chose to engage the British in a regular-style war of sieges and countersieges.[21] Since King William's War, the Troupes de la Marine, Canadian militia, and Indians had kept the English off balance, and despite several costly efforts, the English proved incapable of penetrating the French periphery. Montcalm could have secured the preservation of New France if he had prevented the British from marching into Canada and forcing his smaller army to battle. The Troupes de la Marine were the ideal force to slow and bleed the British forces as they tried to penetrate the periphery. The soundest French strategy therefore would have made use of the Indians and the Troupes de la Marine in the wilderness to bog down British advances up Lake Champlain or into the Ohio Valley and concentrate French regular forces where they could have done the most good – at the mouth of the Saint Lawrence River and Louisbourg. A major, albeit costly, operation to retake Nova Scotia certainly would have complicated British control of the eastern approaches to Canada. At the point when the British finally broke into New France, Montcalm should have turned to a Fabian and scorched earth strategy – another task for which the Troupes de la Marine were ideal. Instead, he chose to play to the British Army's greatest strength and allowed it to march relatively

Early American Imprints, 1639–1800 [New Canaan, CT: Readex, 1981–1982]), microfiche 6488: 21.

18 William J. Eccles, "The French Forces in North America during the Seven Years' War," *DCB*, xvii.

19 Loudoun to Cumberland, August 29, 1756, LO 1626. Jennings, *Empire of Fortune*, 172, wrote that the frontiersmen of Canada "were incomparably superior to the 'American' colonials in their adaptation to wilderness campaigning.'" "Incomparably superior" overstates the case. American rangers proved on many occasions that they too could effectively fight in the American wilderness.

20 Loudoun's memorandum books, July 23, 1757, Huntington Manuscript 1717, Henry E. Huntington Library, San Marino, CA, hereafter HM 1717.

21 William J. Eccles, *France in America*, 2d ed. (East Lansing: Michigan State University Press, 1990), 199–200.

unimpeded into Canada, where it could bring its superior manpower and materiel to bear.

Control of the frontier therefore was the pivot on which British success or failure would turn. As such, the Indians, particularly the Iroquois, were key. If they could win them to their side, the British could use the Iroquois as a barrier against attacks from Troupes de la Marine and French-allied Indians from the *pays d'en haut* (Great Lakes region).[22] The greater value to the British, however, was that if they could neutralize the Indians, British regular forces would have to deal only with the Troupes de la Marine and the wilderness, still no small tasks, before they reached Canada. Last, if all went well for the British, they could turn the Indians loose on Canadian settlements.

The Iroquois, nonetheless, kept their distance. Since 1701, they had maintained strict neutrality in the Anglo–French conflict. The English had coaxed only the Mohawks into service in King George's War. Then, at the outbreak of the war, the Americans managed to antagonize the Mohawks. The 1754 Albany Congress had dissolved without mending the significant fissures concerning land, trade, and mutual defense that increasingly soured colonist–Mohawk relations.[23] To top it off, an alliance with the British raised the specter of a civil war between the New York Iroquois and the French-allied Catholic Mohawks of the St. Lawrence missions. Thus, before they joined the British side, the Iroquois demanded a clear "sign" that Great Britain indeed would win the war. As George Montagu Dunk, earl of Halifax, noted, not until British arms had "done something of consequence for ourselves and them" would the Six Nations "heartily" raise the hatchet for the British.[24]

Britons, however, could point to nothing after Braddock's defeat that would bolster the Iroquois' confidence. Because of the British disaster on the Monongahela, for instance, Peter Wraxall, Assistant Superintendent of Northern Indian Affairs, noted, the French possessed at least a three to one advantage over the British in Indian allies.[25] The surrender of the British garrison at Oswego to the French and Indians was another blow. Not only did the French secure their lines of communication to

---

22 Indian Affairs, February 1756, LO 2476.
23 For the Albany Congress, see Timothy J. Shannon, *Indians and Colonists at the Cross-roads of Empire: The Albany Congress of 1754* (Ithaca, NY: Cornell University Press, 2000).
24 Halifax to Loudoun, August 13, 1756, LO 1478. Jennings, *Empire of Fortune*, 297. The French alliance with the Indian bands of the *pays d'en haut* remained strong even in the face of earlier Indian "rebellions." See Richard White, *The Middle Ground: Indians, Empires, and Republics in the Great Lakes Region, 1650–1815* (New York: Cambridge University Press, 1991), xiv, chap. 6. Loudoun to Cumberland, August 29, 1756, LO 1626.
25 Wraxall to Henry Fox, September 22, 1755, LO 656.

their western outposts, but Iroquois neutrality also tilted toward them. The "mini-massacre" at Oswego, when French officers turned a blind eye as their Indian allies killed British prisoners and plundered the fort, suggested to Indians across the frontier that the French were more amenable to them than were the British. Matters only deteriorated from there as far as the British were concerned. Troupes de la Marine and Indians from the *pays d'en haut* not only devastated the American frontier from New England to North Carolina, but French regular forces destroyed Fort William Henry in 1757 and British commanders snatched defeat from the jaws of victory at Fort Carillon in 1758. In fact, the only Indians the British could depend on were the Stockbridge and other "domesticated" Indians of southern New England. Loudoun's correspondence is rife with complaints about his paucity of Indian allies. His letter to Cumberland in the summer of 1756 pointed to the crux of the British problem. "From the Indians, you see we have no support." "We have at present no Indians but a handful of Mohawks and a few straggling Indians from different tribes," he complained to Henry Fox, "and those at present not useful." "Those that we call friends," Loudoun noted, "are no more than neutrals."[26]

The details of British diplomacy with the Six Nations suggest the precarious position in which the English found themselves. Situated in western Iroquoia, the Senecas' villages would be the first to feel the brunt of French-sponsored raids originating from the *pays d'en haut*. In October 1755, Pierre de Rigaud de Vaudreuil de Cavagnial, the Governor-General of New France, warned the Iroquois that "should any of the Five Nations be found next spring among the English, I will let loose all our Upper and domiciled Nations on them; cause their villages to be laid waste and never pardon them."[27] Yet the Senecas initially were willing to risk war with the French to remain on the receiving end of British presents of arms, food, clothing, and scalp bounties. They agreed to join the British for the summer 1755 campaign in New York on the condition that they receive among the usual presents a hearty supply of rum. The rum, however, "kept them Continually drunk" and made them useless to British commanders.[28] Then, after the French victory at Oswego had driven the bulk of English forces from western New York, British agents discovered English scalps displayed as war trophies at Seneca castles.[29] After British officials called them to account for that fact, the Senecas openly joined the French and threatened the other nations of the League with civil war if

26   Loudoun to Cumberland, August 20, 1756, LO 1525; Loudoun to Fox, November 22, 1756, LO 2263; Loudoun to Fox, August 19, 1756, LO 1522.
27   Dyaderswane to William Johnson, September 24, 1756, LO 1887; M. de Vaudreuil to M. de Machault, October 21, 1755, NYCD, 10: 378.
28   William Shirley to Fox, December 20, 1755, LO 704.
29   Information about the Seneca, March 6, 1757, LO 2976.

they did not follow suit. The Cayugas and Onondagas, stuck between the Senecas and the British, belatedly joined the Senecas. At a hastily called meeting between William Johnson, Superintendent of Northern Indian Affairs, and the western Iroquois, a Cayuga spokesman acknowledged that some of his people had "used the hatchet against our Brethren the English." In the end, the Cayugas "repented" and claimed that they remained "firmly resolved to hold fast the Covenant Chain," but only after Johnson promised more gifts. At that point, the Senecas, Cayugas, and Onondagas professed their neutrality, not fidelity, toward the English.[30]

"Fickleness" and "treachery" like that exhibited by the Senecas led British officers to view all their Indian allies with animosity, making it unlikely that Britons ever would be comfortable in depending on them. Amherst, writing to Thomas Gage late in the war, perhaps best expressed the continued frustration of the British with their Indian allies. Describing the Stockbridge Mahicans – the one band that consistently served faithfully as scouts not only for Amherst, but for Loudoun and Major General James Abercromby as well[31] – Amherst wrote: "I have as bad an opinion of those lazy rum drinking Scoundrels as any one can have." Yet he felt compelled to enlist them in Britain's service for fear that they might join the French. "I shall however take them into his Majesty's service for this next campaign," he told Gage, "to keep them from doing mischief elsewhere." In the end, he hoped that the Stockbridge rangers "may do some good by doing mischief of which we have a great deal to do to be a par with the French." Still, Amherst wrote, "I hate them all."[32]

II. Britons Turn to American Rangers, 1756–1757

In the wake of the British disaster on the Monongahela, Americans from across the colonies formed themselves into companies of rangers. In New

---

30   Loudoun to Johnson, June 9, 1757, LO 3809 and Journal of Sir William Johnson's Proceedings with the Indians, *NYCD*, 7: 254–260. Francis Jennings wrote that the Covenant Chain "had become a shadow of its former self before the war broke out." See Jennings, *Empire of Fortune*, 190, chaps. 3–5.

31   The Stockbridges were descendants of Housatonic and Mahican Indians who in the late 1730s had settled at Rev. John Sergeant's mission and school in western Massachusetts. See T. J. Brasser, "Mahican," *HNAI*, Vol. 15, *Northeast*, 206–208. William Shirley originally planned to raise one company of 30 Stockbridges. Eventually, 45 enlisted under Captain Jacob Cheeksaunkun, Lieutenant Jacob Naunauphtaunk, and Ensign Soloman Uhauamvaumut. See Shirley to Henry Fox, December 20, 1755, LO 704; Shirley to James Abercromby, June 27, 1756, LO 1257; Muster Rolls for Captain Jacob Cheeksaunkun's Company of Stockbridge Indians, November 14, 1756, LO 2211; William Johnson to Loudoun, August 3, 1756, LO 1397.

32   Amherst to Gage, February 20, 1759, Jeffery Amherst MSS, William L. Clements Library, Ann Arbor, MI and Amherst to Gage, March 26, 1759, ibid.

Hampshire, for example, Robert Rogers recruited fellow backwoodsmen from Colonel Joseph Blanchard's militia regiment to raise Rogers's Rangers.[33] In Pennsylvania, John Armstrong began enlisting backwoodsmen to serve in a ranger company under his command. The Virginia House of Burgesses, meanwhile, enlisted three 50-man companies of rangers. Following a tradition that dated back well over half a century, the House of Burgesses promised the rangers a bounty of £10 on the scalp of every Indian above the age of 12. The Virginia bounties drew American frontiersmen to the army. Robert Dinwiddie, Lieutenant Governor of Virginia, reported in January 1756 that over the course of the previous fall and early winter his rangers had sacked several Indian towns.[34]

Frontier communities needed the rangers to defend them, as the French and their allies wasted little time after Braddock's defeat in striking at the American backcountry. In late 1755 and early 1756, war parties fell on isolated American settlements from Georgia in the South to Pennsylvania in the North. By the spring of 1756, for example, Delawares and Shawnees from the Upper Ohio Valley had killed or made prisoner perhaps 700 British subjects along the southern Appalachian range. By the fall, the number had exceeded 3,000. "The last news from Fort Duquesne assure us of the destruction of Virginia, Carolina, and part of New Georgia," French officials in America advised the crown; "all these province are laid waste for forty leagues from the foot of the mountains, in the direction of the sea."[35] The situation, from a British and American perspective, quickly deteriorated. By October 1756, American settlers had abandoned their homes and plantations within 50 miles of Fort Cumberland (at the junction of Wills Creek and the Potomac River in Maryland) for fear of "Flying Parties of the Enemy."[36]

American rangers responded to the enemy offensive in kind. In one of the most famous raids of the war, in 1756, Armstrong's Pennsylvanians set out for the Delaware village of Kittanning on the Allegheny River. The colonists designed the Kittanning raid as much to avenge earlier Delaware attacks on the Pennsylvania frontier as to destroy the town as a forward operating base for French and Indian raiders.[37] In a type of operation that had become commonplace for American rangers, the small force crossed undetected into Delaware territory. In their predawn attack on

---

33 Muster Roll of the Troops Employed in His Majesty's Service on Merrymac River, *Documents and Records Relating to the Province of New Hampshire*, ed. Nathaniel Bouton, 23 vols. (Concord, NH: George E. Jenks, State Printer, 1867–1893), 6: 318.
34 *SAL*, 6: 465, 551; Robert Dinwiddie to William Johnson, January 23, 1756, LO 767.
35 Abstract of Despatches from Canada, n.d, *NYCD*, 10: 424; Abstract of Despatches from Canada, August 30, 1756, *NYCD*, 10: 484.
36 Dinwiddie to Loudoun, October 6, 1756, LO 1977.
37 Jennings, *Empire of Fortune*, 276.

Kittanning, they spared no means in the destruction of the Delawares. They put Kittanning to the torch, immolating men, women, and children in their homes. They pursued wounded and dying Delawares into the woods, determined not to let valuable scalps escape them. After an orgy of destruction that lasted several hours, Armstrong gathered his forces, completed the razing of Kittanning, and then retreated.[38] The Kittanning raid gave the Americans their first tactical victory on the Pennsylvania frontier. It was, however, counterproductive; it occurred at the same time that Pennsylvania's Indian negotiators were trying to bring the Delawares and Shawnees back into the fold of neutrality. Rather than marking a decisive victory, the raid merely stimulated more Indian attacks on the frontier.[39]

Two Britons who long had served in North America and seen firsthand in King George's War the effectiveness of American rangers – William Johnson and William Shirley – determined to make good use of them. Johnson, for instance, insisted that Rogers's ranger company be detached from the New Hampshire provincials and attached to his force. He made them, with the Mohawks under Hendrick (Theyanoguin), the scouting arm of his army in his Lake George campaign in the summer of 1755.[40] Because he could call only on the Stockbridge Indians for allies, William Shirley, once Johnson could spare the rangers, gave them an even larger role in his operations. He had in mind for Rogers's Rangers the same kinds of operations he had seen Gorham's Rangers conduct in King George's War. Shirley ordered Rogers to organize a company of 66 men "used to traveling and hunting," whose primary mission would be to "distress the French and their allies by sacking, burning, and destroying their houses, barns, barracks, canoes, battoes, etc., and by killing their cattle of every kind; and at all times to endeavor to way-lay, attack, and destroy their convoys of provisions by land and water, in any part of the country."[41]

Loudoun followed Johnson and Shirley's lead and was quick to realize that American rangers were "more proper" than British regulars for the kind of campaign that he faced in North America. After surveying the state of military affairs in the colonies, he told Henry Fox, "Whoever is

---

38   John Armstrong, "Col. John Armstrong's Account of the Expedition against Kittanning, 1756," *Pennsylvania Archives*, ser. 1, 2: 767–775.
39   For the efforts of negotiators to halt the bloodshed on the Pennsylvania frontier, see James H. Merrell, *Into the American Woods: Negotiators on the Pennsylvania Frontier* (New York: W. W. Norton & Company, 1999), chap. 6. Intelligence &c. Related by Ogaghradasisha, October 11–18, 1756, LO 2001.
40   Rogers, *Journals*, 1–7.
41   Ibid., 14–15.

Superior in irregulars has an infinite advantage over the other side; and must greatly weaken, if not totally destroy them before they can get to the Point where they can make their Push."[42] "There is no carrying on the Service here for without Rangers," he informed Fox in October 1756, "for it is by them, we can have Intelligence of what motion the Enemy are making, and by them, that we can secure our Camps and Marches from Surprise; from here it appears to me that till we can regain the Indians, which can only be done by beating the Enemy, no Army can Subsist in this Country without rangers."[43]

Loudoun looked to incorporate large numbers of rangers into the British military establishment in the colonies. In September 1757, he publicly called for 1,100 American rangers, or one-fourth of the total enlistees he requested from the northern colonies, for the next year's campaigns. In his private journal, Loudoun wrote that he would have preferred that the colonies enlist 4,000 rangers, perhaps as a response to his fear that there were 4,000 Troupes de la Marine awaiting him in Canada. All told, when pondering the future of his army and the security of the British colonies in North America, he became another in the lengthening line of senior British officers who realized that "the Service cannot be done without them [the rangers]."[44]

Loudoun's staff also came to appreciate the value of the rangers. In December 1757, Loudoun called a conference of his field commanders to discuss, among other issues, how many rangers they would need for the next year's offensives. To that date, fewer than 400 American rangers, the company of Stockbridge scouts then under Rogers's command, and a company of Mohawks were the only pro-British scouts in service.[45] With the Stockbridge Mahicans threatening to abandon the British and return to their homes as a result of the shoddy treatment they had received at the hands of British and American traders, and the spring campaign only months away, the officers responsible for leading the British Army

42 Loudoun to Daniel Webb, August 20, 1756, LO 1808 and Loudoun to Fox, October 3, 1756, LO 1961.
43 Loudoun to Fox, November 22, 1756, LO 2263.
44 The Number of Rangers Required from the Northern Provinces, September 1757, LO 3957 and Loudoun's memorandum book, December 19, 1757, HM 1717.
45 By late 1757, Rogers, John Stark, Charles Bulkeley, and John Shepherd commanded four companies of rangers totaling 317 men. See A Return of His Majesty's Companies of Rangers, November 7, 1757, LO 6802. In April 1756, William Shirley had instructed Major General John Winslow to raise two 100-man companies of rangers under Captains Thomas Speakman and Humphrey Hobbs from the best troops "fit for the Wood Service and to be depended upon" in Nova Scotia. See Shirley to Winslow, April 30, 1756, LO 1091. In August 1756, British commanders, at the recommendation of William Johnson, placed the Stockbridge Indians under Rogers's command. See Rogers, *Journals*, 26.

in the field seconded Loudoun's proposal to increase the American ranger establishment to near 1,000 men.[46]

Loudoun then turned to the backcountry settlers of the northern colonies to fill the ranks of the expanded ranger corps. By late 1757, senior British commanders in North America had come to believe that frontier settlers possessed a corporate knowledge of, and "natural bias" toward, ranging. The frontiersmen of New Hampshire, Loudoun told that colony's governor, Benning Wentworth, were "more used to Ranging" than any other settlers. They were, in Loudoun's estimation, "Stout able Men, and for a brush [fight], much better than their Provincial Troops."[47] In an October 1757 memorial, Rogers had promised to raise 1,000 New England frontiersmen. Loudoun took him at his word and authorized him to raise five companies of rangers that Rogers would command.[48]

Yet even with the need for the rangers clear, Loudoun still had reservations about the rangers and Rogers. Although he acknowledged that the rangers were the ideal troops to "strike a terror into the Enemy," he was reluctant to unleash them against Canadian villages and farms.[49] In August 1756, for example, Rogers had submitted to Loudoun the first of several memorials in which he requested permission to "plunder Canada."[50] When Loudoun failed to respond to his initial request, Rogers rushed off another letter in which he reaffirmed that he was most eager to march against the Indians and *Habitants*. Loudoun, however,

46 Stockbridge Indians to William Shirley, December 16, 1756, LO 5026; Loudoun to Newcastle, December 26, 1756, LO 2416. By the spring of 1758, the Britons and the Stockbridge Indians had patched up their quarrels and the Mahicans again were willing to fight for the British. See Jacob Cheeksaunkun and Jacob Neva Nautphtonk to Loudoun, February 14, 1758, LO 5592. The 1758 Stockbridge force contained 3 officers, 1 sergeant, and 50 privates. Each private was paid 2s.6d per day – the same pay as a provincial private. See Engagement of the Stockbridge Indians, February 1758, LO 5799. For the terms under which the Stockbridge Indians enlisted, see WO 34: 75, 1758, and for their 1758 muster roll, see WO 34: 76, summer 1758. The Stockbridge Indians accompanied Rogers on his St. François raid, and Amherst recruited them into British service in 1760. See WO 34: 51, March 20, 1760 and Loudoun's memorandum books, December 20, 1757, HM 1717.

47 Americanus to Loudoun, December 8, 1757, LO 4971. Loudoun to Benning Wentworth, August 18, 1757, LO 4252; Loudoun to William Pitt, May 3, 1757, *Correspondence of William Pitt*, ed. Gertrude Selwyn Kimball, 2 vols. (1906; reprint, New York: Kraus Reprint Co., 1969), 1: 55.

48 Robert Rogers, Memorial to the Earl of Loudoun, October 25, 1757, LO 4702; Loudoun, Beating Orders to Captain Robert Rogers, January 11, 1758, LO 5391.

49 Loudoun to Cumberland, October 2, 1756, LO 1948. Many Frenchmen also shared Loudoun's concern about the methods their native auxiliaries used, but they too agreed that both the individuals and their methods were a necessary evil. See Louis-Antoine de Bougainville, *Adventure in the Wilderness: The American Journals of Louis Antoine de Bougainville 1756–1760*, ed. and trans. Edward P. Hamilton (Norman: University of Oklahoma Press, 1964), 191.

50 Rogers to Loudoun, August 11, 1756, LO 1467.

hesitated to authorize a campaign that might well degenerate into a scalp-hunting party. A combination of moral repugnance and military necessity informed his attitude toward the rangers' practice of scalping. First, he thought scalping was a "Barbarous Custom" that fell outside the accepted norms of soldierly behavior.[51] Moral scruples aside, Loudoun and the British Army also needed prisoners from whom to gather valuable intelligence. "One Prisoner," he wrote in the fall of 1756, "at present is worth ten scalps."[52] Finally, in November 1756, Loudoun had seen enough of the rangers' scalping and warned that he would no longer reward the killing of enemy captives with bounties.[53]

Loudoun's conviction that the rangers' scalping fell outside the mores of proper military behavior failed to take into account the realities of war in North America. At the center of the rangers' conceptualization of war, one that experience reinforced, was their understanding that quarter and the humane treatment of prisoners were optional and unlikely to be offered them. Rogers possessed no reservations about killing prisoners, although that is not to say he killed every captive he took. Even after Loudoun expressed his concerns about scalping and mistreatment of prisoners, Rogers issued orders to his men to kill captives if the situation dictated it. He described to Loudoun an occasion in early 1757, for instance, when around 200 Frenchmen and Indians ambushed his 50-man company. The rangers were trying to reach British lines with seven captives. Rogers, correctly suspecting that the enemy would attempt to rescue their comrades, directed "those who had charge of the prisoners Should kill them" if the company came under attack. Moments later, a French and Indian force opened fire on the rangers. Rogers, he related in his official report of the skirmish, ordered the fire "returned after killing our prisoners." The ensuing fight was a near disaster for Rogers's command. On a Western European battlefield, the rangers would have been seen as *hors de combat* and entitled to surrender without fear of reprisal. In the war in the American wilderness, however, no such category existed. When a French officer called to Rogers by name and assured him quarter if he surrendered himself and his men, Rogers "absolutely refused to receive their professed Mercy" and yelled back that his rangers would "Cut

---

51 Rogers to Loudoun, August 16, 1756, LO 1501 and Loudoun to James Abercromby, November 11, 1756, LO 2196. Loudoun believed that Montcalm shared his repugnance toward scalping. Yet Montcalm offered a bounty of 60 livres on each English scalp. See Rogers, *Journals*, 22. Of course, British soldiers were not above scalping. See Peter Way, "The Cutting Edge of Culture: British Soldiers Encounter Native Americans in the French and Indian War," *Empire and Others: British Encounters With Indigenous Peoples, 1600–1850*, eds. Martin Daunton and Rick Halpern (Philadelphia: University of Pennsylvania Press, 1999).
52 Loudoun to Phineas Lyman, September 13, 1756, LO 1798.
53 Loudoun to James Abercromby, November 11, 1756, LO 2196.

them to Pieces & Scalp Them."[54] Rather than risk torture and death as captives at the hands of the Troupes de la Marine and their allies, the rangers closed ranks and fought with greater ferocity until the survivors managed to break out of the ambush and reach safety.

Senior British officers other than Loudoun understood that part of the first way of war included "barbarous" acts like scalping and the killing of prisoners. Overall, they ignored such actions and sometimes encouraged them. Major General Abercromby, Loudoun's successor, held no reservations about scalping. Abercromby even took the time to report to his military and civilian superiors in London, including the Secretary of State, the results of minor scalping missions he had sent against the French and Indians. Abercromby's policy on scalping was to send American rangers out to do "as Much Mischief as they" could. One way he judged the extent of the mischief the rangers inflicted on the enemy was by the number of scalps with which the rangers returned to British lines.[55]

By the end of 1757, the British Army's turn to American rangers and its acceptance and legitimization of Americans' first way of war was almost complete. Most Britons in North America had acknowledged the military usefulness of the rangers and were prepared to disregard the excesses that accompanied their raids against the French and Indians. Except for a few holdouts, Britons were on the verge of abandoning the belief that the British Army could win the war in North America without American rangers. Before that happened, however, Britons would make a last and failed attempt to create a British ranger corps.

III. British Attempts and Failure to Replace the Rangers, 1757–1758

British officers often disparaged their provincial auxiliaries as useless, heaping scorn on the typical American's military ineptitude and lack of soldierly bearing. James Wolfe remarked, "Americans are in general the dirtiest, the most contemptible cowardly dogs you can conceive."[56] Amherst, rarely one to temper his contempt for those whom he perceived

---

54 Robert Rogers, Journal of a Scout, January 25, 1757, LO 2704. Rogers made no mention of killing his prisoners in his published journals. Perhaps because he wrote them for a London literary audience, he felt it best to delete such atrocities from his narrative. See Rogers, *Journals*, 40–46, for his published account of the battle.

55 Abercromby to Pitt, May 22, 1758, James Abercromby MSS 280, Henry E. Huntington Library, San Marino, CA, hereafter AB.

56 Wolfe, quoted in Cuneo, *Robert Rogers*, 69. James Wolfe to His Father, May 20, 1758, *The Life and Letters of James Wolfe*, ed. Beckles Willson (New York: Dodd Mead & Company, 1909), 365.

were his social or intellectual inferiors, bemoaned the apparently pathetic state of the provincial soldiers and their unwillingness to fight the French. "If left to themselves," Amherst noted, "[they] would eat fried Pork and lay in their tents all day long."[57]

Regular contempt for the line provincials carried over to the rangers. Although by late 1757 Britons had acknowledged that rangers were indispensable, vocal criticism that the rangers comprised a wild and poorly disciplined lot abounded. "The Ranger officers have no Subordination amongst them," Captain James Abercromby wrote after having accompanied a ranger patrol on a scout of Fort Carillon in November 1757, "& not the least command of their men." "If your Lordship should increase the number of Rangers or even keep them up to the present numbers," he advised Loudoun, "it will be necessary to put some Regular officers amongst them to introduce a great deal of Subordination."[58] Major General Abercromby expressed similar reservations. A week after Loudoun's field leaders had stated that they wanted and needed more rangers, Abercromby told Loudoun, "I hope it was not proposed to increase them to 1,000 men; they seem already numerous enough to govern."[59] As for Rogers, Abercromby saw him as "necessary and useful," but also a scheming American in search of preferential treatment. He mocked the "good share of Nonsense [Rogers] has got into his head" that Loudoun would promote him to colonel and make him "Captain Commandant" of all the rangers.[60] James Wolfe dismissed nearly all the American rangers in late 1758–early 1759 as "Lazy cowardly People."[61]

The rangers in fact lacked discipline, particularly if we judge their behavior by contemporary British professional standards. While desertion rates were in fact much lower within the rangers than among the provincials or regulars, the rangers did not match the eighteenth-century Western European model of the disciplined regular soldier. "The Rangers understood only too well how necessary they were, and they thumbed their noses at authority."[62] Ill will between the rangers and British officers reached a crisis point in December 1757, when rangers stationed at Fort Edward "mutinied" after Britons had flogged two privates in Rogers's

57 Amherst's journal, September 9, 1759, *The Journal of Jeffery Amherst in America from 1758 to 1763*, ed. John C. Webster (Chicago: University of Chicago Press, 1931), 166–167.
58 Captain James Abercromby to Loudoun, November 29, 1757, LO 4915. Captain Abercromby was the aide de camp to his uncle, Major General Abercromby. See Captain Abercromby to Rogers, February 6, 1757, Rogers, *Journals*, 47.
59 Abercromby to Loudoun, December 30, 1757, LO 5159.
60 Abercromby to Loudoun, January 2, 1758, LO 5316.
61 "General Wolfe's Scheme for Improving the Colony," *The Northcliffe Collection, Public Archives of Canada* (Ottawa: F. A. Acland, 1926), 110.
62 "The Rangers": Jennings, *Empire of Fortune*, 208.

company for stealing rum from the garrison's stores. Disconcerted by the floggings, several rangers had gathered outside the guardhouse that held the thieves. Suddenly, the rangers began to demolish the stockade, and one of the mutineers even went as far as to take an ax and chop down the whipping post. Only the arrival of the ranger officers John Shepherd and Charles Bulkeley defused the situation. Shepherd forcibly seized a mutineer's weapon and ordered the "loyal" rangers whom they had brought with them to kill any man who as much as touched the guardhouse.[63]

Although quick action averted bloodshed in the "Whipping Post Mutiny," as the revolt of the rangers came to be called, those regular officers who disliked and distrusted the rangers used it as further proof of the rangers' unfitness for military duties.[64] Colonel William Haviland, British commander at Fort Edward, demanded a court martial. Rogers agreed that one was necessary, though he warned that if British officers inflicted too harsh a punishment on the mutineers, the entire force of rangers might desert – an accurate assessment, but one that only served to convince Haviland that Rogers was no better than his men and was seeking solely to protect them from the punishment they deserved. In Haviland's estimation, it was better that the rangers leave the British camp than to have "such a Riotous sort of people" among the regulars eroding discipline by bad example.[65] Upon hearing of the mutiny, Major General Abercromby penned a note to Loudoun to remind him that he had long thought the rangers were "unfit for service."[66] In January 1758, Loudoun summoned Rogers to Albany and warned him of "the bad consequences of not keeping up discipline and complained to him that these things made me hesitate about augmenting the Rangers so much as I proposed."[67]

---

63   Commanders would inflict as many as 1,500 lashes or a sentence of hanging for theft. Mutiny resulted in execution. See Fred Anderson, *A People's Army: Massachusetts Soldiers and Society in the Seven Years' War* (Chapel Hill: University of North Carolina Press for the IEAHC, 1984), 138–139. Court of Inquiry, December 8–11, 1757, LO 4969.

64   Mutinies on the part of provincials were relatively rare, especially considering the acrimonious relations that existed between them and the regular British officers. Fred Anderson has shown that virtually all of the "troop disorders" resulted from the provincials' conviction that the army had failed to fulfill its obligations to them. See Anderson, *A People's Army*, 187–188, 251–253. The Whipping Post Mutiny, however, originated in the rangers' anger at the severity of the punishment that the Britons had inflicted on the rangers for simple larceny, a crime of which the perpetrators indeed were guilty.

65   The Army convened a court of inquiry, led by Rogers, to assign responsibility for the mutiny. However, since the court could not place blame for the riot, the Army dropped the affair. See Court of Inquiry, December 8–11, 1757, LO 4969 and William Haviland to Abercromby, December 16, 1757, LO 6859. After the Whipping Post Mutiny, Haviland and Rogers rarely spoke to one another.

66   Abercromby to Loudoun, December 11, 1757, LO 4998.

67   Loudoun's memorandum book, January 9, 1758, HM 1717.

In late 1757 and early 1758, as the backlash from the Whipping Post Mutiny began to erode his confidence in Rogers and the rangers, Loudoun faced the unenviable task of reducing the costs of the army in North America. In his effort to impose fiscal economy on British operations, one obvious point jumped out at Loudoun. The rangers were exorbitantly expensive since they demanded higher pay for their service than most troops. The yearly expense of maintaining a 100-man company of American rangers, Loudoun's staff estimated, was £3,251.10.10, or approximately £270 per month. Each ranger also received an annual enlistment bonus, varying between six Spanish dollars and £10. A rough extrapolation thus shows that a two-battalion regiment-sized force of 1,000 rangers, bonuses included, cost around £42,400. For £40,000, the army could pay for nearly 4,000 regulars.[68]

The solution to the problems of discipline and costs that came with the rangers, it seemed to Loudoun, was to train regulars to perform their scouting and security functions. Loudoun was confident that his superiors would approve such a plan. Cumberland had explained to him the relative merits of the American rangers and British regulars. "I hope that you will, in time, teach your Troops to go out upon Scouting Parties," Cumberland wrote, "for, 'till *Regular* Officers with men that they can trust, learn to beat the woods, & to act as *Irregulars*, you never will gain any Intelligence of the Enemy, as I fear, by this time you are convinced that *Indian* Intelligence & that of *Rangers* is not at all to be depended upon."[69]

In the summer of 1757, even before the Whipping Post Mutiny, Loudoun had taken the first step in what he expected would be a long, drawn-out process of training Britons the art of ranging. He called for "Gentleman Volunteers" from the regular regiments to learn "the ranging, or wood service" under Rogers's direction – a striking departure from a tradition that strictly prohibited the placing of British officers under provincial officers' command. As Oglethorpe had earlier, Loudoun understood that if Britons had any hopes of success, they would have to learn ranging from those who knew how to perform it.

---

68 Yearly Expense of a Company of Rangers, December 18, 1757, LO 5039. Monthly maintenance of the 50-man Stockbridge rangers cost approximately an additional £200. See WO 34: 76 and Abercromby to Loudoun, December 30, 1757, LO 5159. Shirley had agreed to pay each ranger private 3s. per day, New York currency (the same pay he gave the Stockbridge scouts), the three sergeants 4s., an ensign 5s., a lieutenant 7s., and Rogers 10s. When Loudoun authorized Rogers to raise the additional companies of rangers in January 1758, he reduced the ranger privates' pay from 3s to 2s.6d per day. See Rogers, *Journals*, 14–15. House of Commons Proceedings, December 1, 1758, *Proceedings and Debates of the British Parliaments Respecting North America 1754–1783, Volume 1, 1754–1764*, eds. R. C. Simmons and P. D. G. Thomas (London: Kraus International Publications, 1982), 269.
69 Cumberland to Loudoun, October 22–December 23, 1756, LO 2065.

Rogers saw the formation of the Gentleman Volunteers as an opportunity to win further favor from Loudoun and raise his standing in the Army. He took the 55 volunteers who presented themselves and began a rigorous program of instruction in what he called the "ranging discipline." He placed the regulars in an independent company and personally trained them "in our methods of marching, retreating, ambushing, fighting, etc., that they might be better qualified for any future service against the enemy we had to contend with."[70]

As a training aid for the volunteers, and as further evidence that he was the Army's best ranger leader, Rogers "reduced into writing" his "rules of ranging." When he had suggested in October 1757 that Loudoun increase the ranger establishment to 1,000, Rogers had also submitted to him an essay on the tactics of ranging.[71] Rogers's essay impressed Loudoun, although in its original form of over 3,100 words it was too long. Loudoun therefore directed Rogers to prepare a "sketch of his methods." Rogers distilled his doctrine first into 28 maxims and then into "Standing Orders" that described the essentials of ranging.[72]

Rogers's Standing Orders were the first formal doctrine of war making composed in North America. They elucidated the key points of ranging, so much so that they remain the foundation of American ranger doctrine to this day.[73] Rogers's doctrine was pragmatic and stood in sharp contrast to the rigid formulations that regular officers employed on the battlefield. "Such in general are the rules to be observed in the Ranging service" Rogers wrote:

> there are, however, a thousand occurrences and circumstances
> which may happen, that will make it necessary, in some
> measure, to depart from them, and put other arts and
> stratagems in practice; in which cases every man's reason and
> judgment must be his guide, according to the practical situation
> and nature of things; and that he may do this to advantage, he

70 Rogers, *Journal*, 56–59.
71 Robert Rogers, "Methods Used in Disciplining...," October 25, 1757, LO 4701. Rogers presented a slightly different version in his *Journals*, 60–69.
72 Rogers to Loudoun, October 27, 1757, LO 4707.
73 David H. Hackworth, in *About Face: The Odyssey of an American Warrior* (New York: Touchstone Books, 1989), 492, notes that in 1965 MACV (Military Assistance Command, Vietnam) issued "little cards to carry around in the jungle and study like the Bible. One was...the 'Standing Orders, Rogers' Rangers,'...Major Robert Rogers' two-hundred-year-old guidelines were as applicable in Vietnam as they'd been in the American colonies during the French, Indian, and revolutionary wars." Today, the Standing Orders have been put in language that is more accessible to the modern reader, although several grammatical errors have been added to give it a "period feel." U.S. Army, *Field Manual 7–85 Ranger Unit Operations* (Washington, DC: Headquarters, Department of the Army, 1987), D-1.

should keep in mind a maxim never to be departed from by a commander, viz. to preserve a firmness and presence of mind on every occasion.[74]

Indeed, Rogers's writings, when compared with Cumberland's insistence that his troops march into battle with no more than 18 inches separating each rank, show which military tradition was more in tune with the realities of war making in the wilderness of North America.[75]

Lieutenant Colonel Thomas Gage, meanwhile, seized the formation of the Gentleman Volunteers, Rogers's doctrine, and the Whipping Post Mutiny as an opportunity for his personal advancement. Cognizant of the discussion within the high command about the necessity of placing a regular officer at the head of the rangers, Gage considered volunteering to accept such a billet. Rather than command rambunctious Americans, however, Gage wanted to lead disciplined and professional British regulars. He found a compromise. In December 1757, he submitted to Loudoun a formal proposal to raise at his own expense a 500-man regiment of "light-armed foot" of British rangers, provided that the crown promised to reimburse him and commission him a colonel.[76]

With the apparent need for British rangers clear, Gage's proposal met with a generally favorable reception from Loudoun's staff. Major General Abercromby, one of the more vociferous critics of the rangers, thought it "extremely advantageous" since British troops would be able to discharge "all the functions of Rangers in a short time better than those at present."[77] Both Colonel Ralph Burton and George Augustus, viscount Howe, agreed it was "the best plan" for bringing discipline to the rangers.[78] Only one officer, Colonel John Forbes, Loudoun's respected and capable Adjutant General, opposed it. As he saw it, the plan was too "lucrative" for Gage, "who is a favourite." More important, Forbes correctly noted, there were few cost savings to be found in raising yet another regiment.[79]

Loudoun overrode Forbes's objections and gave Gage command of the British Army's ranger corps in North America. To Loudoun, Gage's

---

74 Rogers, *Journals*, 70. *Field Manual 7–85* still stresses the pragmatic approach to ranging that Rogers first proposed over two centuries ago. It reads: "This publication does not contain everything the ranger needs to know to successfully execute a unit mission. Rather, it supplements unit training and the ranger unit commander's guidance; it does not supersede it" (p. iv). Rogers's call for "firmness and presence of mind" resembles Jeney's insistence that partisan officers possess *coup d'oeil*.
75 "Exercises for the American Forces," April 18, 1756, LO 1060.
76 Thomas Gage, Proposal to His Excellency the Earl of Loudoun for Raising a Regt. of Light Armed Foot, WO 34: 46A.
77 Abercromby to Loudoun, December 18, 1757, LO 5038.
78 Loudoun's memorandum books, December 11, 1757, HM 1717.
79 Loudoun's memorandum books, December 15, 1757, ibid.

proposal seemed like a panacea that solved all the problems associated with the American rangers. The British troops, he wrote to William Pitt,

> should both make so great a Saving to the Public, in reducing the pay of the Rangers . . . and at the same time have a Corps of Rangers that would be disciplined, which, except a very few, is not the case at present; And as if by this Plan, if it Succeed, I should be Independent of the Rangers, and from thence be able to reduce their expense, besides which, as I am obliged to increase the Rangers, it is necessary to have an Officer at their head, by whom I can communicate the orders to them, and to be answerable for them being executed.[80]

With Loudoun's support in the form of a £2,600 advance, Gage in early 1758 set about raising his regiment. Loudoun of course, could have expected that Gage would turn to the Gentleman Volunteers and students of Rogers's "ranger school" to fill the officer billets in the new regiment. But unlike Colonel Henri Bouquet, who, Forbes noted, attempted to "learn the Art of War, from Enemy Indians or anything else who have seen the Country and War carried on it" while training the 1st battalion of the 60th Regiment for wilderness operations, Gage used the regiment to build his personal patronage base within the army.[81] Gage ignored most of the British officers with ranging experience; of the 19 officers whom he recommended to Loudoun and the War Office for commissions, only 4 had been Gentleman Volunteers. Just as important, he appointed them to the regiment's most junior billets. Gage instead offered the senior commissions in his regiment to the senior company-grade officers in the regular line regiments. In May 1758, the crown, either unconcerned about or unaware of the actual makeup of the regiment or its intended mission, approved Gage's petition, granted him a colonel's commission, and brought the 80th Regiment of Foot into the British establishment.[82]

---

80   Loudoun to Pitt, February 14, 1758, LO 5598.
81   Forbes to Bouquet, June 27, 1758, *The Writings of General John Forbes Relating to His Service in North America*, ed. Alfred Procter James (Menasha, WI: The Collegiate Press, 1938), 125. For Bouquet's "Preparations for an Expedition in the Woods against Savages" see Lewis Butler, *The Annals of the King's Rifle Corps, Volume 1, "The Royal Americans"* (London: John Murray, 1913), 159–162, 330–334.
82   Warrant on Abraham Mortier, January 3, 1758, LO 3664. See also John R. Cuneo, "Factors Behind the Raising of the 80th Foot in America," *Military Collector and Historian* 11 (1959): 97–103. Loudoun to Gage, January 2, 1758, LO 5319. Volunteers for Gage's regiment came from every unit stationed in North America, excluding the troops in the Maritimes and South Carolina. See "Muster Roll," *The Bulletin of the Fort Ticonderoga Museum* 5 (1941): 15–16; *A List of the General and Field Officers as They Rank in the Army* (London: War Office, 1759), 134, hereafter *Army List*; W. Thomas, "Stations of Troops in North America," *JSAHR* 14 (1935): 235–236. *Army List*, 134 and N. B. Leslie, *The Succession of Colonels of the British Army from 1660 to*

It was unlikely that the 80th would replace the rangers. Part of the problem was in the lack of experienced woodland fighters in its ranks and officer corps. A greater part, however, centered on Loudoun's selection of Gage as the regiment's commander. Lieutenant Colonel John Bradstreet, an effective combat leader who understood warfare in North America, had made a similar proposal for creation of a regular–ranger regiment to Loudoun in August 1757. Like Gage, Bradstreet saw command of the regiment as the means to achieve his goal of personal profit and preferment from the British high command. In the end, Loudoun gave Gage – the most senior lieutenant colonel in the British Army then serving in North America – command of the new regiment, much to the disappointment of the more capable but no less ambitious Bradstreet.[83] Gage proved to be a competent organizer who fretted over the details necessary to command a regiment in garrison. But as a combat leader, as John Shy has noted, he possessed "no talent for making war."[84]

the Present Day (London: Gale & Polden, Ltd., 1974), 92. Gage copied the American rangers' equipment. See Beattie, "The Adaptation of the British Army to Wilderness Warfare."

83 See William G. Godfrey, *Pursuit of Profit and Preferment in Colonial North America: John Bradstreet's Quest* (Waterloo, Ontario: Wilfrid Laurier University Press, 1982), 99–100.

84 John Shy has described Gage as "pleasant, honest, sober; a little dull; cautious." See Shy, "The Empire Militant: Thomas Gage and the Coming of War," *A People Numerous and Armed: Reflections on the Military Struggle for American Independence*, rev. ed. (Ann Arbor: University of Michigan Press, 1990), 113. While that passage describes Gage at the outbreak of the American Revolution, it also describes his abilities in the Seven Years' War. "Honest," nonetheless, is an adjective that should be attributed to Gage with caution. Gage was extremely jealous of Rogers's successes and went to no small effort to ruin the ranger's career. While Rogers was a man who rubbed many people the wrong way and seemed at times arrogant, and may have been involved in some inappropriate financial dealings at Michilimackinac, Gage's treatment of him after the war was nonetheless despicable. After the Seven Years' War, when he commanded all British troops in North America, Gage dallied and did not release Rogers from a Montréal military prison in spite of a court marshal acquittal of Rogers on charges of treason and misconduct, charges that Gage unjustifiably initiated. Gage also refused Rogers the pay he deserved for his service during the Seven Years' War. Rogers wrote to Gage that he had been in service as a regular major during Pontiac's War, when he had advanced his rangers £1,700 from his own pocket. He hoped Gage would approve a reimbursement. See Rogers to Gage, March 3, 1764, Robert Rogers MSS, William L. Clements Library, Ann Arbor, MI. Gage informed Rogers that only he, not the rangers, was on the regular rolls, and the rangers therefore would have to receive their pay from provincial sources. See Gage to Rogers, March 19, 1764, Rogers MSS. He then brushed aside Rogers's request for a peacetime command of a frontier garrison by writing, "I am very convinced of your abilities, and knowledge in that particular service, but do not know of any Rangers to be raised at present. . . . Should the opportunity offer itself of employing you to your advantage, I should gladly embrace it." See ibid. Rogers spent the rest of his life trying to repay the debts he had incurred in the service of the crown. In time, his debts landed him in debtor's prison and undoubtedly contributed to his alcoholism, as well as his estrangement from his wife and their eventual divorce.

Indeed, Loudoun's experiment with the 80th gained little for British arms. Creating the regiment had produced no substantial savings. With an outlay of £4,738.18.12 to set up the regiment, plus the monthly cost of £843.16.8 (about £10,100 per year) to keep it operational, the Army could have paid 250 rangers.[85] Since the 80th procured no intelligence above and beyond what the rangers provided, and did not engage the French and Indians in any skirmishes, the money certainly would have been better spent on forming five additional 50-man companies of American rangers.

By the summer of 1758, it was understood and welcomed throughout the army that the 80th would not replace the rangers. The Chief Surgeon of the army, Richard Saunders Huck, noted that "although it has been pretty much in vogue lately to decry all Rangers[,] and Rogers has come in for his Share of Discredit, Parties therefore of regular troops commanded by such Officers as were judged the properest for that [ranging] Service have been sent out to procure Intelligence but returned without effecting any thing, for which they blamed" their troops. Many officers and men alike grew "sick of these Experiments."[86] Even Major General Abercromby, the staunch critic of the rangers, had to concede that he needed them. Despite what may still have been substantial misgivings about the man, he promoted Rogers to provincial major and ordered that when parties of the 80th took the field, Rogers or other American ranger officers were to command them.[87]

After Amherst replaced Abercromby, Gage tried with little avail to convince him that the 80th made up the elite ranger unit of the army. Speaking of engaging Indians in the woods, Gage told Amherst:

> I despair of this being done by Rangers only, Judging from the many Pursuits of these People after Indians during my Service in this Country in which they have never once come up with them. The light Infantry of the Regiment headed by a brisk Officer, with some of the boldest Rangers mixed with Them, to prevent their being lost in the Woods, will be the most likely people to Effect this Service.[88]

Amherst ignored Gage and instead directed the 80th to become adjuncts to Rogers's command. American rangers and British regulars acting in concert, Amherst believed, could strike crushing blows against the enemy. It was important that Americans, who were more adept at ranging, lead

85 Warrant on Abraham Mortier, July 23, 1758, AB 940.
86 Richard Saunders Huck to Loudoun, June 29, 1758, LO 5866.
87 Abercromby to Pitt, August 19, 1758, *Correspondence of Pitt*, 1: 319. Rogers did not receive his official regular commission as a major until 1760 and the Cherokee War.
88 Gage to Amherst, February 18, 1759, Gage Letter Book, Thomas Gage MSS, William L. Clements Library, Ann Arbor, MI.

those operations. As such, he put aside what reservations he may have had about placing Britons under the command of Americans and instead used combined American–British patrols to counter the Canadian and Indian raiders.[89] Amherst also tolerated the use of Americans, with Britons in supporting roles, against enemy noncombatants. British regulars, as noted earlier, accompanied Rogers and the rangers in leveling St. François. In the process, they proved that the real employment of ranger methods – not the cosmetic efforts of Gage – was the key to the British goal of having regulars function like rangers.[90]

James Wolfe, even more than Amherst, made American rangers the cudgel with which he struck his Canadian and Indian foes. Wolfe had served as Cumberland's aide de camp while on "police duty" in Scotland after the '45, where he saw the effectiveness of indigenous troops in crushing enemy opposition. He determined that "Canadian settlements were to receive the same treatment as had the Scottish Highlands after Culloden."[91] As in Scotland 13 years earlier, Wolfe in 1758 had at his disposal indigenous troops to kill and intimidate noncombatants. By thus encouraging what Wolfe saw as the "barbarity which seems so natural" to Americans, whether of Indian or European descent, Wolfe hoped to spare his British regulars from the distasteful tasks of terrorizing the Canadians into submission.

Ironically, Wolfe proved that he possessed the same barbarity for which he criticized the natives of North America. While Amherst laid siege to Louisbourg in 1758, Wolfe ordered his American ranger companies, commanded by Captains Joseph Gorham and Benoni Danks, experienced officers who led war-hardened New England and Nova Scotia rangers, to devastate the Gaspé region.[92] In command of the British Army outside

---

89 Amherst's journal, May–September, 1759, *Journal of Jeffery Amherst*, 108–179.
90 Army administrators in London attempted additional cosmetic changes in 1761. In December of that year, the Army authorized the American-born Joseph Hopkins, formerly a lieutenant in the 48th Regiment of Foot, to raise a 100-man company of American rangers (the Queen's Royal American Rangers) to serve in the regular British establishment. Hopkins recruited his men in Maryland and Pennsylvania and mustered them into service in the summer of 1762. William Alfred Foote argued in his chapter on Hopkins's company ("The American Independent Companies of the British Army 1664–1774" [Ph.D. diss., University of California, Los Angeles, 1966], chap. 16) that with Hopkins's company, "Joseph Gorham and Robert Rogers had a potential rival!" (p. 365). That potential was never realized. Hopkins's company was ordered to the West before he had time to train his men. He lost over half of his command as casualties during Pontiac's War and never effectively deployed his company. In September 1763, Amherst ordered the Queen's Royal American Rangers disbanded and the few remaining men fit for duty drafted into the regular regiments then garrisoning Detroit and Niagara.
91 "Canadian settlements": Eccles, *France in America*, 212.
92 See Journal of a Partisan Officer, 1758, AB 410; *DCB*, s.v. "Danks, Benoni"; ibid., s.v. "Goreham (Gorham), Joseph;" and Ellen D. Larned, "Orderly Book of Sergeant Joshua Perry," *NEHGR* 54 (1900): 70–76.

Québec in 1759, Wolfe increased the scale and scope of his war on Canadian noncombatants. Although he declared at the outset that he and the British Army would not target Canadian civilians, his actions spoke louder than his words.[93] A little over a month after promising them that they could avoid his wrath, he became "indignant at the little regard paid by" the Canadians' refusal to surrender. He ordered Gorham's Rangers to "burn and lay waste the country for the future, sparing only churches," and authorized them to scalp Indians or Canadians dressed like Indians.[94] Gorham's Rangers took Wolfe's order as a license to kill, plunder, and destroy. They conveniently found that most "Canadians dressed like Indians" and used that "fact" as an excuse to take "a few scalps."[95] The rangers were not alone in victimizing the noncombatants of Québec. In the best-known atrocity of the campaign, Captain Alexander Montgomery and a detachment of the 43rd Regiment killed and then scalped a priest and 30 parishioners at St. Anne.[96]

Wolfe's ranger-led war outside Québec, added to Amherst's destruction of St. François, signaled the acceptance within British military circles of American rangers and the kind of war they waged. Britons' experiences with the French and Indians had shown that American rangers indeed were important to British success in North America. Just as important, Britons could not expect their regulars to replace the rangers. In the Indian wars that ran concurrently with and followed the Seven Years' War, British commanders went further in making the first way of war a larger part of their design for victory.

IV. Britons' Adoption of the First Way of War, 1759–1763

The Cherokee War severely strained British military resources in two campaigns and encouraged British commanders to turn to the first way of

---

93 General Wolfe's Proclamations to the Canadians, June 27, 1759, *NYCD*, 10: 1046–1047.

94 John Knox, *An Historical Journal of the Campaigns in North America, For the Years 1757, 1758, 1759, and 1760* (1769; reprint, ed. Arthur G. Doughty, 3 vols. [Toronto: Publications of the Champlain Society nos. 8, 9, 10, 1914]), 1: 438 and General Wolfe's Proclamations to the Canadians, July 29, 1759, *NYCD*, 10: 1047–1048.

95 For the rangers' campaign of destruction outside Québec, see Anon., *Journal de L'Expédition sur le Fleuve Saint-Laurent . . . Extrait du New York Mercury, No. 385, daté de New York, 21 décembre 1759* (n.p.: n.d.), 8–9. For Gorham's Rangers' scalping parties, see Knox, August 11, 1759, *Historical Journal*, 2: 26; August 30, 1759, ibid., 2: 54. Ironically, the rangers were so efficient in destroying Canadian farms and villages that in the winter of 1759–1760 the British troops garrisoning Québec were forced to subsist primarily on old stores of salt pork. Over 1,000 of them succumbed to scurvy over the course of the winter. See Jennings, *Empire of Fortune*, 424.

96 C. P. Stacey, *Quebec 1759: The Siege and the Battle* (Toronto: Macmillan, 1966), 91–92.

war.[97] When word of the outbreak of hostilities on the southern frontier reached Amherst in the spring of 1760, he stripped his regular regiments of their best men and rushed them to Charleston under the command of Colonel Archibald Montgomery. Amherst's orders to Montgomery were clear: quickly punish the Cherokees and then return north for the impending campaign against Montréal.[98] When Montgomery arrived in Charleston with his regulars, he found in place an American plan that would allow him to do just that.

From the opening days of the conflict, Americans and Britons planned to focus their efforts on Cherokee noncombatants. In October 1759, Governor Arthur Dobbs of North Carolina had outlined a strategy to crush the Cherokees. "In Case a War must be proclaimed," Dobbs wrote, "the three Southern Provinces of Virginia and the Carolinas should exert their whole force, enter into and destroy all the Towns of those at War with us, and make as many of them as we should take their Wives and Children Slaves, by sending them to the Islands [West Indies] if above 10 years old...and to allow £10 for every prisoner taken and delivered in each Province."[99]

Montgomery, in May 1760, incorporated Dobbs's plan. Before the Cherokee War, British commanders had parceled out to Americans, Indians, or those British regulars they felt were capable of acting like rangers (the Highland Rangers and the Gentleman Volunteers, for example) the task of terrorizing noncombatants. In Montgomery's case, the entire British force in the Carolinas would act directly against Cherokee noncombatants. Montgomery also knew that his force could not defeat the Cherokees in their own country without American and Indian support and the services that they provided as scouts and guides. Before setting out for the Cherokee towns, he therefore attached to his regulars 300 rangers, 40 handpicked troops from the provincial forces, and 50 Catawba warriors.[100] Meanwhile, the Cherokees remained diplomatically isolated; the

---

97 For accounts of the Cherokee War, see John Oliphant, *Peace and War on the Anglo–Cherokee Frontier, 1756–63* (Baton Rouge: Louisiana State University Press, 2001); Steele, *Warpaths*, 228–234; Tom Hatley, *The Dividing Paths: Cherokees and South Carolinians through the Era of Revolution* (New York: Oxford University Press, 1993), chap. 10; David H. Corkran, *The Cherokee Frontier: Conflict and Survival, 1740–1762* (Norman: University of Oklahoma Press, 1962), 142–272; and Corkran, *The Carolina Indian Frontier* (Columbia: University of South Carolina Press, 1970), 52ff.

98 John Shy, *Toward Lexington: The Role of the British Army in the Coming of the American Revolution* (Princeton, NJ: Princeton University Press, 1965), 103–105.

99 Arthur Dobbs to William Pitt, October 14, 1759, *Correspondence of William Pitt*, 2: 185.

100 Steele, *Warpaths*, 230. For South Carolina's efforts to enlist the Catawbas, see James H. Merrell, *The Indians' New World: The Catawbas and Their Neighbors from European Contact through the Era of Removal* (New York: W. W. Norton & Company, 1989), 197–198.

Creeks and Chickasaws refused to join them, realizing that war would result in their being on the receiving end of a campaign of devastation. With his allies in hand and the Cherokees left to their own devices, Montgomery then set out "to show those savages that it was possible to punish their insolence."[101]

Montgomery's initial advance on the Cherokees' Lower Towns met little opposition.[102] His army first marched on Estatoe, a town of over 200 houses and "all the necessaries of life." They put it to the torch and watched as fires killed those Cherokees who tried to hide from the attackers in their homes. The Britons and their allies, Major James Grant reported, then "proceeded on our march, took all their towns in our way, and every house and town in the Lower Nation shared the same fate with *Estatoe*." One "could not help pitying them a little," Grant wrote. Nonetheless, "after killing all we could find, and burning every house," Grant recalled, they marched westward toward the Middle Towns, where Cherokee resistance stiffened. Outside Etchoe, the Cherokees ambushed Montgomery and his provision train. In the sharp fight that followed, the Indians killed nearly 20 and wounded 90 of the British force and inflicted enormous damage on its pack animals.[103] They had shown Montgomery the limits of his operational capability in the mountains. He sacked Etchoe and then rationalized a retreat by noting that his "correction of the Cherokees had been pretty severe."[104] He ignored the fact that he had not relieved the besieged Fort Loudoun in the Overhill Towns, and withdrew to Charleston and set sail for New York.

In the summer of 1761, it was Grant's turn to lead the armies against the Cherokees. With the northern campaign settled, Amherst could focus on striking the final blow against the Cherokees. In early 1761, he ordered Grant to take an army into the Cherokee towns and spare no effort in annihilating the "miscreants."[105]

Grant struck the Cherokee towns with a combined force of regulars and rangers. Grant saw that the flaw in Montgomery's plan had been his unwillingness to press forward, at all costs, with devastation

---

101 Lieutenant-Governor Henry Ellis to Pitt, March 5, 1760, *Correspondence of William Pitt*, 2: 259; James Grant, Part of a Letter to His Honor the Lieutenant Governor, from Major Grant, *Gentleman's Magazine* 30 (1760): 306.

102 The Cherokees' towns were divided among the Lower, Valley, Middle, and Upper (Overhill) Towns. The Lower Towns were those closest to Charleston.

103 A Particular Account of Col. Montgomery's Expedition against the Cherokees, *Gentleman's Magazine* 30 (1760): 442. See Hatley, *Dividing Paths*, 131.

104 James Grant, Part of a Letter to His Honor the Lieutenant Governor, from Major Grant, *Gentleman's Magazine* 30 (1760): 306.

105 Shy, *Toward Lexington*, 104; Amherst to Pitt, December 8, 1760, *Correspondence of William Pitt*, 2: 360.

of the Cherokee towns. He also knew that the only way to victory "lay in the complete destruction of the Middle Towns and their crops."[106] He moved quickly against Etchoe. Expecting an ambush of his supply train, Grant ordered his rangers to protect it. The Cherokees acted as Grant suspected, attacking the pack train and killing six rangers and nearly five dozen horses. Still, the rangers, with the help of 175 provincials, beat back the attack and allowed the main force to move into the open ground before Etchoe. Grant turned his entire force against the town, destroyed all that remained of it, and then attacked and destroyed Tassee, Nequassee, Joree, and Watoga.[107] His was an outstanding example of the first way of war. Rather than allow a cumbersome supply line to slow him, Grant ordered his troops' rations cut so that they would live off the land and consume more Cherokee crops and livestock. During his 33-day campaign, Grant, burned 15 towns, destroyed 1,400 acres of corn, and made 5,000 Cherokees refugees. "Never was Chastisement more necessary to any Set of Villans or more clearly paid," Amherst wrote.[108] After Grant's juggernaut had ravaged the Lower and Middle Towns, and having exhausted their supplies of powder and shot in the effort to resist Montgomery's invasion, the Cherokees chose peace "in the most submissive Manner."[109]

The rangers' contribution to the campaign's success became clouded in the postwar tiff between the Americans Henry Laurens and Christopher Gadsden. Although it is unlikely that the British force would have advanced with such rapidity into the Carolina backcountry without the rangers, the fight at the pack train, where Grant had to rush provincials to help the rangers fight off the Cherokees, angered him immensely. He went so far as to accuse the rangers of cowardice, and noted (correctly) that some of them had deserted on the march to Etchoe. Gadsden, convinced that Grant had botched the war because he had let the Cherokees off too lightly, published his Philopatrios essays. In them, he excoriated Grant and vigorously defended the rangers. At that point, Henry Laurens, commander of the provincial regiment that accompanied Grant, as well as a rival of Gadsden, took up the defense of his commander's conduct and, by implication, his own. In the end, the sacrifices that the rangers made became less important to the Carolinians than the bickering between Laurens and Gadsden. Clearly, not everyone was a fan of the rangers;

---

106   "Lay in complete": Oliphant, *Peace and War*, 161.
107   Grant's Journal, WO 34: 40.
108   Amherst to Pitt, August 13, 1761, ibid., 2: 464–465; Amherst to Gage, August 1, 1761, Jeffrey Amherst MSS, William L. Clements Library, Ann Arbor, MI.
109   Amherst to Pitt, October 5, 1761, *Correspondence of William Pitt*, 2: 475.

both Britons and Americans, if it advanced their personal agendas, could question their military value.[110]

During Pontiac's War, no questions of the usefulness of the rangers or the first way of war clouded Amherst's view.[111] He spared no effort "to bring them [Pontiac's followers] to a proper Subjection" and realize his wish that "there was not an Indian Settlement within a thousand Miles of our Country."[112] He ordered both his American rangers and regulars to take the field and engage in "Destroying any of the Indian Settlements in that Neighborhood [western Pennsylvania]...Distressing & Punishing the Guilty."[113] After the death of one of his favorite junior officers, Captain James Dalyell, at the Battle of Bloody Run outside Detroit, Amherst, as an "Inducement for a Daring Fellow to attempt the Death of that Villain," placed a £200 reward on Pontiac's scalp.[114]

Amherst proved willing to go beyond the rangers' killing of handfuls of Indian women and children and directed that British forces use the eighteenth-century equivalent of a weapon of mass destruction: smallpox. Infecting one's enemies with smallpox "had an established, if irregular, place in late-eighteenth century warfare."[115] In May 1763, Amherst wrote that the British would "Do well to try to Inoculate the *Indians*, by means of Blankets, as well as to Try Every other Method, that can Serve to Extirpate this Execrable Race." He asked Bouquet, "Could it not be contrived to Send the *Small Pox* among those Disaffected Tribes of Indians? We must, on this occasion, Use Every Stratagem in our power to Reduce them."[116] Two months later, Bouquet responded by noting, "I will try to inoculate

110 Christopher Gadsden, *Some Observation on the Two Campaigns against the Cherokee Indians, in 1760 and 1761: In a Second Letter from Philopatrios* (1762; reprint: *Early American Imprints, 1639–1800* [New Canaan, CT: Readex, 1981–1982]), microfiche 9243 and A Letter signed Philolethes, March 2, 1763, *The Papers of Henry Laurens, Volume III, Jan.1, 1759–Aug. 31, 1763*, ed. Philip Hamer (Columbia: University of South Carolina Press, 1972), 281, 287, 289, 309, 311.

111 For general accounts of Pontiac's War, see Gregory Evans Dowd, *War Under Heaven: Pontiac, the Indian Nations and the British* Empire (Baltimore: Johns Hopkins University Press, 2002); Steele, *Warpaths*, 237–242; White, *Middle Ground*, chap. 7; Jennings, *Empire of Fortune*, chap. 20; Howard H. Peckham, *Pontiac and the Indian Uprising* (1947; reprint, Chicago: University of Chicago Press, 1961).

112 Amherst to Bouquet, June 19, 1763, *HBP*, series 21634, 192. Amherst to Bouquet, August 7, 1763, ibid., series 21634, 232.

113 Amherst to Henry Gladwin, August 28, 1763, Amherst MSS.

114 Amherst to Gladwin, September 9, 1763, ibid. In July, Captain James Dalyell sortied out of Detroit with 400 men to burn the Ottawa towns located about five miles from the fort. The Ottawas, tipped off about the impending attack by Indian spies inside the fort, prepared an ambush for Dalyell's force. In a six-hour engagement at Bloody Run, the British suffered 150 casualties. See Bouquet to Major Allan Campbell, September 7, 1763, *HBP*, series 21653, 219.

115 "Smallpox had an established": Elizabeth Fenn, "Beyond Jeffrey Amherst: Biological Warfare in Eighteenth Century North America," *JAH* 86 (2000): 1553.

116 Memorandum by Sir Jeffery Amherst, May 4, 1763, *HBP*, series 21634, 161.

the bastards with Some Blankets that may fall in their Hands, and take Care not to get the disease myself" in order to "effectually extirpate or remove that Vermin."[117]

With the attempt of Amherst and Bouquet in 1763 to "extirpate" the Indian "vermin" of Pontiac's War, whether with rangers or infectious disease, the British Army's acceptance of the first way of war in North America was complete. Necessity dictated that they put aside their notions about what was proper and improper in war. Great Britain's military heroes to emerge from the North American wars of the late 1750s and early 1760s – Jeffery Amherst and James Wolfe – were in fact the British leaders who ultimately most fully embraced the first way of war. In their wildly violent campaigns to conquer New France and subjugate the frontier Indians, Amherst and Wolfe stood at the head of a British military establishment that, when deemed necessary, would replace the Western European way of limited and regular warfare with the first way of war.

117 Bouquet to Amherst, July 13, 1763, ibid., series 21634, 215. It is impossible to know the complete effect of Amherst's biological war campaign against the Indians. Nonetheless, the rebellion had petered out by the spring of 1765. The failure of Pontiac to capture Fort Detroit, the announcement of the Royal Proclamation of 1763, and peace missions led by Bouquet and John Bradstreet all convinced the Ohio Indians that the war was stalemated and their grievances had been addressed.

5

The First Way of War in the Era of the American Revolution

On Christmas Eve, 1776, George Washington sent a stern warning to the chiefs of Maine's Maliseet–Passamaquoddy nation. "The Cherokees and Southern Tribes," Washington wrote, "were foolish enough to listen to them [the British] and take the Hatchet Against us; Upon this our Warriors went into their Country, burnt their Houses, destroyed their Corn, and obliged them to sue for peace and give Hostages for their future Good Behavior. Now Brothers never let the King's Wicked Counselors turn your Hearts against Me and my Brethren of the Country."[1]

Perhaps intending to remind the Indians to stay the course of neutrality should his next morning's raid on Trenton fail and the Revolutionary cause crumble with it, Washington just as likely sought to spread the word of the Americans' might on the frontier. Washington understood the profound importance of the success of the recent American campaign to destroy the Cherokee's Lower and Middle Towns. Whatever would happen at Trenton, Washington could find solace, and the Indians trepidation, in the knowledge that a major portion of the southeastern frontier was open to American settlement.

Yet within the grand narrative of the War of Independence, the raid against the Hessian outpost at Trenton blots out Washington's Christmas Eve message to the Maine Indians. Students of early American military history should not be surprised. The accepted narrative of the War of Independence gives only minor attention to military operations on the frontier.[2] Similarly, the questions and interpretations that narrative has

---

1 George Washington to the Chief of the Passamaquoddy Indians, December 24, 1776, *The Papers of George Washington, Revolutionary War Series*, ed. Philander D. Chase, 8 vols. to date (Charlottesville: University Press of Virginia, 1985–), 7: 433–434.

2 The grand narrative of the war describes a two-phase course. The first phase, between 1775 and 1778, for example, saw a civil war become a war for independence. That phase of the narrative begins with a popular insurrection and a failed British police action in 1775 and 1776. The war then entered its conventional stage and a period of failed negotiations, which lasted until the American victory at Saratoga in October 1777. Between 1778 and 1781, events entered their second phase, that of the French

produced have remained relatively constant, with Indian affairs receiving usually only secondary or tertiary consideration.[3] The following, then, is an examination not of the War of Independence, but of the American–Indian wars that wracked the late-eighteenth-century southern, western, and New York frontiers.[4] This chapter attempts to put the pattern of frontiersmen violence against Indians during the Revolutionary era in context with the first way of war. Simply put, the Indian wars between 1774 and 1783 were waypoints in the development of the first way of war. In them, we find the same elements – necessity and efficiency, the uncontrollable momentum of extravagant violence, and the quest for the subjugation of Indians – that had defined the first way of war throughout the colonial period.

alliance and a world war. The turning point occurred in 1777 and 1778, after which the French alliance transformed the conflict into a world war and forced the British to defend the home islands, Gibraltar, and their valuable colonies in the West Indies. As a result, British planners had to find ways to suppress the rebellion in America with far fewer resources. They therefore refocused their energies on the Southern colonies, where they believed support for the crown was strongest. Thus began the conquest, pacification, and subsequent ghastly partisan and civil war in the South. After Lord Charles Cornwallis's surrender at Yorktown in October 1781, the war entered its endgame period. Between 1782 and 1783, France and Spain made significant inroads against the British in the West Indies. Weary of war, financially strapped, diplomatically isolated, and defeated on battlefields across the Western Hemisphere, the British acquiesced and gave the Americans their independence. For works that conform to this scheme, see John Shy, "The Military Conflict Considered as a Revolutionary War," *A People Numerous and Armed: Reflections on the Military Struggle for American Independence*, rev. ed. (Ann Arbor: University of Michigan Press, 1990); Piers Mackesy, *The War for America, 1775–1783* (London: Longmans, Green and Co. Ltd., 1964); and Don Higginbotham, *The War of American Independence: Military Attitudes, Policies, and Practice, 1763–1789* (New York: Macmillan Company, 1971).

3   For example, but by no means exclusively, military historians have focused on the contribution of the Continental Army and have asked whether it or the citizen-soldier militia was necessary for American victory. In the same vein, they have questioned whether the French alliance was critical to American independence. Others have moved beyond the affairs of the Continental and British Armies to ask how British pacification policies affected the American population. Similarly, they have wondered why the British chose not to treat America to the same programs as the Highlands during and following the Jacobite Rebellion of 1745. Interspersed within studies that address those questions are a cornucopia of works that contribute to our understanding of Revolutionary era diplomacy, economics, military logistics, common men and women, race relations, republicanism, and Indians. See Shy, "The Military Conflict Considered as a Revolutionary War"; Mackesy, *The War for America*; and Higginbotham, *The War of American Independence*.

4   The best work that addresses the Indian wars during the War of Independence, and their effects on Indian societies, is Colin G. Calloway's *The American Revolution in Indian Country: Crisis and Diversity in Native American Communities* (New York: Cambridge University Press, 1995).

I. The Frontiersmen–Indian Wars on the Western and Southern Frontiers, 1774–1783

Frontiersmen came to dominate the West in the 1760s and early 1770s by sheer weight of numbers – and an unrestrained appetite for land. Because of the expense of garrisoning the frontier, the British Army withdrew from the West and left only small forces at Fort Gage (where the Kaskaskia River empties into the Mississippi River), Fort Michilimackinac, Detroit, Niagara, and Fort Pitt (until 1772) following Pontiac's War.[5] Moreover, the King and his servants at Whitehall assumed that their American subjects would abide by the Proclamation of 1763 and refrain from settling west of the crest of the Appalachian Mountains. The crown designed the proclamation as the first step in an orderly and limited expansion of the West, one intended to put to rest Indians' fear that Americans would soon overrun their homelands.[6] By the early 1770s, however, few in the colonies paid any attention to the Proclamation of 1763. As John Murray, fourth earl of Dunmore (royal governor of Virginia and a speculator with a voracious appetite for western lands), noted, no policy conceived in Great Britain could "restrain the Americans; their avidity and restlessness incite them."[7]

Lord Dunmore's War stood as the first major test of American military prowess since Pontiac's War. In early 1774, the Shawnees responded to Dunmore's provocations and continued encroachments on their hunting grounds in Kentucky with raids on settlers and land surveyors across the Upper Ohio Valley.[8] The frontiersmen proved themselves more than eager to retaliate. At the first word of the Indian attacks, Dunmore raised 150 Virginia rangers and ordered them to fall on Shawnee towns. Meanwhile, he mobilized the Virginia militia for a large-scale invasion of the Ohio country. His orders to his subordinate commanders focused directly on

---

5   John Shy, *Toward Lexington: The Role of the British Army in the Coming of the American Revolution* (Princeton, NJ: Princeton University Press, 1965), 402. According to Walter S. Dunn, Jr., in *Frontier Profit and Loss: The British Army and the Fur Trade, 1760–1764* (Westport, CT: Greenwood Press, 1998), following Pontiac's War the British military effort in the West focused less on protecting colonists than on profiting from the fur trade. The Army expended far greater efforts in building an alliance with the French traders and Indians of the West than in garrisoning the frontier.
6   Eric Hinderaker, *Elusive Empires: Constructing Colonialism in the Ohio Valley, 1673–1800* (New York: Cambridge University Press, 1997), 162–166.
7   Lord Dunmore to Lord [William Legge, second earl of] Dartmouth, December 24, 1774, *Documentary History of Dunmore's War*, eds. Reuben Gold Thwaites and Louise Phelps Kellogg (Madison: Wisconsin Historical Society, 1905), 371.
8   For the machinations among the Americans and British colonial administrators that led to Dunmore's War, see Hinderaker, *Elusive Empires*, 189–192.

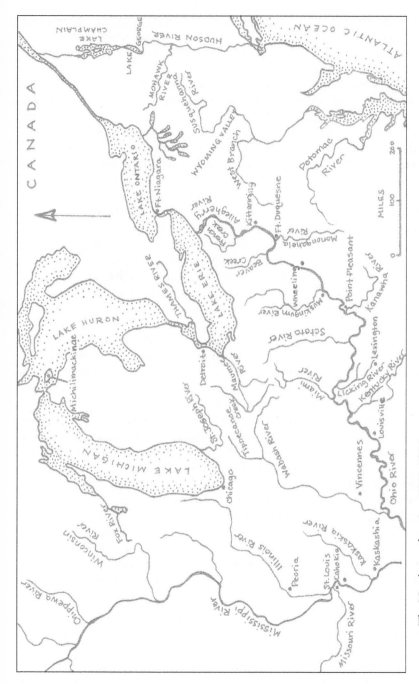

The Northwest frontier, 1750–1815

his intentions for the Shawnees. "Proceed directly to their Towns," he instructed Colonel Andrew Lewis, a veteran ranger of the Seven Years' War, "and if possible destroy their Towns & magazines and distress them in every other way that is possible."[9]

For the Shawnees, it soon became apparent that the "Long Knives" – the western Indians' name for the Virginians – threatened their entire nation's existence. After the Delawares refused to join them, the Shawnees knew that short of besting the Long Knives in a pitched battle, there was little they could do to defend their homes. In October, the outmanned and outgunned Indians therefore offered Lewis battle at the confluence of the Kanawha and Ohio Rivers. At the battle of Point Pleasant, they subjected the frontiersmen to what in the Indians' minds should have been a crushing defeat: at a cost of 30 Indians killed and "some wounded," they made nearly 40 percent (49 killed and 80 wounded) of Lewis's men casualties.[10] Yet the Long Knife army, unlike that of Major General Edward Braddock, upon whom the Indians inflicted a battlefield defeat of similar scale a generation earlier, remained determined to continue its campaign. The frontiersmen were bent on avenging past wounds and seizing the rich lands of the Ohio Valley. They therefore closed ranks, regrouped, and prepared to cross the Ohio.

Failure to halt the American advance at Point Pleasant opened the Shawnees' homelands to almost certain destruction and led the accommodationist-inclined faction within the Shawnees to accept a humiliating peace on the Long Knives' terms. A decade earlier, the Shawnees had made a similar decision for peace when Henry Bouquet had marched west from Fort Pitt and threatened their settlements. In 1774, however, with British officials like Dunmore as hungry for Indian land as the Americans, they found it much harder to placate the Long Knives, who wanted more than a return to the status quo ante bellum. The land speculators and settlers wanted the Shawnees gone. In a crushing blow to their autonomy, Dunmore therefore demanded that the Shawnees give up hostages for their nation's future good behavior and, most damagingly, abandon all claims to their hunting lands in Kentucky.[11] The Battle of Point Pleasant proved an important victory in the impulse toward westward American expansion. As Dunmore explained, "The Event of this Action, proving very different from what the Indians had promised

---

9 Colonel William Preston to Colonel William Christian, June 27, 1774, *Documentary History of Dunmore's War*, 52; Dunmore to Colonel William Preston, July 3, 1774, ibid., 62; Dunmore to Colonel Andrew Lewis, July 12, 1774, ibid., 86.
10 Dunmore to Dartmouth, Official Report, December 24, 1774, ibid., 385.
11 Henry Bouquet to Thomas Gage, November 15, 1764, *HBP*, series 21653, 256 and Dunmore to Dartmouth, December 24, 1774, *Documentary History of Dunmore's War*, 386.

themselves, they at once resolved to make no further efforts against a Power they saw so far Superior to theirs."[12]

Victory in Dunmore's War secured peace along the western frontier for three years. Given the choice between seeing their villages burned and their women and children killed or remaining aloof from the British, the Shawnees chose the latter. "The Virginians are hauty Violent and bloody," British Lieutenant Governor Henry Hamilton noted in 1775, and "the savages have a high opinion of them as Warriors."[13] Indeed, rather than face the onslaught of armies of the Long Knives, all the major tribes of the West agreed to peace when the Patriot government of Virginia approached them. The Americans, meanwhile, held up their end of the bargain and did their best to prevent war on the Ohio frontier, even in the face of sporadic Indian attacks. When in 1777 the "renegade" Indians of Pluggy's Town, for instance, raised their hatchets against Virginia, its assembly responded by authorizing a force of 300 men to march against the town and burn it. Cooler heads quickly prevailed.[14] Congress understood that in striking Pluggy's Town, the Virginians might shatter the fragile peace between the Americans and all the Indians of the Upper Ohio Valley. Congress therefore ordered the expedition halted.

Affairs on the Southern frontier did not bode as well for the Americans. The British and Patriots alike knew that an alliance with the Cherokees could mean the difference between victory and defeat. British officials, with their forces in the South limited to the garrisons at Mobile and St. Augustine, looked to the Cherokees to douse the flames of rebellion. Alexander Cameron, Britain's Deputy Commissioner for Indian Affairs for the Southern Colonies, opened his purse and lavished arms, ammunition, and materiel on the Cherokees. Thomas Brown, the leader of the Loyalist Florida Rangers, wanted to enlist both the Cherokees and Creeks against the Patriots. The Patriots, meanwhile, sent agents to the Cherokees and suggested that they stand aloof from the impending conflict. The Lower and Middle Town Cherokees, after weighing the comparative benefits of neutrality or an alliance with either the British or the Americans, decided that war offered an opportunity to settle old scores. In August 1776, they therefore sent upwards of 600 warriors to destroy American settlements in South and North Carolina. While Great Britain's use of the Cherokees proved to be one of many blunders it made in dealing with the inhabitants of the South – by encouraging the Cherokees to

---

12 *Documentary History of Dunmore's War*, 385.
13 Lieutenant-Governor Henry Hamilton to [Major] General Guy Carleton, November 30, 1775, *The Revolution on the Upper Ohio, 1775–1777*, eds. Reuben Gold Thwaites and Louise Phelps Kellogg (Madison: Wisconsin Historical Society, 1908), 129.
14 Orders of the Virginia Council, March 12, 1777, ibid., 237; Governor Patrick Henry to Colonel David Shepherd, April 12, 1777, ibid., 247.

strike American settlers, British officials galvanized backcountry support for the rebel cause – the decision to side with the British proved a fatal miscalculation for the Cherokees.[15]

By late 1776, an American design for the destruction of the Cherokees had coalesced. "The gross infernal breach of faith which they have been guilty of shuts them out from every pretension to mercy," the North Carolina delegation to the Continental Congress advised, "and it is surely the policy of the Southern Colonies to carry fire and Sword into the very bowels of their country and sink them so low that they may never be able again to rise and disturb the peace of their Neighbors."[16] Despite an accompanying pronouncement that women and children were not to be harmed, the vehemence and color of the Americans' language suggest that a dark cloud had formed over the Cherokee nation.

The American campaign against the Lower and Middle Cherokee Towns in 1776 was both brutal and effective. In the late summer and fall, nearly 5,500 Americans – to date the largest military operation ever conducted in the Lower South – converged in three separate columns on the Indian towns west of the American frontier. Colonel Andrew Williamson's 1,150 South Carolinians approached from the southeast; Colonel William Christian led 1,500 Virginians from the northeast; and Brigadier General Griffith Rutherford took 2,800 troops west-southwest from North Carolina. The results of the campaign never were in doubt. In the face of the advancing host, the Cherokees fled west and left their homes and fields to the mercy of the Americans.[17] The American armies spared nothing in the Lower and Middle Towns. On their march toward the area surrounding present-day Cherokee National Forest, the Americans, one participant recalled, "burned and cut down their corn moving from one town as we destroyed it and marched to another."[18] Along their axes of advance, they also caught Indian women and children, many of whom they killed and scalped rather than make prisoners. Rutherford's North Carolinians alone destroyed 36 Lower Towns, seized runaway African and African-American slaves, and presented North Carolina's Patriot leadership with

---

15 Deputy Superintendent Mr. Henry Stuart's Account of his Proceedings with the Cherokee Indians about Going against the Whites, August 25, 1776, NC Records, 10: 763, 782. For the effects of the British–Cherokee alliance on driving backcountry settlers to the Patriot side, see Rachel N. Klein, Unification of a Slave State: The Rise of the Planter Class in the South Carolina Backcountry, 1760–1808 (Chapel Hill: University of North Carolina Press, 1990), chap. 3. Letter from Charles Roberson and James Smith about the Cherokees, July 13, 1776, NC Records, 10: 665; [North Carolina Assembly] to Gov. Rutledge, of So. Carolina, August 3, 1776, ibid., 11: 337.

16 North Carolina Delegates in the Continental Congress to the North Carolina Provincial Council, ibid., 10: 710.

17 Ibid., 10: xv.

18 James Martin, Petition for Pension, ibid., 22: 146.

plunder valued at over £2,500 to finance the war effort.[19] With their towns and fields in ruins and winter approaching, the Lower and Middle Town Cherokees had little choice but to accept tributary status from the Americans in the treaty of DeWitts Corner.

On the western frontier, meanwhile, desire for revenge for Dunmore's War, coupled with a shrewd calculation of their potential advantage over the Long Knives, motivated the Shawnees to take up the British hatchet in 1777. The peace between the Indians and the Americans, Henry Hamilton had observed two years earlier, was "liable to frequent interruption from more causes than one." "In the inroads of the Virginians upon the savages," Hamilton reported, "the former have plundered, burnt, and murdered without mercy. Tis to be supposed from the character of the savages, that opportunity only is wanting to retaliate."[20] In that mix, Hamilton, expecting a British victory in the East to result from Major General John Burgoyne's invasion of New York, hoped to wage war on the cheap and keep the rebellion off balance in the West. He promised that little harm would come to the Shawnees if they attacked the Americans. In the summer and autumn, Shawnee war parties took Hamilton up on his offer of scalp bounties and struck throughout the Upper Ohio Valley. They drove hundreds of settlers to Wheeling and besieged Fort Henry.[21] Yet just when it seemed that the Shawnees were on the verge of victory, the tide of the war turned against them. Not only had Patriot forces repulsed the British invasion of New York, but Virginia and Pennsylvania frontiersmen raised the siege of Fort Henry. Able to focus resources and attention on the Ohio country, the Continental Congress looked to go on the offensive and extirpate the Shawnee nation.

The American offensives of 1778 became a slaughter of innocents. In February, Congress ordered Colonel Edward Hand of the Continental Army to lead 500 militia and regulars to destroy British-held Sandusky and the Indians wintering there. Bad weather and high waters, however, prevented Hand from reaching Lake Erie and transformed the "Sandusky Campaign" into the "Squaw Campaign." With no Shawnee villages between them and Fort Pitt, Hand's men erased the line between combatants and noncombatants and fell on the neutral Delawares they found in the countryside. Forty-five miles from Fort Pitt, for instance, they killed and scalped four Delawares (one man, two women, and a child) and carried

19 Colonel Andrew Williamson to General Griffith Rutherford, August 14, 1776, ibid., 10: 746–747. North Carolina Council of Safety to Governor Patrick Henry, October 25, 1776, ibid., 10: 861.
20 Hamilton to Carleton, November 30, 1775, *Revolution on the Upper Ohio*, 129–130.
21 Calendar of Letters, October 13–16, 1777, *Frontier Defense on the Upper Ohio, 1777–1778*, eds. Reuben Gold Thwaites and Louise Phelps Kellogg (Madison: Wisconsin Historical Society, 1912), 134, hereafter *Frontier Defense*.

two Indian women into captivity; later they learned that they had killed the brother of the Delaware chief Captain Pipe, "a noted friend to the United States."[22] On another occasion, Hand's troops killed a Delaware boy who was out bird hunting. Hand had to put down a near riot as his troops argued and fought with one another for the right to claim the "honor" of having killed the boy. Later in the "campaign," the Americans fell upon four more Delaware women and a boy making salt; they killed three of the women while the boy escaped. "You be will Surprised in performing the Above great exploits," Hand reported, perhaps intending irony, that during his entire campaign he "had but one man Wounded, & one Drowned."[23] Yet for all of Hand's exploits, all he could point to was a body count of less than a dozen neutral Indians.

Fortunately for the Americans, the Delawares were committed to neutrality; they simply would not allow the murders of a few of their people to thrust them into a destructive war with the Americans. In September, therefore, Delaware leaders George White Eyes, John Killbuck, and Captain Pipe signed a pact of peace and perpetual friendship with the United States at Pittsburg. The Indians agreed that the violence of the previous spring and summer "be mutually forgiven, and buried in the depth of oblivion, never more to be had in remembrance."[24] Of course, the Treaty of Pittsburg did not end all the violence in the Ohio country.

Congress hoped that continued use of the first way of war would destroy the Shawnees. It had replaced the ineffectual Colonel Hand with the equally ineffectual Brigadier General Lachlan McIntosh in July 1778. To strengthen McIntosh's hand, and with the war stagnating in the East, Congress gave him 1,000 more men than his predecessor and explicit orders to "proceed, without delay, to destroy such towns of hostile tribes of *Indians* as he in his discretion shall think will most effectually chastise and terrify the savages, and check their ravages on the frontiers."[25] Little would come, however, from Congress's grand plan. The Shawnees withdrew toward Sandusky, where their women and children would be out of reach of American raiders.

McIntosh's season spent on the Ohio frontier suggested that he was the wrong kind of leader for fighting Indians. McIntosh found that most of his troops' enlistments expired at the end of the year – a circumstance that diminished both his and his men's interest in chasing Indians around

22   Colonel George Morgan to Board of War, July 17, 1778, ibid., 113.
23   Recollections of Samuel Murphy, ibid., 219. Hand to Jasper Ewing, March 7, 1778, ibid., 216.
24   <Kappler/del0003.htm>.
25   Resolution of the Continental Congress, July 25, 1778, *Frontier Advance on the Upper Ohio, 1778–1779*, ed. Louise Phelps Kellogg (Madison: Wisconsin Historical Society, 1916), 121.

the Ohio country. Thus he built two new forts (one of which he named in honor of himself) where he could spend the winter waiting for the war to come to him. Of course, we can only wonder what his troops would have done when their enlistments expired on January 1, 1779, if they had found themselves deep in the midst of Shawnee territory. Far from American settlements or forts, they probably would have inflicted punishment on the Shawnees as they marched home. Instead of forcing his troops to act, however, McIntosh committed the classic blunder of frontier warfare. He garrisoned the newly constructed forts with troops who were safe from all but a want of provisions; as the winter progressed, the garrisons increasingly came to depend on friendly Delawares for food.[26] Shawnee war parties, meanwhile, had a free hand to scour the American frontier. In both January and February 1779 they attacked McIntosh's other fort, Fort Laurens. The American settlers on the frontier did not need Continental regulars satisfied with garrisoning forts, but frontiersmen who would take the fight to the Indians no matter where they were located.

The frontiersmen found such a force in George Rogers Clark's command. In early 1778, Virginia had commissioned Clark a colonel and had given him 200 Virginia rangers to invade the Illinois country. By the fall, Clark, who had fought the Shawnees during Dunmore's War, had moved his force down the Ohio and occupied Kaskaskia.[27] As winter approached, he prepared for an offensive against both the Indians and their putative French allies.

Opinions on the significance of Clark's Illinois campaigns vary. An earlier generation of historians saw them as the centerpiece of a "heroic" tale of how American frontiersmen overcame both the wilderness and Indians to bring civilization to the West. More recently, others have argued that since the British posts in the Illinois country did not threaten American positions in the East, Clark's campaign signified little more than a land grab.[28] Within the context of the development of the first way of

---

26 Lachlan McIntosh to Colonel Richard Campbell, November 3, 1778, ibid., 164. See Recollections of John Cuppy, ibid., 160.

27 Secret Instructions to Clark, January 2, 1778, *George Rogers Clark Papers, 1771–1781*, ed. James Alton James, *Collections of the Illinois State Historical Library, Volume 8, Virginia Series, Volume 3* (Springfield: Illinois State Historical Library, 1912), 34, hereafter *Clark Papers*. For Clark's activities in Dunmore's War, see William Christian to William Preston, November 8, 1774, *Documentary History of Dunmore's War*, 301–302.

28 For works that put Clark in a heroic light, see Lowell H. Harrison, *George Rogers Clark and the War in the West* (Lexington: University of Kentucky Press, 1976); Dale Van Every, *A Company of Heroes: The American Frontier 1775–1783* (New York: William Morrow and Company, 1962); and John Bakeless, *Background to Glory: The Life of George Rogers Clark* (Philadelphia: J. B. Lippincott Company, 1957). Jack M. Sosin, *The Revolutionary Frontier, 1763–1783* (New York: Holt, Rinehart, and Winston, 1967), 117.

war, however, Clark's campaigns mean much more, for in them we see an example of the first way of war's value as a deterrent.

A key to Clark's success in the Illinois country was his initial threat to devastate French and Indian communities, coupled with his subsequent willingness to spare Frenchmen. Since the 1690s at least, Americans had identified the French and Indians as co-conspirators in a grand design to destroy the American frontier. Indeed, antipathy for the "papists" was common among English-speaking Protestants everywhere in the Atlantic world. Clark, however, was a pragmatist who could move beyond labels if it served his interests. He knew that his force would face increased problems if the French inhabitants joined with the Indians against him. Yet he also knew that the Long Knives' reputation as warriors who without hesitation killed women and children preceded them.[29]

Clark capitalized on the psychological advantage of the Americans' reputation. After capturing Kaskaskia, for instance, he dispatched a message to the British-allied Indians wintering outside Detroit. Abandon the British, he told them. "This is the last Speech you may ever expect from the Big Knives," Clark warned, "the next thing will be the Tomahawk. And You may expect in four Moons to see Your Women and Children given to the Dogs to eat, while those Nations that have kept their words with me will Flourish and grow like the Willow Tree on the River Banks under the care and nourishment of their father the Big Knives."[30]

Nowhere did the Americans' reputation for ferocity pay larger dividends than outside Vincennes in February 1779. Henry Hamilton, in a ploy to keep them tied to crown interests, had told the French-speaking residents of Illinois that they "could expect nothing but Savage treatment from the Americans."[31] Clark decided to turn Hamilton's propaganda against him. He first made a public spectacle of the scalping of François Maisonville, a *coureur de bois* (a back-country French trapper) who supposedly had joined Indian war parties. Clark directed Maisonville to be bound in a chair and scalped in plain sight of the town's inhabitants. After partially scalping him, Clark pardoned Maisonville since France and

---

29 Clark to George Mason, November 19, 1779, *Clark Papers*, 119. George M. Waller has noted that the Vincennes campaign suggested to the Indians that the Americans were capable of striking them in their western homelands. See Waller, "Target Detroit: Overview of the American Revolution West of the Appalachians," *The French, the Indians, and George Rogers Clark in the Illinois Country: Proceedings of An Indiana American Revolution Bicentennial Symposium* (Indianapolis: Indiana Historical Society, 1977): 47–66.

30 Clark's Message to the Indians, December 1778, *Clark Papers*, 146.

31 Clark to Mason, November 19, 1779, ibid., 120. For the ambiguous ground the French inhabitants of Illinois occupied, see Donald Chaput, "Treason or Loyalty? Frontier French in the American Revolution," *Journal of the Illinois State Historical Society* 71 (1978): 242–251.

the United States were then allies.[32] Then, when Hamilton refused to accept his demand for the unconditional surrender of Fort Sackville, Clark showed the Americans' darker side. Besides Maisonville, Clark had in his custody four Indians and another *coureur de bois*. He ordered the captives taken into the street opposite the fort's main gate, where its garrison and the town's inhabitants could watch the ensuing events unfold.[33] After sparing the second Frenchman's life as further evidence of his good intentions, Clark ordered the four Indians killed. Hamilton described the scene:

> One of the others was tomahawked either by Clark or one of his Officers, the other three foreseeing their fate, began to sing their Death song, and were butchered in succession. A young chief of the Ottawa nation called *Macutté Mong* one of these last, having received the fatal stroke of a Tomahawk in the head, took it out and gave it again into the hands of his executioner who repeated the Stroke a second and a third time, after which the miserable being, not entirely deprived of life, was dragged to the river and thrown in with the rope about his neck where he ended his life and tortures.[34]

Clark's execution of his Indian prisoners convinced Hamilton, as well as the reluctant French allies of the British, that they should accept whatever terms the Americans offered. While eighteenth-century besiegers often threatened their enemies with death if they did not surrender, Clark's demonstration of ruthlessness must have made the threat seem uncomfortably real to Hamilton. When the respective commanders met outside the fort's walls to discuss terms, Clark announced that he would consider only unconditional surrender. As Hamilton argued for lenient terms, Clark began to wash his hands and face, "still reeking" in Macutté Mong's blood, then reiterated his threat to put the entire garrison to death if it did not surrender immediately. A shaken Hamilton returned to his quarters, conferred with his officers, and opened the fort's gate the next morning. Upon entering the fort, Clark ordered the "Famous Hair Buyer General" arrested, shackled, and transported to Williamsburg. There, Thomas Jefferson ordered him detained not as a gentleman and prisoner of war, but as a war criminal.[35]

---

32 John D. Barnhart, *Henry Hamilton and George Rogers Clark in the American Revolution, with the Unpublished Journal of Lieut. Gov. Henry Hamilton* (Crawfordsville, IN: R. E. Batta, 1951), 182, hereafter *Hamilton's Journal*.
33 *Clark Papers*, 167.
34 *Hamilton's Journal*, 182–183.
35 Ibid., 184. Clark to Patrick Henry, February 3, 1779, *Clark Papers*, 97.

"Hair buying" had long been part of Americans' military culture and remained so after the capture of Hamilton. For instance, when American advances had come to a halt in the Ohio country, Pennsylvania decided to take matters into its own hands and promised to pay generous bounties on the scalps of Indian women and children. Little had changed in the 50 years between Massachusetts in Dummer's War and Pennsylvania in its current Indian war. The implications for the Indians were, of course, frightening. When the neutral Delawares, their towns situated between the Pennsylvania settlements and the Shawnee homelands, protested that scalp hunters might waylay and kill innocent Delawares, American officers refused to do anything to allay their fears. The best that they could offer was a warning that the Delawares must avoid both the literal and metaphorical "warrior paths" and keep clear of Americans.[36]

At about the same time, the British began encouraging the Indians to follow the same warrior paths. The early months of 1780 were dark days for the British effort in the West. The frontiersmen had driven British forces to the trading posts at St. Joseph, Michilimackinac, Detroit, and Sandusky, and because of Clark's successes, their Indian allies were leaving them in droves. Although Clark had condemned Hamilton as "the Hair Buyer," Hamilton in fact had limited Indian participation out of Detroit to only occasional scouting and scalping parties.[37] His superiors in Canada, particularly Guy Carleton, feared that a general Indian conflagration in Ohio would drive settlers to the Patriot cause. But Carleton's replacement, Major General Frederick Haldimand, could no longer afford not to use his resources to their fullest potential. He therefore gave Colonel Arent Schuyler De Peyster, Hamilton's successor, permission to use the crown's western Indian allies as he saw fit.[38]

De Peyster ordered Colonel Henry Bird and 150 regulars and Loyalist rangers to join with 700 Indians to attack Fort Nelson, the Patriot outpost at present-day Louisville, Kentucky.[39] On the march south from Detroit, Bird's Shawnee, Wyandot, and Ottawa auxiliaries learned that Clark knew of their target and had prepared an ambush for them. The Indians then suggested that Bird instead attack the thinly defended settlements along the Licking River in Kentucky. Bird reluctantly diverted

36 Summary of a Letter of Pres. Joseph Reed to Col. Daniel Brodhead, April 29, 1780, *Frontier Retreat on the Upper Ohio, 1779–1781*, ed. Louise Phelps Kellogg (Madison: Wisconsin Historical Society, 1917), 176, hereafter *Frontier Retreat*. Colonel Daniel Brodhead to the Delawares, May 27, 1780, ibid., 184.
37 For Hamilton's Indian policy, see Waller, "Target Detroit," 50 and Jack M. Sosin, "The Use of Indians in the War of the American Revolution: A Re-Assessment of Responsibility," *Canadian Historical Review* 46 (1965): 101–121.
38 Waller, "Target Detroit," 48.
39 Captain Killbuck to Colonel Daniel Brodhead, June 7, 1780, *Frontier Retreat*, 191.

his column and in June reached the Kentucky settlements. The slaughter the Indians and rangers perpetrated was unprecedented; as Bird's Indians and Loyalists advanced down the Licking Valley, they killed hundreds of people. At Ruddle's Station, for instance, they massacred 200 men, women, and children. In a particularly brutal act, even by frontier standards, Bird's allies won the vehement hatred of the Patriots when the few survivors who managed to escape the carnage reported that the Indians had made sport of throwing John Ruddle's infant and wife, while still alive, into a bonfire. Bird, nonetheless, deserves some credit at least for trying to limit the scale of the slaughter. With over 340 captives in hand, and worried that he would not be able to protect them indefinitely from the Indians and rangers, he ordered a hasty retreat to Detroit and thereby spared vulnerable Lexington.[40]

As Great Britain's first major victory in the West, the Licking River raids crushed the frontiersmen's morale. Many Kentuckians, with "doubts and fears" in their minds, quit the frontier. "From what I have seen of the situation of the Enemy's Country," American Colonel John Floyd reported, "they can at any time they please carry on a campaign against this part of the country with equal success to" Colonel Bird's.[41]

Not to be outdone, the frontiersmen retaliated in late summer 1780. Clark led 800 Virginia frontiersmen against the Shawnee towns of southern Ohio. After they crossed the Ohio River, "small raiding parties spread out over the countryside to inflict maximum damage."[42] For over a month Clark's raiders destroyed and plundered Indian villages and fields. Upon his return to Louisville, Clark claimed to have crisscrossed Shawnee territory for 480 miles, put to the torch over 800 acres of fields, and, most significantly, scalped 40 Indians.[43] The frontiersmen and Indians again found themselves locked in a mutual embrace of death and destruction.

At that point, another Indian problem erupted on the Southern frontier. The frontiersmen's victory over the Cherokees in 1776 left only a passing impression on Dragging Canoe (Tsi'yugunsi'ny), an Overhill Cherokee who had led his followers and handfuls of survivors from the Lower and Middle Towns west to villages near Chickamauga Creek. In 1779, in loose coordination with a renewed British focus on the South, Chickamauga warriors began raiding the American settlements that had inched into

40 Captain Killbuck and the Delaware Council to Col. Daniel Brodhead, July 19, 1780, ibid., 220.
41 Colonel John Floyd to Colonel William Preston, August 25, 1780, ibid., 266.
42 Rev. John Heckewelder to Col. Daniel Brodhead, August 14, 1780, ibid., 245; Summary of Letter of Col. Brodhead, September 5, 1780, ibid., 271; "Small raiding parties": Harrison, *Clark and the War in the West*, 91.
43 Clark to Thomas Jefferson, August 22, 1780, *Clark Papers*, 451.

the Tennessee Valley.[44] By 1780, it was clear to Americans that Dragging Canoe and his Chickamauga band demanded attention.

The frontiersmen planned to subject the Chickamaugas to a repeat of the devastations of 1776. Upon the first warnings of hostilities, North Carolina had rushed 500 mounted rangers to burn Chickamauga towns and "chastise that nation and reduce them to obedience."[45] The next year, Virginia and North Carolina pooled their military resources to muster an overwhelming force to send against the Indian villages. The idea behind this Virginia–North Carolina plan was to "transfer the War without delay" to the Chickamauga towns and destroy "their habitation and provisions."[46] Arthur Campbell's army therefore spent late 1780 cutting a wide swath of destruction through the Overhill towns. After the Chickamaugas retreated west in the face of Campbell's onslaught, Lieutenant Colonel John Sevier, after winning an important victory in the War of Independence at King's Mountain, gave chase. In 1781, he led 700 Virginians and North Carolinians into present-day middle Tennessee and northern Alabama, where they burned Indian towns and massacred entire Indian families. The next fall, Sevier took the field at the head of an army of frontiersmen who wiped the headwaters of the Coosa River clean of hostile Indians. The blows the American raiders inflicted were too much for the Chickamaugas. Some fled to middle Tennessee, northwestern Georgia, and northern Alabama, where, for the next 15 years, they continued to be a thorn in frontiersmen's side; most agreed to another peace dictated by victorious American armies.[47]

While Sevier spent 1781 focused on the Southern Indians, frontiersmen in the North again turned on the Delawares. In March, several Delaware bands, believing that they could not live in peace with the Americans, traveled the warrior paths and raided American settlements. In retaliation, Colonel Daniel Brodhead, commander of the American forces in the Upper Ohio Valley, ordered settlers to their blockhouses and flooded the frontier with rangers and scalp hunters.[48] In April, he crossed the Ohio River with 300 Continental Army regulars to destroy the Delaware town of Coshocton near the forks of the Muskingum and Tuscarawas Rivers. "The savages," recalled C. W. Butterfield, one of Brodhead's raiders, "had received no warning of the approach of an enemy." In a driving rainstorm,

44   For the Chickamaugas' raids on American settlements, see William Flemming to Thomas Jefferson, January 19, 1781, CVSP, 1: 446.
45   Governor Martin to Brig. Gen. McDowell, n.d., NC Records, 16: 697.
46   Arthur Campbell to Thomas Jefferson, January 15, 1781, CVSP, 1: 434–437.
47   James Mooney, Myths of the Cherokee (1900; reprint, London: Johnson Reprint Company, Ltd., 1970), 59–60. William Christian to Thomas Jefferson, April 10, 1781, TJP, 5: 395.
48   Col. Daniel Brodhead to Col. David Shepherd, March 8, 1781, Frontier Retreat, 242–243.

the Americans attacked Coshocton and laid it waste. Brodhead then led his men against Lichtenau, a Moravian mission town; there they killed 15 men and took another 20 old men, women, and children as hostages, but spared the town because it had been a Christian settlement. After retreating across the Ohio to Fort Pitt, Brodhead convened a council of war to determine the fate of his Indian prisoners. "Brodhead, himself a humane and chivalric officer," Butterfield later recalled, "only acted upon the idea of a complete justification according to the usages of war. The warriors [not the women and children – this was an operation of the Continental Army, not a band of frontiersmen] were bound, taken a little distance below the town, and dispatched with tomahawks and spears, and then scalped."[49]

The momentum of violence continued to build and set the stage for one of the most atrocious acts in American military history. Colonel David Williamson's company of frontiersmen, frustrated that the Continentals had failed to repeat the Coshocton slaughter elsewhere, embarked on a search-and-destroy mission against hostile Delawares. Upon failing to find any such Indians, Williamson instead turned against the Christian and friendly Delawares at the Moravian mission at Gnadenhütten.[50] There Williamson's troops gathered nearly 100 Indians, tried them in a kangaroo court, and sentenced them to death. In the ensuing slaughter, many of the victims passed their last moments on earth holding hands and singing Christian hymns while their executioners methodically beat their brains out with tomahawks. They then put the mission to the torch.[51]

Atrocities, frequent before the Gnadenhütten massacre, became commonplace thereafter. Although the War of Independence was near its conclusion – a combined French and American army had bottled up General Charles Cornwallis's British force on the York Peninsula in Virginia – participants in the frontiersmen–Indian struggle in the West made it clear that they still had scores to settle. In August, near present-day Blue Lick Springs, Kentucky, a Shawnee–Delaware war party ambushed an American detachment and massacred the 77 men who had surrendered upon the promise of quarter. The reciprocal killings continued through the

---

49 C. W. Butterfield's Narrative of Brodhead's Coshocton Expedition, ibid., 376–379.
50 A year earlier, Brodhead had suggested to the Moravian Delaware leaders that they move their settlements close to Fort Pitt, where he could offer them protection. See ibid., 377. Many of the Delawares at Gnadenhütten were thus there seeking American protection from the ravages of war. For the frontier militia's animosity toward the regular officers of the Continental Army, see Leonard Sadosky, "Rethinking the Gnadenhutten Massacre: The Contest for Power in the Public World of the Revolutionary Frontier," *The Sixty Years' War for the Great Lakes, 1754–1814*, eds. David Curtis Skaggs and Larry L. Nelson (East Lansing: Michigan State University Press, 2001), 187–214.
51 Richard White, *The Middle Ground: Indians, Empires, and Republics in the Great Lakes Region, 1650–1815* (New York: Cambridge University Press, 1991), 390.

fall of 1782, nearly a year after Yorktown. Finally, Clark marshaled an overwhelming force of over 1,000 frontiersmen and led it into southern Ohio. The Americans razed six Indian villages and killed dozens of Indian women and children.[52] The frontiersmen's campaign had no strategic value for the outcome of the War of Independence, but it avenged Indian attacks and helped solidify Americans' claim to the Ohio country.

II. The Frontiersmen–Indian War on the New York Frontier, 1777–1781

Most studies of the clash between Patriots and Loyalists in present-day upstate New York put the struggle in the context of an internecine war, much like the civil war in the Carolina lowlands and the partisan war in Connecticut, lower New York, and New Jersey.[53] However, it is important to remember that as Patriots and Loyalists skirmished and killed one another along the New York frontier, frontiersmen were in the midst of a larger war of conquest, and Indians were in a ferocious war of anticolonialism, on the same frontier.[54] Indeed, all parties – American, Indian, and British – subsumed western New York's Patriot–Loyalist struggle in a larger and more ghastly frontier Indian war. British commanders' decision to employ the Loyalists of the Mohawk Valley no differently than Indians, and thereby treat Patriots in the same ways that they previously had dealt with their Indian and Canadian enemies, ordained that the first

---

52 Waller, "Target Detroit," 69–70.
53 For book-length studies of the civil/partisan/guerrilla war in the South, see Harry M. Ward, *Between the Lines: Banditti of the American Revolution* (Solihull, UK: Helion & Company, Ltd., 2002); Wayne E. Lee, *Crowds and Soldiers in Revolutionary North Carolina: The Culture of Violence in Riot and War* (Gainesville: University Press of Florida, 2001); John S. Pancake, *This Destructive War: The British Campaign in the Carolinas, 1780–1782* (Birmingham: University of Alabama Press, 1985); Ronald Hoffman, Thad W. Tate, and Peter J. Albert, eds., *An Uncivil War: The Southern Backcountry during the American Revolution* (Charlottesville: University Press of Virginia for the United States Capital Historical Society, 1985); John Morgan Dederer, *Making Bricks without Straw: Nathanael Greene's Southern Campaign and Mao Tse-Tung's Mobile War* (Manhattan, KS: Sunflower University Press, 1983); Jerome J. Nadelhaft, *The Disorders of War: The Revolution in South Carolina* (Orono: University of Maine at Orono Press, 1981); and Russell F. Weigley, *The Partisan War: The South Carolina Campaign of 1780–1782* (Columbia: University of South Carolina Press for the South Carolina Tricentennial Commission, 1976). For the partisan war in the Middle Colonies, see Mark V. Kwasny's *Washington's Partisan War, 1775–1783* (Kent, OH: Kent State University Press, 1996).
54 See Max Mintz, *Seeds of Empire: The American Revolutionary Conquest of the Iroquois* (New York: New York University Press, 1999), and Barbara Graymont, *The Iroquois in the American Revolution* (Syracuse, NY: Syracuse University Press, 1972), for studies that contextualize the war on the New York frontier as a frontiersmen–Indian war.

way of war would dominate their handling of the conflict on the New York frontier. Meanwhile, frontiersmen's understanding of the war as first and foremost an Indian war guaranteed that the American effort, regardless of whether individual companies of rangers or the Continental Army conducted them, would be indistinguishable from the kinds of military operations that Americans had executed along the frontier since the early seventeenth century.

The British Army had the Mohawks at its disposal as early as 1775. All parties understood that the Iroquois League would play an important role in any war fought on the New York frontier. George Washington, for instance, noted that the failure of the Patriots to secure at least neutrality from the Senecas and Mohawks "would be a most fatal stroke."[55] Both the British and Patriots rushed emissaries to the Iroquois council houses in hopes of winning the support of the League. Even then, however, the highest levels of the British cabinet fêted Mohawk leader Joseph Brant (Thayendanegea), common-law brother-in-law of the late Sir William Johnson, in London. The Patriots as such stood little chance of securing either Mohawk support or neutrality. Upon receiving Lord George Germain's pledge to investigate Brant's claims that American settlers had encroached upon Mohawk lands, Brant promised to help the British resolve the "troubles in America."[56] The Senecas, traditionally the most antagonistic of the Iroquois toward the British but now fearing the Americans, followed the Mohawks' lead. Only the smaller nations – the Cayugas, Tuscaroras, and Onondagas – showed any disposition to support the rebels, probably reflecting fear of the Americans as well as historical Iroquois tendencies to seek a neutral position from which to play off Europeans against one another. The Oneidas, many of whom had taken to heart the proselytizing of American Protestant missionaries, chose the Americans.

The British, nevertheless, chose not to play the Iroquois card for two years. Although the British had shown how they dealt with rebellious subjects after the Jacobite Rebellion in 1745, moderation ruled in the British camp.[57] For British commanders, the Americans' dread of Indian

---

55 Washington to Philip Schuyler, April 19, 1776, *Papers of Washington*, 4: 90.
56 For the American efforts to bring the Iroquois over to their side, see Proceedings of the Commissioners of the Twelve United Colonies with the Six Nations, August 15, 1775, *NYCD*, 8: 606. For the British side of Iroquois–British diplomacy, see Journal of Colonel Guy Johnson from May to November, 1775, *NYCD*, 8: 658. Answer of Captain Brant to Lord George Germain, May 7, 1776, ibid., 8: 678.
57 Within the British officer corps, Stephen Conway writes, there were "conciliators" and "hardliners." "The conciliators," Conway argues, "were convinced that mild treatment of civilians was essential if the British were to gain a worthwhile victory," while "hatred, fear, anger, and frustration all help to account for the predilection for severity" among the hardliners. See Conway, "To Subdue America: British

war seemed enough to keep most colonists in line. Thus, Major General Burgoyne resorted only to threats when he proclaimed that he would "give stretch to the Indian forces" under his direction and threatened "devastation, and famine and every concomitant horror" to New Yorkers who aided the rebels.[58]

Most Britons were content to keep the "unreliable" Senecas and Mohawks in camp and use the Army to put down the rebellion. As late as October 1777, Burgoyne, soon to face disaster outside Saratoga, chastised the Americans for allowing their Oneida, Cayuga, and Stockbridge allies to mistreat British captives. Perhaps he was hoping to set the conditions that he and his men would face should they have to surrender to the Americans and their Indian allies. Just as likely, "Gentleman Johnny Burgoyne" simply believed that proper officers did not allow their troops – or even their allies – to abuse their prisoners. George Washington, on the other hand, took no exception to his Indian allies' harsh treatment of their British captives. He knew that if the Americans looked the other way as their Indians maltreated their prisoners, the Indians might be more likely to join the Patriots on future campaigns. "Perhaps in point of policy," he suggested to John Hancock, "it may not be improper to overlook these infractions on their [the Indians'] part."[59]

The British disaster at Saratoga and the French alliance that ensued changed the character of the war, especially on the New York frontier. Just as in the Seven Years' War, necessity forced the British to turn to American rangers and the Iroquois. British commanders in Canada, with the loss of 7,000 regular troops and no prospect of acquiring a replacement for Burgoyne's army, found that they had too few men on hand to use in other than defensive roles. They therefore had no choice but to use the rangers for offensive operations. Indeed, as British planners diverted troops slated for North America to the defense of the West Indies, there seemed no alternative to sending the Iroquois and Loyalist rangers against the Patriot frontier. In what then must have added further insult to the injury many British officers felt their reputations had received in the Saratoga campaign, they had now abdicated control of the war's behavior and outcome to Indians and backwoods Loyalists.

The British planners' change in strategic direction made sound operational sense, however. The Iroquois historically had proven themselves

Army Officers and the Conduct of the Revolutionary War," *WMQ* 43 (1986): 382.

58 Burgoyne's proclamation can be found in *For Want of a Horse, Being a Journal of the Campaigns against the Americans in 1776 and 1777 Conducted from Canada, by an Officer Who Served with Lt. Gen. Burgoyne,* ed. George F. G. Stanley (Sackville: New Brunswick Historical Society, 1961), 103–104.

59 George Washington to John Hancock, October 5, 1776, *Papers of Washington,* 6: 475.

effective warriors when properly motivated. The Americans, similarly, had shown in previous conflicts that they were effective rangers and had a particular talent for cowing enemies, whether Indians, Canadians, or Acadians, into submission. Of course, few doubted that the bands of marauding raiders would lay waste to the New York frontier. But with the growing belief that the Northern colonies "were not worth the effort of recovering," so much the better for the defense of Canada and the British trading and military outposts in the West if the New York frontier had to become a military no-man's-land.[60]

The summer of 1778 thus saw the beginning of the Iroquois–Loyalist onslaught against the Patriot frontier, and with it a larger frontiersmen–Indian war. In July, Colonel John Butler commanded a combined force of over 1,000 Loyalist rangers and Senecas under Cornplanter (Ki-ontwog-ky), which, together with one company of British regulars, fell on the Wyoming Valley along the north branch of the Susquehanna River. Butler later would claim that after his troops had overwhelmed the militia protecting the Wyoming settlements, he tried to restrain Cornplanter's Senecas from plundering and scalping. Nevertheless, the Senecas killed and scalped over 70 Patriots, including women and children. "Man, woman, and child were either cut down or carried off with us," one of Butler's ranger officers later recounted, "the dwellings plundered, devastated, and burned."[61]

Butler's rangers were as culpable as the Senecas in perpetrating the "Wyoming Massacre." Evidence suggests that the Americans who joined the Senecas fought and behaved just as Indians and previous generations of American frontier fighters had. When Captain Johann Ewald of the Hessian *Jägers* inquired if he too had killed and scalped, the Loyalist ranger who described the scene of the massacre replied, "Oh Yes! In the same affair I had worked with my tomahawk and scalping knife that my arms were bloody above the elbows." His excuse: "I was born and brought up among these people, and am trained in their customs. He who lives with the Indians and to enjoy their friendship must conform to them in all respects, but then one can depend upon these good people."[62] Tradition, military necessity, and an inexorable momentum of violence had led to a particularly ferocious act.

The Wyoming Massacre was only the first of a series of attacks that racked the Northern frontier in 1778. In September, Brant's Mohawks joined with Captain William Caldwell's Loyalist rangers to destroy the

---

60 "Were not worth": Mackesy, *The War for America*, 158.
61 Ewald's diary entry, June 6, 1779, *Diary of the American War: A Hessian Journal*, ed. and trans. Joseph P. Tustin (New Haven, CT: Yale University Press, 1979), 166.
62 Ibid.

Patriot settlement at German Flats, New York.[63] For most of October, they roamed Ulster County, burned farms, and killed anyone they could catch. Then, in November, Brant's Mohawks left Caldwell to link up with 200 rangers under Captain Walter Butler and a band of Senecas under Little Beard (Sequidonquee) for an attack on Cherry Valley. After capturing all the settlers except for those who managed to retreat to a blockhouse, Little Beard's Senecas killed and scalped their prisoners – about 30 in all. Like his father after the Wyoming Massacre, Walter Butler disclaimed responsibility for the one his force perpetrated at Cherry Valley. In one sense, of course, it made little historical sense to expect Loyalists or British officers to restrain the Iroquois, on whom they relied, from responding to the cultural imperatives of the Iroquois way of war. As the ranger officer told Ewald, when the Indians (and the rangers) were "far from their homeland" they rarely offered quarter to their vanquished foes. Whatever the modern judgment, by the end of 1778 and after the Cherry Valley Massacre, Butler's Rangers had become, from the Patriots' perspective, an "infamous corps of murderers" and deserving of any fate that befell them.[64]

The Indian–Loyalist raids against the Patriot frontier continued into the first half of 1779. Brant's Mohawks ranged as far as Minisink on the Delaware River, where they destroyed a Patriot detachment sent to ambush them, put the settlement to the torch, and killed some of their militia captives.[65] Only a Patriot offensive, carried into the heart of Seneca country, offered a temporary reprieve from the devastation the Loyalists and Indians were inflicting on the New York frontier. In the end, Seneca women and children would be made to pay for their warriors' and the Loyalists' destruction of American settlements.

In early 1779, Congress determined that the disaster on the New York frontier demanded that an army of overwhelming strength turn its full fury on the Senecas. The ensuing Sullivan–Clinton campaign thus showed the first way of war in action. In one of the most complex American operations of the War of Independence, Congress directed that three separate armies – under Major General John Sullivan, Brigadier General James Clinton, and Colonel Daniel Brodhead – sweep across New York and converge near Tioga.[66] From Tioga, the combined army, Sullivan noted, would "totally

---

63 Colonel Guy Johnson to Lord George Germain, September 10, 1778, *NYCD*, 8: 752.
64 Butler had assumed command of the rangers after his father fell ill. *DCB*, s.v., "Thayendanegea," "Butler, John," "Butler, Walter." *Ewald's Diary*, June 6, 1779, 166. Albert Hazen Wright, ed., *The Sullivan Expedition of 1779: Contemporary Newspaper Comment and Letters*, 4 vols. (Ithaca, NY: A. H. Wright, 1943), 2: 37–38, hereafter *Sullivan Expedition*.
65 *DCB*, s.v. "Thayendanegea."
66 Alexander Flick, "The Sullivan–Clinton Campaign in 1779," *Proceedings of the New Jersey Historical Society* 15 (1930): 66–67. See also Joseph R. Fisher, *A Well-Executed*

extirpate the unfriendly nations of the Indians, to subdue their country, destroy their crops, and drive them to seek habitations where they would be less troublesome to us and our allies."[67] The state governments of New York and Pennsylvania enthusiastically backed the plan and offered rangers to augment the Continentals. Pennsylvania went as far as to place a bounty on the scalps of Senecas, regardless of sex, as an enlistment bonus for its troops.[68]

American forces – Continental regulars and scalp hunters alike – used the late summer of 1779 to devastate huge tracts of Seneca lands. With the Iroquois Confederacy torn asunder by infighting and the Oneidas allied with the Continental Congress, American armies could march unimpeded across western New York and directly against the Seneca towns. Although Brodhead's force failed to make the rendezvous at Tioga, Sullivan's and Clinton's columns, totaling 4,500 troops, linked up near the border of New York and Pennsylvania. In August, Sullivan's troops brushed aside the last obstacle to their path when they bested a party of Senecas and Loyalist rangers at the battle of Newton outside present-day Elmira, New York.[69] The Patriots then poured into the Seneca homelands, killed Indians, and destroyed hundreds of houses and thousands of acres of crops in the field. By the end of the summer, the Seneca villages were in "great heaps of ruin."[70] Guy Johnson reported to his superiors in London that Patriots had destroyed "almost all the Villages and cornfields of the Six Nations" and forced the survivors to flee to British-held Niagara.[71]

The Sullivan–Clinton campaign fueled the Senecas' fury and redoubled their commitment to the British. While it had resulted in a temporary cessation of raids against the frontier in the winter of 1779 and 1780, by the spring, Sir John Johnson had welcomed a large force of Seneca warriors at Niagara. After augmenting it with Butler's Rangers and Loyalists from his own King's Royal Regiment of New York, the combined British–Indian force advanced toward the Patriot settlements and American–allied Iroquois villages in the Mohawk Valley.[72] What had been severe factionalism before the Sullivan–Clinton expedition had become a full-blown civil war after it. Brant's Mohawks destroyed the villages of the Oneidas and

---

Failure (Columbia: University of South Carolina Press, 1997), for a critical view of the campaign.
67 John Sullivan's Address to the Oneidas, *Sullivan Expedition*, 1: 6.
68 Rufus B. Stone, "Sinnontouan, or Seneca Land, in the Revolution," *Pennsylvania Magazine of History and Biography* 48 (1924): 211.
69 Extract of letter from Camp, August 30, 1779, *Sullivan Expedition*, 3: 7.
70 September 25, 1779, ibid., 3: 11.
71 Colonel Guy Johnson to Lord George Germain, October 11, 1781, *NYCD*, 8: 813.
72 Governor [James] Robertson to Lord George Germain, July 1, 1780, *NYCD*, 9: 793. For the hardship endured by the Senecas at Niagara, see Calloway, *American Revolution in Indian Country*, chap. 5.

Tuscaroras. Besides destroying the Iroquois confederacy that had stood for a century, the Mohawks denied the Patriots much of their intelligence network. Johnson's troops meanwhile swept across western New York. By June, he could report that his Indians and rangers had killed or made prisoner 156 Patriot settlers. Throughout the summer, Indians and Loyalists remained in the field. In the fall, they swept down on Canajoharie and Schoharie and laid waste to those settlements and the stores of grain without which the Patriots would suffer famine in the winter. Upon assessing the impact of his campaign, Guy Johnson judged the 1780 offensive as one of the major accomplishments of the British war effort on the New York frontier.[73]

By 1781, after three seasons of the Indian war, New York's frontier had become a no-man's-land. Few settlers remained in their communities, as most had fled east toward the relatively more secure confines of Schenectady.[74] Thus, there remained standing no Patriot targets worthy of a major effort. Guy Johnson nonetheless continued to probe for advantage with his rangers. In October, he instructed Major John Ross of the 35th Regiment of Foot and Captain Walter Butler to take 1,200 Indians, rangers, and regulars and sack Schenectady, the largest standing Patriot outpost on the New York frontier. At the battle of Johnstown, however, the Patriot militia managed to situate itself between Ross and his target. Since his mission was not to fight the Americans in the open but rather destroy their settlements, Ross began an orderly withdrawal to Niagara. For most of the retreat, American rangers and Oneida scouts nipped at Ross's flanks. On October 30, an Oneida war party captured Walter Butler, executed him, and brought to an end the war on the New York frontier. "The rebels of the Mohawk Valley," it has been said, "rejoiced more over the news of his death than they did at the surrender of Cornwallis at Yorktown."[75]

In the final analysis, the frontiersmen–Indian war on the New York frontier was more than a civil war. It, and the frontiersmen–Indian wars in the South and the West that paralleled the War of Independence, saw the first way of war explode to the surface and lead to horrific violence. Indeed, the actions of Americans in those wars, if we examine them from a perspective that takes into account traditions and practices from the colonial period, were predictable. For 175 years, first Americans, and

73 Mr. Heron's Information on a Conversation at New York, September 4, 1780, *NYCD*, 8: 806. Colonel Guy Johnson to Lord George Germain, July 26, 1780, ibid., 8: 797.
74 For a fictional account of the fear that the Senecas, Mohawks, and Loyalist rangers inspired along the American frontier in New York, see Walter D. Edmonds's classic of American historical fiction, *Drums Along the Mohawk* (1936; reprint, Syracuse, NY: Syracuse University Press, 1997).
75 *DCB*, s.v. "Butler, John."

then Britons had found the first way of war useful. It should be of little surprise, then, that when conflict erupted on the frontier during the Revolutionary era, both Americans and Britons turned to it. In that sense, the wars between frontiersmen and Indians and their Loyalist allies that paralleled the War of American Independence belong as another chapter in the history of the first way of war.

6

The First Way of War in the 1790s

In September 1792, in response to ongoing Creek and Chickamauga raids on American settlements in the Old Southwest, Robert Anderson penned a terse letter to his state's governor. With the Indians capitalizing on their "skulking, wolfish advantages" to pillage outlying farms, Anderson contended that it was "hazardous, and distressing, to carry on a defensive war" against them. He therefore proposed that Georgia, South Carolina, and North Carolina pool their militias – men "well calculated for such enterprise" – to put over 5,000 infantry and 500 cavalry in the field. The states' militias could then "march through and destroy the disaffected Cherokee (Chickamauga) towns, which would be just on their way, and meet in the Creek country, destroy what they could, and so return." Since the Indians were not "so well calculated to oppose a spirited attack in their country," Anderson believed that two months of hard campaigning would compel them to sue for peace.[1]

The full-scale, coordinated invasion of the Creek country for which Anderson called never materialized. Although Governor Edward Telfair of Georgia was willing to commit a portion of his militia to such a campaign, the leaders of North and South Carolina did not offer up their troops. The federal army, meanwhile, consisted of only a small fighting force. The South, moreover, was not a priority; the War Department had stationed the great majority of federal troops near the Ohio country to counter the Indian threat there.

Anderson's plan, however, should not be discounted as the grumbling of a frustrated commander. It gives us a clear sense of how late-eighteenth-century American frontiersmen conceptualized warfare. Anderson reminded the Governor that he and his fellow frontiersmen, "having had so much experience in the ways of Indian warfare," knew better than others how to deal with the Indians.[2] Victories over the Indians were won by

---

1 Robert Anderson to the Governor of South Carolina, September 20, 1792, *ASPIA*, 1: 317–318.
2 Ibid.

marching directly against their villages, burning their homes, destroying their fields, and killing and capturing their old men, women, and children. The key to defeating Indians was the first way of war.[3] The kind of war Anderson championed thus leads us to ask: where did the first way of war fit in the 1790s and what impact did it have on the military affairs of the early Republic? In the 1790s conflicts with the Indians (the Franklin–Chickamauga War of 1788–1794, the Creek Troubles of 1792–1793, and the Ohio Indian War of 1790–1795), American frontiersmen carried the first way of war as their preferred means of making war into the age of the early Republic. They also compelled the United States Army, much like the British Army in North America of earlier generations, to use it against Indians on the frontier. The permanence of the first way of war on the 1790s frontier reinforced the tensions that arose as some Americans sought to build a new military tradition, one based on their recent experience with the Continental Army in the War of Independence, and others, particularly frontiersmen, remained wedded to the colonial military experience. In the details of federal, state, and Indian relations in the post-Revolutionary period, we see how the supporters of a new tradition that began at Saratoga and Yorktown tried to control rangers' place in Americans' military establishment, whether through forbidding frontiersmen to wage their variety of war, limiting their participation, or assigning them roles of secondary importance. Only the Army's

3 Anderson's plan seems out of place in the historiographic consensus that shapes the Federalist Era's military history. The reigning scholarly synthesis defines the first years of the Army's existence as its "Building Period," when the Army set the foundation for a regular and, most important, limited conceptualization of war. In the 1780s and 1790s, the argument runs, Americans grappled foremost with civil–military relations. They focused primarily on the place and role of a professional army in American society, as well as the standing of militia forces in the nation's military structure. How Americans conquered the Indians of the Transappalachian West receives only secondary consideration. Indeed, one might come away from surveys on the military history of the Building Period convinced that its salient points touched only on esoteric debates on regulars versus militia and a few minor campaigns against the Ohio Indians.
    For the elucidation of the Building Period synthesis, see Jerry K. Sweeney, *A Handbook of American Military History: From the Revolutionary War to the Present* (Boulder, CO: Westview Press, 1996), 1–42. Among the voluminous literature on military affairs of the early Republic, surveys include Francis Paul Prucha, *The Sword of the Republic: The United States Army on the Frontier, 1783–1846*, rev. ed. (Lincoln: University of Nebraska Press, 1987); Allan R. Millett and Peter Maslowski, *For the Common Defense: A Military History of the United States of America* (New York: Free Press, 1984), chap. 4; Walter Millis, *Arms and Men: A Study in American Military History*, rev. ed. (New Brunswick, NJ: Rutgers University Press, 1981), chap. 1; Richard H. Kohn, *Eagle and Sword: The Federalists and the Creation of the Military Establishment* (New York: Free Press, 1975); Russell F. Weigley, *The American Way of War* (Bloomington: Indiana University Press, 1973), chap. 3 and *History of the United States Army* (New York: Macmillan Company, 1967), chap. 5; Maurice Matloff, gen. ed., *American Military History*, rev. ed. (Washington, DC: Office of the Chief of Military History of the United States Army, 1973), chap. 5.

acquiescence to waging and acceptance of the first way of war prevented several frontier communities from seceding from the United States at the exact moment when it was trying to form a new nation. Moreover, partial acceptance of the first way of war became the key to the Army's success over the Indians of Ohio.

I. The Franklin–Chickamauga War, 1788–1794

Eastern Tennessee was ripe for war in 1788. As recently as 1786, John Watts (Kunoskeskee) and his Chickamauga followers had raided the settlements near present-day Knoxville. John Sevier responded by leading backcountry rangers in the destruction of three Indian towns.[4] The fear from both New York City and the peace-inclined Cherokee towns was that a cycle of retribution would engulf innocents and neutrals in a larger campaign of murder and retaliation. Little Turkey, a Cherokee peace advocate, reported to the government's Indian agent in North Carolina, Richard Winn, that his followers were "much afraid of them (Sevier and his followers) fearing they will return and do us an injury as they did before (during the Revolution)."[5] His hope, of course, was that the American government would contain the hostilities.

Containing the war, however, proved difficult. At the core of the problem was the backcountry settlers' hostility toward both the federal government and the Chickamaugas. Since 1784, when frontiersmen led by Sevier had seceded from western North Carolina and established the State of Franklin, the government had had virtually no control over the American settlements in the eastern Tennessee Valley.[6] Indeed, settlers rose in armed opposition when North Carolina attempted to reassert its authority over them. The main reason for Franklin's existence, meanwhile, was to provide backcountry settlements with a government that would protect them from what the settlers perceived as the equally threatening

---

4   James Mooney, *Myths of the Cherokee* (1900; reprint, London: Johnson Reprint Company, Ltd., 1970), 63. For a brief biography of Sevier, see Secretary [for the Territory of the United States South of the Ohio River] [Daniel] Smith to John Sevier, February 17, 1791 *Terr. Papers*, 4: 46.
5   Little Turkey to Winn, October 12, 1788, *ASPIA*, 1: 46.
6   Franklin's boundaries were never precisely delineated but encompassed the eastern portion of present-day Tennessee. At the end of 1788, North Carolina agreed to cede its western lands to the United States in return for an end to the Franklin–North Carolina civil war. In 1796, the federal government absorbed the area that had comprised Franklin into the new state of Tennessee. See Lester J. Cappon, gen. ed., *Atlas of Early American History: The Revolutionary Era, 1760–1790* (Princeton, NJ: Princeton University Press for the Newberry Library and the IEAHC, 1976), 89a1, and Samuel Cole Williams, *The Lost State of Franklin* (Philadelphia: Porcupine Press, 1974). The Franklinites' desire for land motivated their rebellion.

John Sevier bronze statue in the National Statuary Hall, U.S. Capitol
Building

Indian menace and government programs to limit their settlement on
Indian lands. In the summer of 1788, therefore, Sevier, acting as President
of Franklin, ordered a preemptive attack on the Chickamauga towns.
Franklinites killed 30 Indians and drove the survivors farther south down

the Tennessee Valley. Chickamauga warriors responded in kind by taking 30 captives from the settlements situated between the Holston and French Broad Rivers. Affairs had deteriorated so badly by December that agent Winn reported to Secretary of War Henry Knox that Tennessee was aflame in a war of mutual raids and murders.[7]

The war became the Washington administration's problem when North Carolina ceded its western lands to the federal government in 1789. Strapped for both cash and forces (the Army's strength was a mere 700 officers and men), Knox did his best to prevent the outbreak of a full-scale Indian war in Tennessee. Containing hostilities was a task of the first importance. The government already faced an Indian adversary in the Old Northwest, and while Watts's and Sevier's followers engaged in their personal vendettas, a *petite guerre* between the Creeks and Georgia was on the verge of degenerating into a general bloodletting. Knox counseled patience: the steady development of settlements and conversion of Indian hunting grounds into farms, he believed, would slowly but no less effectively overwhelm the Indians. All the frontiersmen had to do, he advised, was establish their farms and watch the Indians "be reduced to a very small number" as they moved west.[8] The Indians, all the while, could not help but see the ongoing development of Franklinite settlements as proof that Sevier and his followers were "determined to extirpate the Indians, and to claim the sole property in their lands."[9]

Amid the confusion that followed the imposition of federal governance in eastern Tennessee, President Washington gave the Franklinites mixed signals. He first offered them a carrot for American suzerainty and pardoned them for any past transgressions they may have committed in their rebellion. Then, brandishing the stick, he declared that the federal government would prosecute any United States citizen who violated the terms of the 1785 Treaty of Hopewell with the Cherokees. At Hopewell, the United States had agreed to restrict American settlement to the east of the Blue Ridge Mountains.[10] That, of course, was unacceptable to the 3,000 American families who had occupied and improved over three-quarters

7 Governor Samuel Johnston [of North Carolina] to Winn, August 31, 1788, *ASPIA*, 1: 45; Winn to Knox, October 13, 1788, ibid., 1: 45; Winn to Knox, August 5, 1788, ibid., 1: 28; Winn to Knox, December 8, 1788, ibid., 1: 29.

8 Knox, Report on Southern Indians, July 6, 1789, ibid., 1: 14–15 and Return of the Depredations Committed by the Creek Indians since the Commencement of Hostilities in the State of Georgia, October 5, 1789, ibid., 1: 77.

9 Joseph Martin to Knox, February 2, 1789, ibid., 1: 48; Knox to George Washington, July 7, 1789, ibid., 1: 52 and Bennet Bullew, Agent for the Cherokees, to President Washington, August 22, 1789, ibid., 1: 56.

10 For text of the treaty, see <Kappler/che0008.htm>. In 1785 and 1786, the Cherokees abandoned any claims to the lands within Franklin at the Treaties of Dumplin Creek and Choata Ford. See Cappon, ed. *Atlas of Early American History*, 61 and North Carolina Cession of Western Land Claims, December 22, 1789, *Terr. Papers*, 4: 3–8.

of a million acres of land west of the Blue Ridge. Knox then took a harder line with the settlers. Opposed to the unregulated settlement of the frontier, he saw the Franklin settlements as a test case for the imposition of governmental authority in the West. "The disgraceful violation of the treaty of Hopewell with the Cherokee," he wrote, "requires the serious consideration of Congress. If so direct and manifest contempt of the authority of the United States be suffered with impunity, it will be in vain to attempt to extend the arm of government to the frontiers." Sevier and the Franklinites, meanwhile, waited until a more opportune time appeared to settle their scores with the Chickamaugas.[11] We can only speculate, but the Franklinites, if they knew of them, would have seen pronouncements like Knox's as proof that the far-distant federal government did not have their best interests at heart.

The spring and summer of 1791 was a tense period from which either war or peace would emerge. In April, 29 Franklinites, to the consternation of Governor William Blount, who was in the midst of delicate treaty negotiations with the Cherokees and Chickamaugas, made an armed reconnaissance down the Tennessee Valley and briefly established a blockhouse at Muscle Shoals (near present-day Florence, Alabama). Blount understood what the Franklinites planned. In 1784, he and Sevier had unsuccessfully lobbied Georgia's assembly, which at that time held title to the lands near Muscle Shoals, for the right to lay out a new county there.[12] The most recent foray, therefore, suggested that the Franklinites were determined to present the government with a fait accompli and expand their settlements to the west at both the Indians' and the government's expense. In June, as tensions settled down, a second party of Franklinites murdered a peaceful Indian "trespasser" on lands that clearly belonged to the Cherokees.

The Franklinites' actions, however, did not derail the peace talks. Both Blount and the Cherokees desperately needed peace and in July concluded the Treaty of Holston. The main provisions of the treaty centered on the Cherokees' abandonment of any claims to land on which the Franklin settlements sat in return for an annual annuity of $100,000. Washington's administration was willing to pay huge sums of money for peace. The

---

11 Thomas Jefferson [Secretary of State] to Congress, November 8, 1791, *American State Papers. Class VIII, Public Lands,* 9 vols. (Washington, DC: Gales and Seaton, 1832–1834), 1: 23. Proclamation by the President, August 26, 1790, ibid., 4: 34 and Knox to Washington, July 7, 1789, ibid., 1: 53. For Knox's general attitude toward frontier settlement, see Alan Taylor, *Libertymen and Great Proprietors: The Revolutionary Settlement on the Maine Frontier, 1760–1820* (Chapel Hill: University of North Carolina Press for IEHAC, 1990), 37. Address from the People of Greene County to Judge Campbell, November 2, 1790, *Terr. Papers,* 4: 38.
12 Ulrich Bonnell Phillips, *The Course of the South to Secession* (Gloucester, MA: Peter Smith, 1958), 38.

Chickamauga war faction, however, saw the treaty as a betrayal of their interests by their Cherokee cousins. Led by Watts and a reluctant Bloody Fellow (Nenetooyah, as he was known to the Indians, had received a "peace medal" from George Washington), they must have realized that any treaty between them and the Americans would address only the latter's concerns.[13] The Franklinites, meanwhile, understood that the treaty had done little to remove the threat poised by the hostile Chickamaugas.

By the autumn of 1792, Watts had decided that the time had come for the Chickamaugas to act or face certain destruction at the hands of the American frontiersmen. Little Turkey reported in September that Watts had convinced all the Chickamauga towns to join the Lower Creeks on the warpath and personally was leading 500 Chickamaugas, Creeks, and Ohio Shawnees under Cheeseekau (the older brother of the leader the Americans later would know as Tecumseh) to destroy the frontier settlements in Knox County. "This declaration of war," Blount wrote, seemingly oblivious to the reality of Franklin–Chickamauga relations, "was very unexpected, and has given great alarm to the frontiers."[14] Still, the frontiersmen at Buchanan's Station outside Nashville blunted the Indian assault long enough to convince Watts that he had lost the element of surprise. After a siege of a few days in which Watts suffered gunshot wounds in both thighs and Cheeseekau was killed by a bullet that shattered his skull, Watts led his raiders back to their villages.[15] The fight at Buchanan's Station, meanwhile, convinced the Franklinites that only a war would settle the issues with the Chickamaugas.

Blount found himself in a difficult position. On the one hand, he faced a frontiersman war party that was becoming increasingly boisterous in its demands for an offensive war against the Chickamaugas. On the other hand, he had neither support for such a war from his superiors nor any federal troops with which to execute it. His only option, it seemed, was to stall and see the course that events took. The one thing he could do, however, was to remind the Chickamaugas of the consequences of their actions. He presciently told them that wars with the Americans "are always dreadful, not only to the warriors, but to the innocent and helpless women and children, and old men."[16]

The Franklinites were well past talking. Actions, they told Blount, spoke louder than words, and the Chickamaugas had already shown their

---

13   William Blount to Secretary Smith, April 17, 1791, *Terr. Papers*, 4: 55; James Robertson to Secretary Smith, June 6, 1791, ibid., 4: 59; <Kappler/che0029.htm>.
14   Blount to Knox, September 11, 1792, *ASPIA*, 1: 276.
15   Blount to Knox, October 2, 1792, ibid., 1: 294 and Blount to Knox, September 26, 1792, ibid., 1: 288. For the Shawnees' alliance with the Chickamaugas, see John Sugden, *Tecumseh: A Life* (New York: Henry Holt and Company, 1997), chap. 5.
16   Blount to the Glass, a Chief of the Cherokees, September 13, 1792, *ASPIA*, 1: 281.

intentions. In the previous 22 months, Indian warriors – Chickamaugas, Creeks, Shawnees, and some Cherokees – had killed 122 settlers in Davidson, Sumner, and Tennessee Counties (the Mero District) alone. Dozens of frontiersmen, meanwhile, had presented themselves to Blount and expressed their willingness to march against and destroy the Chickamauga towns. Indeed, perhaps Blount's sole consolation in what seemed the inexorable advance toward a general war was his knowledge that the Tennessee frontiersmen would provide him with men "equal, in Indian warfare, to any other" in America should he have to fight.[17]

Blount came to believe that he had little choice but to put Franklin troops in the field to protect the frontier. He therefore ordered Sevier, based on his "high character in Indian warfare," to form a company of rangers to guard the settlements.[18] Blount's orders to Sevier, however, were to remain on the defensive. The number of Indian raids dramatically decreased after Sevier's rangers took the field. Whether that was because of Indian aversion to campaigning in difficult winter conditions or the presence of Sevier's men on the frontier we can only speculate. One thing, however, was certain. The Franklinites had yet to see the government do anything offensively to solve the Chickamauga problem.

In January and February 1793, the anger of the Franklinites with the government's unwillingness to undertake a winter campaign against the Chickamaugas almost erupted in open rebellion. After he forbade Americans from committing any hostile act against the Indians, Blount had to order the militia to disperse a mob of 300 settlers with "a mistaken zeal to serve their country" who had gathered to destroy "as many as they could of the Cherokee (Chickamauga) towns." As if that had not been enough to antagonize the Franklinites, Blount then exacerbated their rancor toward him and the federal government by ordering the militia to patrol the frontier to protect the Indian towns from American raiders. Blount even considered convening a special tribunal to prosecute Holston "treaty violators." Only the objections of local Franklinite judges that they had "no authority to try offenders of that description" led Blount to pull back from a political blunder of the first order.[19]

When Blount refused to convene a legislative assembly to address the Chickamauga troubles and what they viewed as exorbitant taxes, the settlers began grumbling that they would be better off managing their own affairs. Allowing them a public forum to air their grievances certainly

---

17 A Return of Persons Killed, Wounded, and Taken Prisoners, from Miro District, since the 1st of January, 1791, ibid., 1: 329–331; Blount to Knox, November 8, 1792, *Terr. Papers*, 4: 208–214.
18 Governor Blount to the Secretary of War, September 27, 1792, ibid., 4: 175.
19 Proclamation of Governor Blount, January 23, 1793, ibid., 4: 235 and Blount to Knox, February 1, 1793, *ASPIA*, 1: 434–435.

would have complicated Blount's task. He therefore stalled and promised to call an assembly later. In a ploy to win the support of Sevier, whom he rightly saw as the natural leader of any new rebellion, he played the patronage card and entrusted the trade goods by which the government hoped to secure peace with the Chickamaugas to Sevier's son, Joseph.[20]

Stalling and patronage, of course, were only temporary fixes. Blount had to do something to calm the mass of the frontiersmen. In March, he mustered a full-time company of rangers for "quieting of the people, whose sense of injuries is such, that it is with the utmost difficulty they can be restrained from embodying, going and destroying the Cherokee towns." This force of rangers proved effective salve for the Franklinites' anger when militia Colonel John Tipton (the same man who had sacked Tilassee the day after Christmas 13 years earlier but had fought Sevier's forces in the Franklin–North Carolina civil war) blustered that he would raise 900 frontiersmen and personally lead them against the Chickamaugas. When only five would-be raiders answered his call – clearly, Sevier, not Tipton, spoke for the frontiersmen – Blount dodged a potential crisis.[21]

Yet just when it seemed that tensions were decreasing within the American community, events took a dramatic turn for the worse. In April, Blount had ordered Major John Beard and 125 rangers to pursue Indians who had struck the Mero District. Beard's men, unable to apprehend the Mero raiders, instead murdered 15 friendly Cherokees who had approached them under a flag of truce. One of those killed was the wife of Hanging Maw (Scolacutta), one of the leaders of the Cherokee peace movement. At a time when war with the Chickamaugas seemed imminent, Beard's murders threatened to shatter the tenuous peace with the Cherokees. Blount, of course, ordered Beard arrested, but could do nothing when a jury of Franklinites acquitted him of any wrongdoing.[22]

By early summer, Blount suspected that the Franklinites' actions had doomed any hope for peace. He therefore flip-flopped and began to advocate federal intervention in the war. "A vigorous *national* war," he now advised, "only can bring the Indians to act as they ought, and that I hope we shall have this Fall."[23]

In July, Territorial Secretary Daniel Smith, a political ally of Sevier, authorized Sevier to lead a 150-man armed reconnaissance of the Indian towns. The Indian fighter had circumvented Blount and had written directly to Smith to express his willingness "to explore as low down

---

20 Blount to Sevier, May 31, 1793, *Terr. Papers*, 4: 264–265 and Blount to Sevier, June 2, 1793, ibid., 4: 267–268.
21 Blount to Knox, March 20, 1793, *ASPIA*, 1: 436.
22 Blount to Beard, April 18, 1793, ibid., 1: 453 and Mooney, *Myths of the Cherokee*, 74.
23 Blount to Acting Governor Smith, June 17, 1793, *Terr. Papers*, 4: 274.

as the lower Cherokee (Chickamauga) towns." Smith saw merit in Sevier's proposal and encouraged Knox to support the Franklinites. For the first time in their conflict with the Chickamaugas, the Franklinites had a sponsor within the federal government who supported their war aims.[24]

Sevier moved against the Chickamaugas in September 1793, and when he did, altered his mission from reconnaissance to destruction. Forbidden to attack Chickamauga villages, he ordered his rangers to roam the countryside and burn and destroy outlying Indian fields. With winter approaching, he knew that destroying the Indians' provision grounds would reduce their ability to make war. "We took and destroyed near three hundred beeves," he reported, "many of which were of the best and largest kind. Of course, their losing so much provision, must distress them very much."[25] He was right. With the Indians scrambling to stockpile supplies to ride out the approaching winter, Blount reported to Knox that the territory enjoyed "an unexpected cessation of Hostilities, the Indians as yet not having committed a single murder since the visit General Sevier paid the nation."[26]

The Chickamauga War reached its denouement the next fall. Sporadic killings, one and two at a time, had recommenced in the spring.[27] With the success of Sevier's raid still fresh in mind, General James Robertson decided that the moment of decision had arrived. In an ominous note to Watts, he warned, "Our people will not go to war against your towns any more, if you come in and make peace. We shall wait long enough for you to come with a flag; but if you do not come, our people will be sure to come again to war; and we have men enough to fight, and destroy you all, and burn your towns."[28] Robertson's offer was disingenuous but his threat was real: two weeks earlier, he had ordered Major James Ore "to destroy the Lower Cherokee towns."[29] Robertson had decided that if the federal government would not wage war on the Chickamaugas, the settlers would go it alone.

Ore led 750 Franklin rangers against the Chickamauga towns in October. Capitalizing on their skills as woodsmen, Ore's rangers marched over difficult terrain, around the Chickamauga town of Running Water, and took Nickajack by surprise. In a repeat of so many other similar raids, the rangers assaulted the village, engaged the Indian warriors in a brief but sharp firefight, killed those slow to flee, and then torched the buildings

24 Acting Governor Smith to Knox, July 19, 1793, ibid., 4: 282.
25 Sevier to Blount, October 25, 1793, *ASPIA*, 1: 469–470.
26 Blount to Knox, November 21, 1793, *Terr. Papers*, 4: 311.
27 Mooney, *Myths of the Cherokee*, 76–77.
28 Robertson to Watts, September 20, 1794, *ASPIA*, 1: 531.
29 Robertson's Orders to Major Ore, September 6, 1794, ibid., 1: 530.

and fields. With Nickajack burning behind them, they swung north and marched four miles upriver to sack Running Water.[30]

Settlers across the Tennessee frontier waited to see if Ore's raid had been enough to push the Chickamaugas into submission, or if it had left them enraged and resolved to strike with greater ferocity. Blount, hoping to capitalize on the shock of the raid, sent the Chickamaugas a final warning:

> quit your towns and remove your stock, and other property, to the woods, leaving your houses and such of your corn as you cannot remove.... Too much blood has been shed already, and if more is shed, it will increase the difficulty of securing blessings of returning peace. War will cost the United States much money, and some lives, but it will destroy the existence of your people, as a nation, forever.[31]

The raid and Blount's threat worked. Watts and Bloody Fellow, with only 400 warriors spread across the remaining towns, knew that Ore or Sevier could return at any moment and bleed the Chickamaugas even more. They and their warriors therefore agreed to meet Blount to discuss peace. In a rare gesture of magnanimity from victorious Americans, Blount, never a strong advocate for the war, offered the Chickamaugas equitable terms. He demanded only that they honor the Treaty of Holston and, in return, provided them with provisions and trade goods to get through the winter.[32] The logic of revenge nevertheless required one last pointless act of violence: four days after Watts and Bloody Fellow signed the treaty, renegade Chickamaugas attacked Sevier's plantation and killed five people, including one of the General's children.[33] With the Indians essentially eliminated as a military threat, however, few on the Franklinite side looked to restart hostilities. Thus President Washington could report to Congress two months later that hostilities with the Chickamaugas "have ceased and there is a pleasing prospect of permanent peace."[34]

The implications of the Franklin–Chickamauga War were many. The most important one, of course, was that frontiersmen maintained their own conception of how best to deal with what they saw as a band of "merciless savages."[35] When the government, with its insistence on diplomacy

---

30   Blount to Robertson, October 1, 1794, *Terr. Papers*, 4: 357.
31   Blount to Double-head, and other Chiefs and Warriors, November 1, 1794, *ASPIA*, 1: 534.
32   <Kappler/che0033.htm>.
33   Anthony Crutcher to William Crutcher, November 12, 1794, *ASPIA*, 1: 542.
34   Washington quoted in William G. McLoughlin, *Cherokee Renascence in the New Republic* (Princeton, NJ: Princeton University Press, 1986), 25.
35   Colonel Winchester to Blount, November 9, 1794, *ASPIA*, 1: 539.

and negotiation rather than force, could not protect them, the frontiersmen turned to the first way of war. Frontier communities had no shortage of men like Sevier, Robertson, or Ore who held little compunction about sacking Indian villages and leaving Indian women and children to perish from disease, starvation, and the elements. Only after they had driven the Indians from their lands or crushed them completely as a military threat would the frontiersmen consider coexistence with both the Chickamaugas and the federal government.

II. The Creek Troubles, 1792–1793

Open warfare was never far below the surface of American–Creek relations. Although the collective Creek nation officially had adopted neutrality in the War of Independence, individual Creeks seized the opportunities afforded by the war between the British and Americans to purloin slaves and horses by raiding settlements in Georgia, Tennessee, and South Carolina. After Great Britain's defeat, the Creeks turned to Spanish Florida for protection and assistance in stemming the tide of American settlement. Spain, its Governor in New Orleans noted, encouraged the Creeks as "a vanguard for the protection of the Mississippi and these other dominions [Florida] of our King, [from] the insatiable and turbulent ambition of the Americans' menace."[36] Indeed, by 1787 American frontiersmen across the South accepted it as fact that the Creeks, Spaniards, and British worked together to block the settlement of western Georgia and present-day Alabama.[37] The Creeks consequently became the objects of the greatest antipathy from the backwoods settlers of Georgia.

36 [Arturo] O'Neill to [Marqués de] Sonora, July 11, 1787, John Walton Caughey, *McGillivray of the Creeks* (Norman: University of Oklahoma Press, 1938), 156, hereafter *McGillivray*. Since the late seventeenth century, the Spanish had been concerned with the advance of American settlement toward their possessions in western Florida. See Herbert E. Bolton, "Spanish Resistance to the Carolina Traders in Western Georgia," *GHQ* 9 (1925): 115–130. See also Jane M. Berry, "The Indian Policy of Spain in the Southwest, 1783–1795," *Mississippi Valley Historical Review* 3 (1917): 462–477.

37 The Creek nation consisted of the Lower and Upper Towns, the former on the trade paths that led to Georgia and the latter on the paths that led to South Carolina. In 1789, Knox reported that the Upper Towns consisted of 60 villages on the Alabama River and the Lower Towns of 40 villages on the Chattahoochee and Appalachicola Rivers. See Knox, Report from H. Knox, Secretary of War, to the President of the United States, Relating to the Southern Indians, July 6, 1789, *ASPIA*, 1: 15. In 1797, Benjamin Hawkins, United States agent to the Creeks, listed 12 Lower Towns on the Chattahoochee River and 25 Upper Towns on the Tallapoosa and Coosa Rivers. See Benjamin Hawkins, *A Sketch of the Creek Country in 1798 and 1799* (1848; reprint, New York: Kraus Reprint Company, 1971).

Governor George Matthews of Georgia would tell the Creeks:

> We wished, and still do wish, we could forget the many and repeated injuries you have done us during and since the late war with Great Britain. It is in vain to talk of satisfaction.
>
> Your conduct towards us long since has authorized our putting flames to your towns, and indiscriminately killing your people.
>
> Now open your ears *wide*, and hear what we tell you: Should any act of hostility, or depredations, be committed on our people by your nation, be perfectly assured we will not hesitate to do ourselves ample justice, by carrying war into your country, burning your towns, and staining your land with blood. You will then be compelled to fly for refuge to some other country.[38]

War, naturally, was not the only alternative. Alexander McGillivray (the "Beloved Man" of the Upper Creeks), the son of a Scots trader and a French–Creek woman, spent the late 1780s trying to find a way for the Creek nation and Americans to coexist peacefully. Although he had served as British Deputy for Indian Affairs and encouraged the Upper Creeks to fight the Americans during the Revolution, by the late 1780s McGillivray had realized that continued armed opposition to the Americans would lead to if not the Creeks' ruin, then at least his own.[39] McGillivray wanted to find a "Middle Ground" between the Americans and Creeks; he strove to reestablish the system of trade and mutual economic dependence that had been the foundation of peace between the Americans and Creeks throughout the eighteenth century. Yet he was not so naive as to depend solely on the economic interests of the South Carolinians and Georgians to keep them in line. Thus, as he held one hand out to the United States, he offered the other as a secret partner to an Anglo–Scottish mercantile firm (Panton, Leslie, and Company) of exiled Loyalists operating from Pensacola. Beyond the personal gain that came from occupying the central position in a three-way Anglo–Creek–American trade network,

38 [Governor George Matthews of Georgia] to the Fat King and Other Head-men of the Lower Creeks, August 7, 1787, *ASPIA*, 1: 33. For the ill will that characterized Creek–American relations in the Confederation Period, see Randolph Downes, "Creek–American Relations, 1782–1790," *GHQ* 21 (1937): 142–184.

39 McGillivray was not above raising the collective Creek hatchet if it served his personal interests. In 1787, for instance, he sent 500 Creek warriors against the American settlements on the Cumberland River to prevent the establishment of a trading post there. Also in 1787, he directed the murder of Georgian and potential trade competitor William Davenport. See Claudio Saunt, *A New Order of Things: Property, Power, and the Transformation of the Creek Indians, 1733–1816* (New York: Cambridge University Press, 1999), 78.

a Creek–Spanish–British tripartite alliance offered McGillivray a trump card to play against the Americans should they not act as he wished.[40] McGillivray's scheme rested on the flawed assumption that the Americans and all the Creeks would welcome a return to the Middle Ground. Most problematic for those who hoped to see the Georgians and Creeks living in peace was the shattering of the trade system during the late war. The War of Independence wrought significant changes on the Deep South: "by the time peace was achieved the decades-old pattern of trade that linked Georgia and the Creeks had been destroyed. New Georgians, eager to till the land so recently gained from the Creeks, changed the character of the backcountry."[41] The Creeks had a special name for the Georgians: "Ecunnaunuxulgee" – "people greedily grasping after the lands of the red people."[42] McGillivray thus complained to American treaty negotiators that although his followers were prepared to accept peace, Georgians continued to plunder Indian hunting camps. Many of the Creeks, McGillivray warned, therefore came to see both his and the Americans' talk of peace and trade as "only deceitful snares to lull them into security, whereby the Americans may more the easily destroy them."[43]

The demise of the Middle Ground meant war. By 1788 Georgians had, in McGillivray's description, "usurped" Indian rights by killing game on Creek lands and torching Indian hunting camps. Creeks responded by attacking Georgia's outlying settlements.[44] At first, all went well for the Creeks, who, McGillivray boasted, had been so "Victorious in every quarter over the Americans . . . there is so good a prospect of Compelling the Americans to relinquish all Idea of Encroachments."[45] His claims certainly would have rung true to the frontiersmen of Georgia. In the span

---

40 Like the Indians of the *pays d'en haut*, some Creeks believed that trade "defined peace, bound peoples together, and provided the foundation for political relationships." See Kathryn E. Holland Braund, *Deerskins and Duffels: The Creek Trade with Anglo-America, 1685–1815* (Lincoln: University of Nebraska Press, 1993), xi. McGillivray's standing among the Creeks was a product of his skill at serving as the conduit through which all trade flowed between the Indians and the British, as well as his familial lineage. For a brief biography of McGillivray that puts his trading activities at the forefront of his career, see James H. O'Donnell, "Alexander McGillivray: Trading for Leadership, 1777–1783," *GHQ* 49 (1965): 172–186.

41 "By the time": Braund, *Deerskins and Duffels*, 169. Edward J. Cashin has written, "Whatever else the American Revolution meant to Americans, for those in the Georgia backcountry it meant the end of a British policy that favored Indians retaining their hunting grounds and the beginning of the American policy of Indian removal." Cashin, ed., *Colonial Augusta: "Key of the Indian Country"* (Macon, GA: Mercer University Press, 1986), 123.

42 Colin G. Calloway, *The American Revolution in Indian Country: Crisis and Diversity in Native American Communities* (New York: Cambridge University Press, 1995), 20.

43 McGillivray to Richard Winn, Andrew Pickens, and George Matthews, September 15, 1788, *ASPIA*, 1: 30.

44 McGillivray to [Juan y Vicente] Folch, April 22, 1789, *McGillivray*, 227.

45 McGillivray to [Vizente Manuel de] Zéspedes, January 5, 1788, ibid., 165.

of 12 months, Creek warriors killed 72 settlers, wounded another 29, and captured 30 more; they absconded with 110 black slaves, nearly 650 horses, and 1,000 head of cattle; and they burned 89 houses.[46]

Each Creek raid, however, encouraged the Georgians to turn to the first way of war. The American peace negotiators to the Creeks (Benjamin Lincoln, Cyrus Griffin, and David Humphreys) pleaded with the federal government to allow Georgia to undertake a war of conquest. They suggested that Knox first send an ultimatum to the Creeks demanding that they cease the raids. When the Indians explicitly refused the terms, the United States would muster 3,500 infantry and 500 cavalry at Augusta and "carry arms to the very heart of the Creek country."[47] No one needed to say, of course, what those troops would do when they entered Creek villages.

Nevertheless, the intervention of the federal government allowed for a reprieve. President Washington, far from his land speculator days and now an established leader responsible for the welfare of the entire nation, believed that the best way to ensure peace on the frontier was to bring the Indians into the trading orbit of the United States. He therefore summoned the Creeks to New York in 1790 for treaty negotiations. The Creek delegation, led by McGillivray, welcomed the terms that Washington offered; they understood the need to "prevent the Calamities" that awaited them in an American–Creek war.[48] Thus, in return for 800 square miles between the Ogeechee and Oconee Rivers – lands that Georgia already had acquired from the Creeks in the 1783 Treaty of Augusta – the Creeks won the amity of the federal government. The United States agreed to enforce the Oconee as the western border of Georgia, thereby establishing a frontier well east of the Creek towns on the Chattahoochee River and providing the Creeks with a secure hunting ground. More important, the treaty established the economic interdependence that both Washington and McGillivray sought. By a secret provision, the United States agreed to send $60,000 annually in duty-free trade goods, through McGillivray, to the Creeks' villages.[49] The goods would aid the Creeks in diversifying their economy and strengthen the position of McGillivray – now the leading Creek peace advocate – among the miccos (Creek civil headmen). The Treaty of New York in fact offered everything for which McGillivray could have hoped. The Creeks could continue the deerskin trade with the British through McGillivray's connections with Panton, Leslie, and Company. At the same time, they could build a trade in agricultural products

---

46 Return of Depredations Committed by the Creek Indians since the Commencement of Hostilities in the State of Georgia, October 5, 1789, *ASPIA*, 1: 77.
47 Lincoln, Griffin, and Humphreys to Knox, November 20, 1789, ibid., 1: 78.
48 Benjamin Hawkins to McGillivray, March 6, 1790, *McGillivray*, 257.
49 Braund, *Deerskins and Duffels*, 176 and <Kappler/cre0025.htm>.

and slaves with the Americans to the East.[50] The Spaniard Estevan Miró knew the Creeks' game: McGillivray and his allied miccos would "keep on the good side of both parties, and that they will maintain themselves in our [Spain's] friendship, the former [McGillivray] receiving his pension [$2,000 in 1791] and the others presents, while at the same time they enjoy all the advantages furnished them by the [United] States."[51]

The balls in McGillivray's diplomatic-economic juggling act soon began to fall on his head. Many Creeks saw no need to back down to the Americans. Twice soundly having defeated American armies in the Ohio country, Shawnee delegates arrived from the North to encourage the Creeks to raise their hatchets and drive the Americans from their lands. In addition, many young Creek males wanted, just as earlier generations had, to prove themselves on the battlefield.[52] Complicating matters for McGillivray, only a select few Creek miccos shared in the Americans' largess after the New York negotiations. William Bowles – an exiled Loyalist adventurer and trader (his connections were with a Bahamian firm) who hoped to supplant McGillivray as Beloved Man – did his best to remind young, less-established Creeks of that fact.[53] Lower Town miccos challenged the authority of the mestizo McGillivray to speak for them. The frontiersmen, of course, did their part to inspire rancor among the Creeks. They ignored the treaty's provisions and moved their cattle herds across the Oconee to graze on Indian lands; beyond having their cattle destroy deer habitat, Georgians took to actively slaughtering hundreds of deer and ruining the livelihood of many Creek warriors.[54] "To bring peace and stability to the Old Southwest required more people than Knox and McGillivray at the conference table."[55] Thus, it should have come as no surprise when 80 Creek warriors joined the Chickamaugas on an attack of the Cumberland district of Tennessee in February 1792 and others crossed the Oconee and hit the Georgia settlements.[56]

50 J. Leitch Wright, Jr., "Creek–American Treaty of 1790: Alexander McGillivray and the Diplomacy of the Old Southwest," *GHQ* 51 (1967): 379–400.
51 Miró to [Don Luis de] Las Casas, October 16, 1790, *McGillivray*, 285.
52 For the traditional division within Creek society between young and old on issues of war and peace, see Saunt, *A New Order of Things*, chaps. 1 and 2.
53 Claudio Saunt has examined the economic inequality that pervaded post–Revolutionary Era Creek society. He notes how historians are apt to describe Indians – like McGillivray – who lived in brick houses, owned slaves, and appeared to be white. That focus looks past the mass of Indians whom the new economies left behind. See Saunt, "Taking Account of Property: Stratification among the Creek Indians in the Early Nineteenth Century," *WMQ* 57 (2000): 737–738. The marginalized Creeks naturally provided a ready pool of supporters for Bowles's campaign to oust the wealthy McGillivray as leader of the Creeks.
54 Randolph Downes, "Creek–American Relations, 1790–1795," *Journal of Southern History* 8 (1942): 362.
55 "To bring peace": Wright, "Creek–American Treaty of 1790," 386.
56 Blount to James Robertson, April 1, 1792, *Terr. Papers*, 4: 133.

Knox moved to avert war. He directed James Seagrove (United States agent to the Creeks) to remind the miccos that the United States had no further designs on their lands and to encourage them to rein in their warriors. He also hoped to capitalize on the same divisions within the Creeks that Bowles had seen. Knox suggested that the United States could offer employment to the less-established Creeks if they chose to raise their hatchets against the Chickamaugas. If he could get "their active young men, possessing strong passions for war," on the Americans' side, he could defuse most of the tensions not only in Tennessee, but in Georgia as well.[57]

Events in Georgia, however, had already progressed well beyond the stage where Knox's alliance building could have worked. Bowles and the Spanish had gone far to erode the confidence of the Creeks in the Americans. First, the Americans learned that Bowles had shipped his supporters a cache of arms. Then, in the summer, the Georgians also learned from the Cherokee spy Richard Finnelson that McGillivray planned to lead his followers in a Spanish-supported war against the Americans. At New Orleans, the Spanish governor showed Finnelson "a very large quantity of guns, ammunition, hatchets, and other goods for Indians" that he had earmarked for the Southeastern Indians. He then informed Finnelson that McGillivray, in return for a gift of $1,500 from Spain, had "turned to be a new man" and renounced, at least to the Spanish, his treaty with the Americans.[58] Word of McGillivray's machinations spread quickly. Andrew Pickens wrote to the Governor of South Carolina that he had learned from several Chickasaws and Choctaws that "the Creeks are on the eve of going to War with us."[59]

Blount, already occupied with the Franklin–Chickamauga War, now had to face the unenviable task of quieting the war cries among the Georgia frontiersmen. In August, he advised Knox that the United States must focus its efforts on "the young and unruly part of" the Creeks. "The leading chiefs," Blount told Knox, "most earnestly wish for peace & friendship but to punish them with a View to giving peace to the Frontiers would be like lopping off a bough from a tree for the purpose of killing it, the root of the evil is the numerous and insolent Creeks and it is they who encourage and lead forward the too willing young." Knox answered that he understood that the Creek raiders were "a Banditti,

---

57 Knox to Seagrove, April 29, 1792, *ASPIA*, 1: 253–254.
58 A Talk Delivered by James Seagrove, May 18, 1792, ibid., 1: 299. Information by Richard Finnelson, n.d., ibid., 1: 288. When Seagrove confronted the Spaniards on their "interference" in Creek–American relations, the Spanish Governor denied any complicity. See Translation of Governor Quesada's Letter to James Seagrove, June 14, 1792, ibid., 1: 303.
59 Andrew Pickens to the Governor of South Carolina, September 13, 1792, *Terr. Papers*, 4: 169.

and do not implicate the whole nor any considerable part of that Nation. The hostilities of the Individuals arise from their own disposition, and are not probably dictated, either by the Chiefs, or by any Towns or other respectable classes of the Indians."[60] The frontiersmen nevertheless were well past differentiating between friendly and hostile Creeks. It was in that context that Anderson wrote the letter, quoted at the outset of this chapter, to the Governor of South Carolina. Besides distilling the collective experience of frontiersmen with Indian warfare, he resorted to a thinly veiled threat to turn to a foreign power for protection if the government in the nation's capital continued to ignore their concerns. "But now, sir," Anderson wrote, "you may rest assured, that the moment has arrived, when the most spirited exertions of Government are necessary, and I am truly sorry that the citizens cannot be permitted to defend themselves in the best way, without the approbation of Government." If the government failed to act, Anderson warned, "we may as well dissolve the Union, as to pretend to hold it together, because Georgia will be ruined, perhaps this state [South Carolina], and several others much injured. Indeed, I am of opinion (if they see Congress tardy or relax in their exertions, as they have been against the Northern tribes) they well soon have Spain to contend with; and perhaps one or more of the European powers."[61]

The government had to act to quiet the war cries from the frontiersmen. The best for which the antiwar factions on either side could hope was that the Georgians would show some restraint and attack only hostile Creeks. Seagrove therefore rushed a report to New York in which he identified the five Creek towns that he believed held the majority (500) of the hostile Creeks.[62] Knox, meanwhile, ordered "the most expert and hardy woodsmen" of the Georgia militia into federal service. If the rangers were under government control, the Georgia army would be without its vanguard. In the same set of orders, Knox reminded Major Henry Gaither – commander of federal forces in Georgia – that the Army's primary task must be "to induce the Indians to continue the peace, and to calm every attempt to raise a storm."[63]

---

60 Blount to Knox, August 31, 1792, ibid., 4: 166 and Knox to Blount, November 26, 1792, ibid., 4: 221–222. Knox's use of the phrase "respectable classes of Indians" is telling, especially in terms of the economic cleaves within Creek society.
61 Robert Anderson to the Governor of South Carolina, September 20, 1792, *ASPIA*, 1: 317–318.
62 List of the Unfriendly Towns in the Creek Nation, and Those that the Friendly Chiefs Recommend Should be Punished; also Their Number of Fighting Men, April 30, 1793, ibid., 1: 392.
63 Knox to Gaither, April 29, 1793, ibid., 1: 367. For the shortage of federal forces in Georgia, see Return of Non-commissioned Officers and Private Belonging to the Legion of the United States, June 5, 1794, *ASPMA*, 1: 67.

The storm, however, was about ready to break. On May 8, Edward Telfair advised Knox that "such is the havoc and carnage making by the savages, in every direction on our frontier, that retaliation by open war becomes the only resort." Telfair therefore had ordered 700 Georgia militia – six troops of cavalry and three battalions of infantry – under General John Twiggs to establish a forward operating base on the Ocmulgee River. Only flooded rivers, Telfair reported, had prevented the Indians from continuing their attacks; the implication, of course, was that as soon as the waters subsided, the Georgians would push off for the Creek towns. He then advised Knox of the ground rules of the coming campaign: "Let no idea of peace so far amuse as to divert the necessary and immediate preparations for war. Every information you may receive tending thereto must proceed from ignorance or design. The field is now taken; the people must be protected, and a failure, in this juncture, will affect the operations of Government in a serious degree."[64]

Agent Seagrove feared for the Creeks. "There is seven-eighths of the Creek nation that is really friendly to us," he lamented, "and will remain so, unless they are injured by parties from Georgia going in." He predicted the result of the Georgians' war: "there will be no discrimination; and should they fall on the friendly towns, a general war is inevitable." He also feared that the point had arrived at which the Georgians could no longer be stopped but only controlled. He told Knox that the only alternative to a massacre of the Creeks was to send 1,000 federal troops (at a time when the Army had only 200 troops in the South) under "a cool, prudent commander" to destroy the hostile towns. Knox must appoint the commander of such an expedition from the regular establishment. Georgia's officers, Seagrove suspected, "would go into a war of this kind with ideas that a discrimination of friend from foe among Indians was ridiculous and absurd."[65]

Knox did what he could to prevent bloodshed. He reminded Telfair that because of "considerations of policy," particularly the ongoing American negotiations with Great Britain over the forts it occupied in the Old Northwest, "it is deemed advisable to avoid, for the present, offensive operations against the Creeks." However, to bolster Georgia's defenses, Knox agreed to reinforce the regular establishment in the state with more federally paid troops. President Washington, he told Telfair, had agreed to take an additional 100 cavalry and 100 infantry from Georgia's ranks and place them under federal control. Acknowledging that blockhouses offered "a very imperfect security to the frontier," in an absurd gesture that only infuriated frontiersmen, Knox recommended that Telfair keep two-man scout parties at 12-mile intervals along the frontier. The government,

64   Telfair to Knox, May 8, 1793, *ASPIA*, 1: 369.
65   Seagrove to Knox, May 24, 1793, ibid., 1: 387.

Knox noted, would pay the scouts five-sixths of a dollar a day for their service.[66]

Then, in the spring and summer of 1793, a series of events combined to calm, at least temporarily, the settlers' passion for war. First, the Americans learned in late April that McGillivray had died on February 17 at Pensacola.[67] Since the Georgians believed that most of the "seeds of the present troubles were sown by McGillivray," there was a real chance that the war faction within the Creek towns would lose influence with its leader gone to meet his Maker. Seagrove reported as much in July.[68] The Georgia troops then deserted. They had rushed to the frontier assuming that they would have the opportunity to pillage Creek lands. Instead they found themselves on onerous fatigue duty constructing a string of blockhouses along the Ocmulgee River. By midsummer, they were leaving the Ocmulgee camps in droves.[69] At that juncture, further intelligence arrived from Timothy Barnard (Seagrove's deputy) that the miccos had agreed to "take every step in their power to make a peace and settle matters with the United States." The miccos had gone as far as to gather all the horses stolen from Americans and return them to the Georgians. When the leaders of Coweta (Creeks under Bowles's influence) refused to comply, the miccos bullied them into submission. The show of force on the miccos' part, Barnard reported, "seems to have put a stop to hostilities." He knew of no raiders heading for Georgia; all that was out were a few individual horse thieves whom the miccos would handle in due course.[70]

From the federal government's perspective, it seems it had settled affairs with the Creeks. Diplomacy, despite the efforts of the Georgians to derail it, had avoided driving the Creeks into the arms of the Spanish, who "would naturally align them with the Choctaws and Chickasaws [until] they would become a worse terror in Georgia than the Shawnees are to the Northern States."[71] Reports kept trickling in suggesting that the Creeks indeed wanted an end to the hostilities. In August, John Galphin – a mestizo horse and slave thief who hoped to improve his standing with the Americans and perhaps replace McGillivray as leader of the Creeks in the Americans' eyes – promised that the Creeks would abide by the Oconee

---

66 Knox to Telfair, May 30, 1793, ibid., 1: 364.
67 Seagrove to Knox, April 19, 1793, ibid., 1: 378. McGillivray's obituary notice from the August 1793 issue of *Gentleman's Magazine* is printed in *McGillivray*, 362. *Gentleman's Magazine* described him as a Creek chief and stated that his death was "very much lamented by those who knew him best."
68 Seagrove to Knox, May 24, 1793, *ASPIA*, 1: 388. Seagrove to Knox, July 6, 1793, ibid., 1: 392.
69 For the revolt of the Georgia militia, see Twiggs to General Jared Irwin, April 26, 1792, and Twiggs to Telfair, May 25, 1792, in John Twiggs, "The Creek Troubles of 1793," *GHQ* 11 (1927): 275, 277.
70 Barnard to Gaither, June 21, 1793, *ASPIA*, 1: 422.
71 Ibid.

border. Galphin had "given strict orders to our warriors, to commit no hostilities on the other side of the Oconee." In that context, President Washington, Knox reminded Telfair in September, "utterly disapproves" of a war with the Creeks.[72]

Many frontiersmen, nonetheless, remained determined to settle the Creek Troubles in their own way. At the height of the tensions, Telfair had given militia commanders blanket permission to pursue Indian horse thieves wherever that pursuit might carry them. In September, Lieutenant Colonel William Melton used that order as a pretext to attack Oakfuskee. There his company scalped six Creek men, left the town's 10 buildings in ashes, and took eight Creek women prisoners. Melton's actions served as a message to both the Creeks and the federal government. "Ever since the English war," he told the miccos, "our Father of New York has kept our hands tied up, to keep us from ever retaliating the many wrongs we suffered from you every spring."[73]

Melton's raid snowballed into greater problems for Seagrove. He learned that five other militia commanders had organized 90 men for a second raid across the Oconee. More personally ominous for Seagrove, they had ordered their men to abduct anyone – American or Indian – who might try to treat for peace. Georgians then began to talk openly of assassinating Seagrove. "Major Seagrove and his deputy, Mr. Barnard," Major Jonathan Adams reportedly said,

> should both be sacrificed; that, instead of pacifying the Indians, they were only encouraging and paying them to destroy our frontier inhabitants; and, as Congress are a set of rascals, and the Secretary of War an enemy to his country, if he had his power, he would drown them in the sea; observing, at the same time, that he was confident, the Executive officers of the Federal government wished that the Indians might destroy the whole State of Georgia. The Federal troops, he supposes, are of no service in protecting the frontier, and laughs at the two hundred men which the Governor is authorized to raise.[74]

It is little wonder that Seagrove began to fear for his life from both the Creeks and frontiersmen.[75]

---

72 Galphin to Irwin, August 21, 1793, ibid., 1: 371. Knox to Telfair, September 5, 1793, ibid., 1: 365.
73 Buckner Harris to Seagrove, October 2, 1793, ibid., 1: 412; Seagrove to Telfair, September 22, 1793, ibid., 1: 411; Seagrove to Telfair, October 3, 1793, ibid., 1: 412; Melton to the Head-men and Warriors of Donally's Town, Flint River, September 22, 1793, ibid., 1: 372.
74 Frederick Dalcho to Seagrove, September 25, 1793, ibid., 1: 414.
75 Constant Freeman to Knox, September 18, 1793, ibid., 1: 426.

Georgia rangers struck the Creek towns on the Chattahoochee River a second time in September 1793. When Seagrove complained to Telfair, the Governor answered with silence. "As usual," Seagrove wrote, "I have no reply to my request, or any notice taken of so serious an application."[76] Only their rebuff at Chiaja on the Flint River – a town where the raiders expected to seize a number of slaves and instead suffered four casualties – dampened their desire for more raids.[77] With winter approaching, the frontiersmen returned to their homes while Seagrove traveled to the Creek Country in hopes of negotiating an end to the raiding.[78]

The winter of 1793–1794 proved a fruitful one for those who wanted peace. Seagrove managed to convince the miccos that war sentiment among the Georgians was confined to a few hotheads. Thus, the miccos agreed to continue to do their part to control their young warriors. At about the same time, George Matthews replaced Telfair as Governor. Although six years earlier he had taken a belligerent stand toward the Creeks, in the spring of 1794 he believed peace was in the state's best interest. This did not represent a sudden surge of idealism on his part. Matthews was a land speculator who, like Knox, was averse to the unregulated settlement of the frontier by those who held his personal pecuniary interests in little regard. Soon to become known as the governor who signed the act that instituted the "Yazoo Fraud" – the corrupt deal in which the Georgia legislature, in return for lavish bribes, sold over 35 million acres of land near the Yazoo River (in Mississippi) to the Yazoo Company for one and a half cents per acre – Matthews had a vested interest in ensuring that the frontiersmen had only choices he controlled by which to satisfy their hunger for western lands.

It was in this setting that the Georgia frontiersmen finally took matters into their own hands. Angered that Seagrove and Matthews had done nothing to chastise the Creeks, Elijah Clarke led a motley group of landless but armed frontiersmen across the Oconee. Clarke had been a major general in Georgia's militia during the Revolution; he was convinced that his old troops would never take arms against him. On the west bank of the Oconee, Clarke's followers first constructed a blockhouse that they called Fort Defiance and then proceeded to declare the independence of their own republic. Matthews's government brought charges of treason against the rebels in Wilkes County; when the backcountry jury dismissed the state's indictment of Clarke, the Governor responded

---

76 Seagrove to Constant Freeman, September 28, 1793, ibid., 1: 428.
77 Seagrove to Knox, October 31, 1793, ibid., 1: 469.
78 Michael D. Green, *The Creeks: A Critical Bibliography* (Bloomington: Indiana University Press for the Newberry Library, 1970), 34 and Daniel M. Smith, "James Seagrove and the Mission to Tuckaubarchee, 1793," *GHQ* 44 (1960): 41–55.

forcefully.[79] He ordered General Jared Irwin (another land speculator who would become Governor in his own right) to apprehend Clarke and raze the rebels' settlements. Facing the possibility that Irwin's infantry might be inadequate for the task, Matthews ordered a company of artillery from Savannah to blast Clarke and his followers off the Creek lands. It did not come to that; the confrontation between the state troops and the rebels was bloodless. Irwin promised Clarke and his followers that if they submitted peacefully to the state's authority, he would guarantee the protection of both their persons and their property. When Clarke consented, Irwin ordered Fort Defiance razed.[80]

Matthews's actions were a stark warning that he would not tolerate a continuation of the frontiersmen's war with the Creeks. Moreover, the federal government seemed finally to have had enough of the Georgians. Both frontiersmen and Creeks, Alexander Hamilton observed in a letter to Matthews, were culpable for the affairs of the previous years. He wrote: "It cannot be denied, that frequent and great provocations to a spirit of animosity and revenge are given by them (the Creeks); but a candid and impartial survey of the events which have from time to time occurred, can leave no doubt that injuries and provocations have been too far mutual; that there is much to blame in the conduct of the frontier inhabitants, as well as in that of the Indians." Unable to control the Indians, he could at least influence the settlers' behavior. Thus, he made it clear that he would tolerate no more "hostilities, by an irregular and improper conduct" from them.[81] Secretary of War Knox, at a time when most Americans still held a strong aversion to standing armies, blustered that the government would post 1,500 men on the frontier to keep war from consuming it.[82]

Not all was lost, however, for the frontiersmen. The miccos had their restless young men under control, and the Indian raids had stopped. The federal government then backed away from the hard line and offered a conciliatory plan to the frontiersmen. First, the War Department sent Benjamin Hawkins to replace Agent Seagrove, whose even-handed approach to Creek–Georgian relations had made him universally detested along the frontier. Hawkins, amply supplied with gifts, quickly became a Beloved Man among the Creeks, ensuring that the miccos heard American more than Spanish or British positions at their councils. McGillivray's legacy too played a role in building the peace. In 1795, the government

---

79　Discharge of General Clark by the Justices of Wilkes County, *ASPIA*, 1: 496; Knox to Matthews, July 28, 1794, ibid., 1: 501; Matthews to Knox, October 12, 1794, ibid., 1: 499.
80　Constant Freeman to Knox, September 29, 1794, ibid., 1: 500.
81　Copy of a Letter from the Secretary of the Treasury to his Excellency the Governor of Georgia, September 25, 1794, *ASPIA*, 1: 502.
82　Downes, "Creek–American Relations, 1790–1795," 372.

finally opened trading factories along the Creek–Georgia border, thereby fostering ties of mutual economic interdependence between Indian and frontiersman. In the long term, the trading posts would further fracture Creek society; in the short term, they drew many Creeks more deeply into the American economy and away from the Spanish and the British trading firms.[83] The Yazoo Act, meanwhile, promised the imminent opening of a new frontier of "unsettled" lands in Alabama and Mississippi.

The Creek Troubles deeply affected the subsequent history of the Old Southwest. Although Knox's and Washington's policy of avoiding the use of force worked and prevented mass bloodshed and suffering, many in the South would remember that the federal government had tied their hands when they wanted to wage what was to them a just war against the Creeks. Clearly, the government's policy was better thought out and certainly more humane. "Though peace had been established with the Creeks, not to be seriously interrupted until the outbreak of the War of 1812, Georgia looked upon the Federal government more as an enemy than a friend in these dealings with the Indians; and she had come to feel that if the Indians were ever driven out of her borders she would have the task of doing it."[84] The Georgians were only partly right. In the Creek War of 1813–1814, Tennessee frontiersman Andrew Jackson, commanding both regular Army troops and frontiersmen, personally guaranteed that the Creeks would feel the full brunt of the first way of war. Before discussing how Jackson took it upon himself to complete the extirpation of the Creeks that Georgia frontiersmen had started in the 1790s, however, we need to examine the first way of war's role in the last of the Federalist Era's Indian wars.

III. The Ohio Indian War, 1790–1795

The most demanding military and diplomatic crisis to face George Washington's first administration was with the Indians of the Ohio country.[85] During the Confederation period, American–Indian relations in the

---

83 Braund, *Deerskins and Duffels*, 177.
84 "Though peace": E. Merton Coulter, *Georgia: A Short History* (Chapel Hill: University of North Carolina Press, 1947), 184.
85 Larry L. Nelson and David Curtis Skaggs view this conflict as the fifth installment in what they have termed the "Sixty Years' War for the Great Lakes." They note that this war has no formal name; the United States Army refers to it as the "Miami Campaign." Some historians have taken to calling it the "Northwest Indian War," while Nelson and Skaggs prefer the term "Miami Confederacy War." See Nelson and Skaggs, eds., *The Sixty Years' War for the Great Lakes* (East Lansing: Michigan State University Press, 2001), 10. The confusion over what to call the war, or for that matter campaign, points to the general confusion about the place of the early frontier wars in American military

Northwest had deteriorated to the point where the Indians stood on the verge of halting American expansion at the Ohio River.[86] With the British occupying forts in the Great Lakes region, those Indians whom the Americans labeled "discontented" – virtually all the nations of the Old Northwest – found a willing supplier of arms and materiel.[87] The Indians, of course, needed little external encouragement. The 1780s had seen an Indian political movement, first led by Joseph Brant, long an opponent of the Americans, sweep across the Northwest that called for Indian peoples to retake their homelands. Thus while American frontiersmen in the South clamored for federal assistance in staking out new frontiers in Tennessee and western Georgia, the Washington administration had to find a way to maintain the American presence in the Northwest, one that stood on the brink of being overwhelmed by an Indian confederacy as determined and as powerful as Americans had ever seen.[88]

As we have seen, Washington, like Knox, initially believed that Americans could best win the West through peaceful means. He saw the purchase of Indian lands, rather than their expropriation through military conquest, as the "cheapest . . . least distressing way of dealing with them." "There is nothing to be obtained by an Indian war," Washington told Congress, "but the soil they live on, and this can be had by purchase at less expense, and without . . . bloodshed."[89]

The government's conciliatory messages to the Indians – diluted by settlers' murders of peaceful Indians and attacks on Indian villages – had failed miserably. In 1789, Shawnee raiders held the Americans' declarations of peace in such contempt that they crossed the Ohio to raid Kentucky.[90] The responses that had characterized the Kentucky settlers' efforts to subdue the Indians – from the disaster at Blue Licks in 1783 to

historiography. I suggest that "Ohio Indian War of 1790–1795" is more appropriate since the war was with most of the Indian nations of Ohio. Also, I see a need to differentiate it from the "Northwest Indian War of 1810–1813" in the Old Northwest that overlapped the War of 1812.

86 Expansion was the lifeblood of the early Republic. See Drew R. McCoy, *The Elusive Republic: Political Economy in Jeffersonian America* (Chapel Hill: University of North Carolina Press for the IEAHC, 1980). There were those who believed that territorial expansion and the energies it unleashed eventually would destroy the Republic. See Eric Hinderaker, *Elusive Empires: Constructing Colonialism in the Ohio Valley, 1673–1800* (New York: Cambridge University Press, 1997), 268–269.

87 Report from Henry Knox, Secretary of War to the President of the United States, Relating to the Several Indian Tribes, June 15, 1789, *ASPIA*, 1: 12.

88 Washington to Congress, August 7, 1789, ibid., 1: 12.

89 Washington quoted in Wiley Sword, *President Washington's Indian War: The Struggle for the Old Northwest, 1790–1795* (Norman: University of Oklahoma Press, 1985), 27.

90 Knox to Washington, June 15, 1789, *ASPIA*, 1: 13. Since 1783, one estimate had Americans killed in Kentucky at 1,500. See Judge Harry Innes to Knox, July 7, 1790, ibid., 1: 88.

George Rogers Clark's and Benjamin Logan's raids in 1786 against the Shawnees' Ohio towns – had been fruitless in stemming the tide of Indian "aggression."[91]

Once it had become clear that only arms, not diplomacy, would suppress the Indian confederacy, Washington and Knox wasted little time in deciding upon the course of action they would take. They both believed that Congress needed to increase the size of the regular army (Knox recommended at least 2,500 men). In April 1790, Congress heard the administration's pleadings and funded an army of just over 1,200 men.[92] Washington thereupon mobilized the militia to serve as adjuncts to the regulars, and Knox ordered Brigadier General Josiah Harmar to take the new army to Fort Washington (present-day Cincinnati). The Secretary's instructions to Harmar were clear: "To extend a defensive and efficient protection to so extensive a frontier, against solitary, or small parties of enterprising savages, seems altogether impossible. No other remedy remains, but to extirpate, utterly, if possible, the said Banditti."[93]

Extirpating the Indians, however, proved more difficult than was first imagined. Harmar bungled the campaign from the moment he moved north. On October 14, for example, a group of the Kentucky rangers under Colonel John Hardin pushed ahead of Harmar's main force to attack the Miamis' villages. In what should have raised a warning flag to Harmar, Hardin found the villages deserted. Harmar, nonetheless, seemed oblivious to the dangers that faced him and set about establishing his base amid the ruins of the Miami village.

Harmar's complacency played directly into the Indians' hands. He first held out the hope that his army might stumble on an Indian army that would consent to join it in battle. When that failed to produce any appreciable results, Harmar decided that dallying in abandoned Indian villages was doing little to extirpate the Indians. He divided his force into smaller units with which to seek them out. Some of his troops would stay behind and destroy the Indians' fields, while others, in parties of 50 regulars augmented with 200 to 500 militia, would conduct search-and-destroy missions. It was a recipe for disaster. First on October 19 (at Eel River) and then three days later (at Kekionga, modern-day Fort Wayne, Indiana), Miamis under Little Turtle (Me-she-kin-no-quah) and Shawnees under

91 For the war between the Kentuckians and Ohio Indians in the early 1780s, see John Mack Faragher, *Daniel Boone: The Life and Legend of an American Pioneer* (New York: An Owl Book, 1992), chap. 7. See also, Sword, *President Washington's Indian War*, chap. 5.

92 Knox to Washington, *ASPIA*, 1: 13. Weigley, *History of the United States Army*, 90.

93 Knox to Harmar, June 7, 1790, *ASPIA*, 1: 97. Besides Harmar's column, Major John Hamtramck was to ascend the Wabash River from Vincennes and destroy Indian towns. After marching only 150 miles, however, Hamtramck's militia refused to proceed any further and returned to Vincennes. See Matloff, *American Military History*, 111.

Blue Jacket (Weyapiersenwah) ambushed and overwhelmed the joint regular–militia companies.[94] In both cases the militia – who had joined the expedition expecting plunder and booty, not hand-to-hand combat with Indian warriors – panicked and deserted the regulars. The regulars followed their training and formed into lines to exchange volleys of fire with their opponents. At the end of both days, 178 American troops had fallen. Harmar then regrouped his shaken army for the march back to Fort Washington. One can only imagine the sense of foreboding that his troops (for whom Braddock's expedition was probably not too distant a memory) must have felt as they began their retreat. The Miamis and Shawnees were nonetheless content with their victories and had left the field to celebrate driving the Americans from their homelands. Back at Fort Washington, Harmar claimed victory and noted that his troops had burned 300 buildings, destroyed 20,000 bushels of corn, and broken up the Indians' "head quarters of iniquity."[95] Of course, much of the destruction was a result of Little Turtle's scorched-earth bait to draw the American army into an ambush, bait that Harmar eagerly took.[96]

In the Army's garrisons, few acknowledged the real cause of the debacle: the Army's inability to operate effectively in the wilderness. The postbattle investigative report was strikingly similar to the one that Lieutenant Colonels Thomas Dunbar and Thomas Gage had prepared in the wake of Braddock's defeat 35 years earlier. Like the British regulars of 1755, the American officers of 1790 exonerated their commanding officer and excoriated their troops. The militia (nearly 80 percent of the army), as observed at the start of the campaign, "were not such as might be expected from a frontier country, viz. the smart, active woodsmen well accustomed to arms, eager and alert to revenge the injuries done them and their connections."[97] But reflecting the regulars' traditional contempt for rangers, Harmar and his subordinate officers had done little to correct the inadequacies they saw in their men. The easiest thing for the regulars to do was to figuratively close ranks and assign the blame for the losses to the militia.

If anyone had bothered to look, meanwhile, the frontiersmen of Kentucky offered the Army a model on which to reform the tactics and operations of the next force it would send against the Indians. While the Kentuckians were unruly and difficult to discipline, they proved to

---

94 For the role of the Shawnees, and Blue Jacket particularly, in defeating Harmar, see John Sugden, *Blue Jacket: Warrior of the Shawnees* (Lincoln: University of Nebraska Press, 2000), 97–106.

95 Court of Inquiry on General Harmar, September 21, 1791, *ASPMA*, 1: 20–30 and Harmar to Knox, November 4, 1790, *ASPIA*, 1: 104.

96 Michael S. Warner, "General Josiah Harmar's Campaign Reconsidered: How the Americans Lost the Battle of Kekionga," *Indiana Magazine of History* 83 (1987): 41–64.

97 Court of Inquiry on General Harmar, September 21, 1791, *ASPMA*, 1: 21.

be effective Indian fighters. In March 1791, Knox had directed Brigadier General Charles Scott to hand-pick 500 Kentucky mounted rangers "from men of reputation in Indian affairs" and destroy the Indian towns lying on the Wabash River. Knox intended that two forces would depart from the mouth of the Kentucky River, cut across the Wabash Valley, and reenter American lines at Vincennes. Beyond burning wigwams and fields, Scott was to capture "a considerable number of women and children" to hold as hostages for the Indians' good behavior.[98] Scott's rapid sweep through Indian country suggested the damage a determined ranger force could inflict on the Indians. Scott sacked two of the Miamis' largest towns; in addition, he gathered up 41 women and children as captives.[99] He then sent what should have been a dire warning to the Ohio Indians: "your warriors will be slaughtered, your towns and villages ransacked and destroyed, your wives and children carried into captivity, and you may be assured that those who escape the fury of our mighty chiefs, shall find no resting place on this side of the great lakes."[100]

In the late summer of 1791, however, Scott's threats carried little weight. Knox entrusted the second cavalcade to Brigadier General James Wilkinson of the regular army. "Wilkie," perhaps the most unscrupulous officer ever to serve in the United States military, was more interested in intrigue and self-aggrandizement than in fighting Indians. With both himself and his troopers reluctant to press too deeply into enemy territory, Wilkinson chose to trace much of Scott's path and revisit the villages that Scott's column previously had destroyed. Wilkinson, upon his return to Kentucky, wrote a glowing report of his operation. With incompetents like Wilkinson appointed to the command of troops in the field, the Army clearly lacked the ability to prosecute an Indian war.

Still, Indians across the Ohio country wondered if the Americans finally had returned to their old ways of sending rangers to torch Indian villages and towns and kill women and children. Cornplanter, the Seneca war leader who had fought the Americans in the late 1770s, remembered the Americans as "town destroyers." He described how Seneca "women look behind them and turn pale, and our children cling close to the necks of their mothers" when the destruction and suffering that American troops inflicted on the western Iroquois were recounted.[101]

---

98 Instructions to Brigadier General Charles Scott, March 9, 1791, *ASPIA*, 1: 129.
99 Paul David Nelson, "General Charles Scott, the Kentucky Mounted Volunteers, and the Northwest Indian Wars, 1784–1794," *Journal of the Early Republic* 6 (1986): 219–251.
100 Report of Brigadier General Scott, June 28, 1791, *ASPIA*, 1: 131 and [Scott] to the Various Tribes of the Piankeshaws, and all the Nations of Red People, lying on the waters of the Wabash River, June 4, 1791, ibid., 1: 133.
101 The Speech of Cornplanter, Half-Town, and the Great Tree, Chiefs and Councillors of the Seneca Nation, to the Great Councillor of the Thirteen Fires, n.d., ibid., 1: 140.

There was little chance, however, that the Americans would send waves of rangers into the Indian country, for the Army was determined to win the war with its regulars. Not only was the Army's reputation at stake, and with it the prestige of the new federal government, but in January, Knox reported – just as the British regulars of 1757 had done – that the troops most capable of hurting the Indians, the frontier rangers, were too expensive for the government's taste. His department estimated that each 500-man regiment of rangers would cost the treasury $49,454; each 600-man regiment of regulars, however, would cost only $12,240.[102] The Army could find a further cost reduction, Knox related, in "levies," men enlisted into the regular service for six months. Congress therefore decided to raise a second regiment of regulars, augment it with levies, and attach the militia to it.[103] The rangers, although clearly necessary and authorized by Congress despite their high costs, were few and far between in the remodeled American army. The Army, of course, got what it paid for with its 600 regulars, 800 levies, and 600 militia when Major General Arthur St. Clair set out for the Wabash Valley in the fall of 1791.

As an example of how to fight Indians, St. Clair's campaign made Braddock's and Harmar's look like masterpieces. The rheumatic and choleric St. Clair had neither a sense of urgency nor, it seems, any basic understanding of the enemy he faced.[104] On the night of November 3, outside what he suspected were Indian towns, St. Clair paused to give his army rest but failed to take even the most rudimentary security precautions to protect it against an Indian attack. Little Turtle's Miamis and Blue Jacket's Shawnees struck about 30 minutes before sunrise the next morning in what St. Clair called "as unfortunate an action as almost any that has been fought." As Indian warriors broke St. Clair's line into more digestible pieces, St. Clair could think of little else to do but order a bayonet charge. The charges drove the Indians from the disintegrating American front until the warriors "returned, and the troops were obliged to give back in their turn." St. Clair, on the brink of suffering a frontier Cannae, was saved only when his surviving troops shed their weapons and accoutrements and fled headlong to Fort Jefferson, 29 miles to the south.[105] There were plenty of scalps (637 Americans eventually died and another 263 were wounded) to collect on the battlefield, and the Indians gave only

---

102 A General Estimate, January 22, 1791, ibid., 1: 121.
103 Knox to Washington, January 22, 1791, ibid., 1: 112.
104 Leroy V. Eid, in his "American Indian Military Leadership: St. Clair's 1791 Defeat," *Journal of Military History* 57 (1993): 71–88, has argued that "St. Clair was not peculiarly incompetent." St. Clair, Eid argues, "primarily lost the battle because the consensual approach to leadership employed by his opponents functioned so well" (p. 72). Indeed, St. Clair was not peculiarly incompetent. He was just as incompetent in the art of Indian fighting as most of his regular Army brethren.
105 St. Clair to Knox, November 9, 1791, ibid., 1: 137.

short chase. When all was said and done, and a congressional committee had interviewed St. Clair and his subordinates, the blame for the Army's second disaster – its worst ever at the hands of Indians and its most costly in terms of losses until the Civil War – was settled on the "want of discipline" among the levies and militia.[106]

The Indian victory at the Battle of the Wabash shattered any American hopes for quickly subjugating the Ohio Indians. It was clear that the days of the regular Army's offensives north of the Ohio had ended. There was also the fear that the emboldened Indian confederacy might try to push the American frontier back to the Appalachian Mountains.[107] Knox therefore rushed directives to the westernmost frontier counties to call out their rangers. The settlements, he advised, needed "the most expert hunters or woodsmen, to serve as scouts or patrols" to warn of Indian raids.[108] In a similar vein, Knox asked that Congress give the President carte blanche to pay for and equip the rangers. He also asked for permission on behalf of Washington to conduct direct negotiations with the few remaining nonhostile Indians in the West. Washington, in such a time of emergency, Knox noted, should "be authorized to stipulate such terms as he shall judge right."[109] It would have been too little too late if the Indian confederacy had not been content to drive the American invaders across the Ohio for a second time. Fortunately for the settlers of Kentucky, western Pennsylvania, and Virginia, only a few Miamis and Shawnees crossed the Ohio to attack American settlements.

The unenviable task of rebuilding the regular army, in the meantime, fell to Major General "Mad" Anthony Wayne. Ironically, George Washington never thought highly of Wayne – he opined that Wayne was "open to flattery; vain; easily imposed upon; likeable to scrapes" and "addicted to the bottle." He made him commander of the new Legion of the United States because he had no other alternative.[110] Nonetheless, Wayne built a disciplined force of regulars well augmented with experienced rangers. Wayne also embraced the first way of war, the kind that focused on purposeful and direct attacks on the enemy's most vulnerable and important

106 Causes of the Failure of the Expedition against the Indians, in 1791, under the Command of Major General St. Clair, May 8, 1792, *ASPMA*, 1: 38.
107 The Indians, naturally, considered such an option. See Joseph Brant to Israel Chapin, July 28, 1792, ibid., 1: 243. For the American public's panicked response on both the frontier and in settled areas to St. Clair's defeat, see William P. Walsh, "The Defeat of Major General Arthur St. Clair, November 4, 1791: A Study of the Nation's Response, 1791–1793" (Ph.D. diss, Loyola University of Chicago, 1977).
108 Knox to the Lieutenants of the Counties of Westmoreland, Allegheny, and Washington, in the State of Pennsylvania, December 29, 1791, *ASPIA*, 1: 217.
109 Statement Relative to the Frontiers Northwest of the Ohio, n.d., ibid., 1: 198.
110 Quoted in Kohn, *Eagle and Sword*, 125. Yet, historians, including Weigley in *History of the United States Army*, 93, have heaped many well-deserved encomiums on Wayne as the "Father of the Regular Army."

center of gravity – agricultural resources and noncombatant populations. For those operations to succeed, forces had to be capable of operating stealthily and effectively in enemy territory and, just as important, dictating the terms of battle. It needed rangers. The army that Wayne assembled between 1792 and 1794 was that kind of army.

Wayne built the first United States regular army that could operate without fear of defeat in Indian country. When he set out to destroy the Indian villages on the Maumee River in the summer of 1794, he made sure he had adequate rangers to screen and protect his army from ambush. In October 1793, for instance, he told Knox that he needed more than the 396 scouts and rangers he currently had with him.[111] He went on to note that the greatest impediment to American success in the Northwest was finding sufficient escorts – traditionally the role of rangers – to protect the supply columns his army would need.[112] He therefore bristled with anger to learn that Scott's hard-charging Kentucky rangers had dwindled in strength to only 200 men. Although eager for battle, Wayne would not risk taking the field without a proper accompaniment of rangers that could screen the force until he could bring its full weight to bear on the Indians. "You may rest assured," Wayne told Knox, "that I will not commit the Legion Unnecessarily & unless more powerfully supported than I at present have reason to expect."[113] Indeed, Wayne set out for the Maumee River towns only after Charles Scott arrived with 1,500 mounted rangers.[114] Then William Wells appeared at Wayne's camp. Wells was a particularly valuable man to have on one's side for a fight with the Indians. Captured by them at age 13, Blacksnake, as the Miamis knew him, had lived with the Indians for nine years and had even fought with distinction under his father-in-law, Little Turtle, at the Battle of the Wabash. In 1792, Wells traveled to Vincennes to negotiate for the Miamis. There, he met his brother, from whom he had been separated for nearly a decade. His brother convinced him to return to Kentucky, where he entered the service of the American army as a scout.[115]

Wayne's regulars, guided by Wells's scouts and protected by Scott's Kentucky rangers, entered the Maumee Valley in July 1794. They found the settlements at the Glaize (at the junction of the Auglaize and Maumee Rivers) hastily evacuated. One Ottawa warrior remembered years later

---

111   Wayne to Knox, October 5, 1793, *ASPIA*, 1: 360.
112   Wayne to Knox, October 23, 1793, ibid., 1: 361.
113   Wayne quoted in Paul David Nelson, *Anthony Wayne: Soldier of the Early Republic* (Bloomington: Indiana University Press, 1985), 244.
114   Wayne to Knox, July 7, 1794, *ASPIA*, 1: 487.
115   For Wells's career, see Paul A. Hutton, "William Wells: Frontier Scout and Indian Agent," *Indiana Magazine of History* 74 (1978): 183–222. See also Harvey Lewis Carter, "A Frontier Tragedy: Little Turtle and William Wells," *The Old Northwest* 6 (1980): 3–18.

that upon receiving the warning that the Legion had managed to enter the valley undetected – Wayne had approached the Maumee by a circuitous route rather than marching straight at the Indians' villages, like Harmar and St. Clair – the Indians fled in panic. "Old women, burdened with immense packs strapped to their shoulders," he recalled, "followed their retreating families with all the haste their aged limbs would permit."[116] "Thus," Wayne reported, "we have gained possession of the grand emporium of the hostile Indians of the West, without loss of blood."[117] Amid those fields of plenty, Wayne first constructed four blockhouses that he called Fort Defiance. He then made one last peace overture. "In pity to your innocent women and children," he told the Shawnees, "come and prevent the further effusion of your blood."[118]

After Blue Jacket refused to talk, Wayne set about methodically destroying Indian villages and fields. On August 20, the Indians interrupted the burning campaign when they offered battle against the regulars at Fallen Timbers. Thanks in part to the scouts and rangers who had guided and escorted the Legion safely through the wilderness, Wayne could focus the full strength of his regulars on the Indians. The Legion, facing an Indian foe who had agreed to stand in place and fight a battle for which the regulars were better trained and equipped, drove the Indians from the field with a bayonet charge. Historians have noted how, after the battle, the British refused the Indians entry to Fort Miami. With their abandonment by the British, so goes the traditional narrative, the Indians knew their cause was lost and sued for peace.[119]

The American conquest of southern Ohio, formalized in the Treaty of Greenville a year after the battle, however, was more a product of Wayne's unleashing the first way of war and less the result of the British abandoning the Indians at Fallen Timbers. While it is true that after 1795 and Jay's Treaty the Indians stood alone against the Americans, in the summer and fall of 1794, Jay's Treaty was not a driving factor in the Indians' decision to make peace. News of the treaty signing was not reported until the

---

116 Quoted in Sword, *President Washington's Indian War*, 288.
117 Wayne to Knox, August 14, 1794, ibid., 1: 490.
118 To the Delawares, Shawnese, Miamies, and Wyandots, August 13, 1794, *ASPIA*, 1: 490.
119 Richard White, for instance, has written, "As Wayne marched toward the Maumee, it became apparent that what he did mattered less than what the British did, for only the British could unite and supply the Indians" (p. 467). White also has written, "The real defeat came during the retreat; for when the Indians fell back to Fort Miami, the garrison shut the gates on them and refused them aid" (p. 468). See White, *The Middle Ground: Indians, Empires, and Republics in the Great Lakes Region, 1650–1815* (New York: Cambridge University Press, 1991). In a similar light, Armstrong Starkey in his *European and Native American Warfare 1675–1815* (Norman: University of Oklahoma University Press, 1998), 154, has argued, "The Indian defeat lay in the collapse of their British alliance and in the dissolution of Indian unity."

end of January 1795, and its terms were not made public until July.[120] Throughout their negotiations with the Americans, the British had told the Indians that they were their steadfast allies. The Indian military leaders, of course, were not as naive or inexperienced as to accept British pronouncements without question. Thus, when they considered the question of war or peace in 1794, they had only themselves on whom to depend.

Thus the battle at Fallen Timbers, much like the Battle of Point Pleasant in Lord Dunmore's War, showed the Indians that they were powerless to stop the Americans from ravishing their homelands. Even if the British had allowed Blue Jacket's warriors into the fort, it would have done little to prevent the Americans from marching at will across the Maumee Valley. The British garrison comprised fewer than 200 men and certainly was in no position to sortie out and meet the Americans in battle. Thus, after witnessing the devastation of the Maumee Valley, each nation within the confederacy had to wonder when it too would feel the fury of the Legion's destructive energies.

Indeed, the most overlooked event in the chain of events between the battle on August 20 and the Indians' capitulation at Greenville a year later is the campaign of devastation that followed Fallen Timbers. The Legion, Wayne reported, remained for three days on the banks of the Maumee to destroy all the Indian houses and cornfields. The British and the few Indians inside Fort Miami were compelled "to remain tacit spectators to this general devastation and conflagration." On August 27, a week after the battle, the Legion set out on a march to ravage the Auglaize Valley. The Americans returned to Fort Defiance "by easy marches, laying waste the villages and cornfields for about *fifty miles on each side of the Miami.*"[121] Thus, having seen their villages wiped from the face of the earth, the Ohio Indians wisely chose to end, at least temporarily, their resistance to the Americans. Once again, Americans had used the first way of war to compel their enemies to accept an American peace and American conquest.

That the "Father of the Regular Army" adapted so thoroughly the first way of war should not be surprising. Wayne was an innovative soldier who throughout his career proved capable of adapting to any situation that he faced. He had made victory over the Indians – an achievement of the first order given the Army's earlier record against them – possible because he saw the need to instill discipline and training within the Legion. Moreover, like the frontiersmen of Tennessee and Georgia, he also knew to

---

120   Stanley Elkins and Eric McKitrick, *The Age of Federalism: The Early American Republic, 1788–1800* (New York: Oxford University Press, 1993), 417.
121   Italics mine. Wayne to Knox, August 28, 1794, *ASPIA*, 1: 491.

strike directly at the Indians' points of greatest vulnerability: their villages, fields, and noncombatants. Rangers helped make those direct attacks possible and, in the end, became an integral part of the army with which he obliterated Indian resistance to American conquest of the southern Ohio Valley. The Father of the Regular Army, in that sense, became only one of many American soldiers whose actions and deeds carried the first way of war out of the colonial period into the 1790s.

7

The First Way of War and the Final Conquest of the Transappalachian West

The Americans' peace terms ending the Creek War stunned the miccos of the Creek nation in the summer of 1814. As punishment for the "unprovoked, inhuman, and sanguinary war waged by the hostile Creeks against the United States," Major General Andrew Jackson, the sole American negotiator with the Indians, demanded no less than the destruction of the Creek nation. Jackson's harshest provision, one that the Creeks had little choice but to accept, required that the Creeks give the United States 23 million acres as war reparations.[1]

Several miccos hoped that they might persuade Jackson to accept a return to the peace of the late 1790s, one based on trade and reciprocity rather than reparations. The recently ended conflict had been as much a civil war between pro- and anti-American Creeks as a struggle between the United States and the Creek nation. Many of their people under the Creek leader William McIntosh, the miccos reminded Jackson, had joined the Americans to fight against their fellow Creeks, the Red Stick faction of the Upper and Lower Towns.

At the Treaty of Fort Jackson, however, Jackson refused to distinguish between pro-American Creeks and Red Sticks. When the accommodationist miccos prostrated themselves before him, Old Hickory remained unbending; he would brook no compromise concerning the land cessions. Jackson stated that even McIntosh's followers would have to sign away their lands. The reparations, Jackson said, were a lesson to all who might oppose the Americans. He told the Creeks "We bleed our enemies in such cases to give them their senses."[2]

---

1 Articles of Agreement and Capitulation, *ASPIA*, 1: 826–827.
2 Jackson to Big Warrior, August 7, 1814, *The Papers of Andrew Jackson*, ed. Sam B. Smith and Harriet Chapelle Owsley, 5 vols. (Knoxville: University of Tennessee Press, 1980), 3: 110. For a study that focuses on Jackson's harsh handling of the Creeks during the treaty negotiations, see Frank Lawrence Owsley, Jr., *Struggle for the Gulf Borderlands: The Creek War and the Battle of New Orleans, 1812–1815* (Gainesville: University Press of Florida, 1981), chap. 8 and Claudio Saunt, "Taking Account of Property: Stratification among the Creek Indians in the Early Nineteenth Century," *WMQ* 57 (2000): 733–760.

Jackson's "bleeding" of the Creeks marks a culminating point in American military history as the end of the Transappalachian West's Indian wars.[3] The first half of the 1810s saw two conflicts – one in the Old Northwest (the Northwest Indian War of 1810–1813) and a second, the Creek War of 1813–1814 – in which American frontiersmen and Indians clashed. Unlike the War of 1812, with which they overlapped, these conflicts did not end in a return to the status quo ante bellum, but rather in so thorough a destruction of Indian power that the United States completely subjugated the Indian peoples of the Transappalachian West.[4] The conquest of the West was not guaranteed by defeating the British Army in battle in 1815, but by defeating and driving the Indians from their homelands. Thus, when combined, the Northwest Indian and Creek Wars produced the first way of war's most significant contribution to American history: the American conquest of the lands of the Transappalachian West.

I. The Northwest Indian War, 1810–1813

By the 1810s, many Old Northwest Indians had seen enough of settler encroachments on their lands to know that the time had come for them to make a stand. Starting in the early 1800s, the Shawnee brothers Tecumseh and Tenskwatawa (the Open Door), also known as the Prophet, began consolidating what one observer called "a very general and extensive movement among the savages" of the West.[5] From Prophet's Town, near the confluence of the Tippecanoe and Wabash Rivers, Tenskwatawa

---

3   One could argue that the Indian wars of the 1810s were the last gasp of a half-century-long Indian war for independence from the Americans. See, for example, Gregory Evans Dowd, *A Spirited Resistance: The North American Indian Struggle for Unity, 1745–1815* (Baltimore: Johns Hopkins University Press, 1992).

4   For the most part, the Indian wars of the first half of the 1810s are seen as component parts of the War of 1812. Donald R. Hickey, in his essay on the conflict, has shown how historians have focused the overwhelming proportion of their studies on the regular side of the war and relegated Indian fighting to secondary importance. Hickey, in that tradition, judges the Old Northwest theater of operations as "probably the least important [compared to the Niagara frontier, the St. Lawrence and Lake Champlain front, the Chesapeake Bay, and the Old Southwest and Gulf Coast] because it was so far removed from the centers of power, population, and commerce further east" (p. 749). The Old Southwest is considered important because Andrew Jackson won his victory over the British at New Orleans. See Hickey, "The War of 1812: Still a Forgotten Conflict?" *Journal of Military History* 65 (2001): 741–769.

5   Extracts of Letters Addressed to the War Department, May 24, 1807, *ASPIA*, 1: 798. Historians disagree over the degree of influence that Tenskwatawa or Tecumseh had in the Indian movement at the various stages of its development. Whatever the answer, by the middle of the first decade of the 1800s, Westerners feared that they faced a new Indian confederacy. See John Sugden's *Tecumseh: A Life* (New York: Henry Holt and Company, 1997) and R. David Edmunds's, *The Shawnee Prophet* (Lincoln: University of Nebraska Press, 1983).

and his followers proselytized for a return to the ways of the "Great Spirit" and a repudiation of European ways. His brother, meanwhile, traveled the West in a diplomatic mission to spread the cause of Indian unity. At the core of Tecumseh's compelling orations was his call for Indian co-ownership of all the lands of the West. Although the argument for common ownership of Indian lands by all Indians did not originate with Tecumseh – other Indian leaders, including Pontiac in the 1760s and Joseph Brant in the 1780s, had made similar arguments – his was the most dangerous for Americans since he combined Indian religion and politics in his movement. Moreover, Tecumseh was more ambitious in his goals. He hoped to unite all the Indians of the West in his confederacy, not just the nations of the North. For Tecumseh and his followers, ending the land sales was the cure-all to American interference in Indian life and society.

The burgeoning confederacy of western Indians that emerged on the Tippecanoe River threatened to block the course of American land acquisitions in the Old Northwest. Since the conclusion of the Ohio Indian War, Indians who once had led the resistance to the Americans, men like Little Turtle and Blue Jacket, had become "agency chiefs" who had mortgaged the future of their people. The pacified Indians became dependent on American trade goods and annual annuities and quickly fell into a morass of indebtedness that, in turn, fed the need for more land sales. A younger generation of Indians, however, believed that conceding their independence to the Americans was the foolish and harmful policy of soft old men who had lost both their dignity and their will to fight. Thus began a contentious debate within the Indian villages of the West, a debate with the Shawnee brothers and their message of Indian resistance and independence at the center. As Indian anger and frustration grew, especially as the Americans clamored for more land and the influence of the agency chiefs waned, the number of supporters for a new anti-American Indian union swelled.[6]

That, from the frontier settlers' perspective, made the situation critical. Though by 1810 it had not yet declared war or sent raiders against settlements, the nascent confederacy inspired near panic among the American residents of the Indiana and Illinois Territories. At about the same time, tensions between the United States and Great Britain were close to boiling

6   War was not the only option on the Northwest frontier. Many Americans and Indians looked to mutual accommodation and maintenance of a Middle Ground. See Colin G. Calloway, "Beyond the Vortex of Violence: Indian–White Relations in the Ohio Country, 1783–1815," *Northwest Ohio Quarterly* 64 (1992): 16–26. Elizabeth A. Perkins argues that the wars on the Northwest frontier, while terrible events, also offered a "process of mutual discovery" in which combatants on both sides saw the humanity of their adversaries. See Perkins, "War as Cultural Encounter in the Ohio Valley," *The Sixty Years' War for the Great Lakes, 1754–1814*, eds. David Curtis Skaggs and Larry L. Nelson (East Lansing: Michigan State University Press, 2001), 217.

over into open war. The American settlers of the Old Northwest feared that at any moment the British would outfit Indian war parties to send against the American frontier. In July 1811, therefore, dozens of them met at Vincennes to draft a petition to President James Madison demanding that the government act to prevent a calamity on the frontier. "The safety of the persons and property of this frontier," the petitioners wrote, "can never be effectually secured, but by the breaking up of the combination formed by the Shawnee Prophet on the Wabash."[7]

Indiana's Territorial Governor, William Henry Harrison, at first proved reluctant to heed too closely the settlers' panicked messages to Washington. The Governor was convinced that most of the Indians of the Northwest would reject Tenskwatawa and Tecumseh. His face-to-face meetings with Tecumseh, however, changed that belief. First, in 1810, Tecumseh vociferously, and at times almost violently, protested the previous year's treaty of Fort Wayne. There, Harrison had convinced several destitute Delaware, Miami, and Potawatomi chiefs to abandon their claims to most of southern Indiana for an annuity of just over $5,200.[8] Both Tecumseh and Harrison left their first meeting warily eyeing each other for the next move. The canoes loaded with Kickapoos, Wyandots, Peorias, Ojibwas, Potawatomis, Winnebagos, Shawnees, and other western Indians whom Tecumseh brought with him for the second round of diplomacy at Vincennes in 1811 pointed unmistakably to the extent of Indian frustration with the Americans and Harrison. After weeks of talks that settled none of the issues dividing the two sides, Tecumseh left the negotiations for a preplanned trip to the South. Before leaving Vincennes, he informed Harrison that he was traveling to the South to bring the Creeks, Choctaws, and Chickasaws into the Indian confederacy. That was all the excuse Harrison needed.

Harrison determined to destroy Prophet's Town. He believed that leveling Tenskwatawa's village would destroy support for the Prophet and discredit his brother among the neutral and peace-inclined Indians. It would stand as a dire warning to the Indians to remain docile in their relations with the United States. Destroying the physical center of the confederacy would present the Indians with two options: continue to cede lands or suffer greatly at the Americans' hands. With Tecumseh in the South, there was probably no better time for a campaign against the Indians' headquarters.

7 Memorials from the Inhabitants of the Indiana and Illinois Territories, Addressed to the President of the United States, July 1811, *ASPIA*, 1: 802.
8 For the terms of the treaty, see <Kappler/del0101.htm>. In subsequent amendments to the treaty, Harrison doled out additional annuities. The Miamis could consider themselves lucky compared to other Indians; they received a $200 annuity, plus $500 worth of domestic animals. See <Kappler/mia0103.htm>.

No Harmar- or St. Clair-like disasters would hinder Harrison's march into Indian country. The Governor had served as Anthony Wayne's aide de camp in the Fallen Timbers campaign and clearly understood the precautions he needed to take on his advance against Prophet's Town.[9] He first marshaled a mixed force of Indiana and Kentucky frontiersmen and United States regulars. Making a slow but steady advance up the Wabash Valley, his backcountry rangers examined "every place which seemed calculated for an ambuscade."[10] Stopping at present-day Terre Haute, Indiana, Harrison constructed Fort Harrison on contested lands. The fort showed any Indians who might have misunderstood that the Americans intended to take the Wabash Valley as their own. Most important, should misfortune befall the army outside Prophet's Town, it would have a strong point to which to retreat and rally.

The Indians in Prophet's Town, meanwhile, waited for the right moment to strike. Tecumseh had warned his brother not to allow the Americans to draw him into a fight; the time was not yet right to start the war for the Indian reconquest of the Old Northwest. Thus, although Tenskwatawa's followers observed the Americans' advance, none attacked Harrison's column. When the Americans arrived unmolested outside the village on November 6, Tenskwatawa's emissaries came forth and announced that the Prophet would parley with them the next morning. Harrison, expecting subterfuge, had his men sleep with their weapons loaded and ready. Seeing little else he could do, Tenskwatawa put aside his older brother's instructions. The Indians struck a little before 4:00 A.M. on November 7. The Prophet told his warriors that he had imbued them with special powers that would protect them from the Americans' bullets. Whether from belief in those powers or from the knowledge that they faced a desperate situation, when the warriors struck "they manifested a ferocity, uncommon even with them," Harrison later reported. Only after suffering nearly 200 casualties did Harrison's troops drive the Indians from the field and through the village. Harrison then set about accomplishing the aim of his expedition. He burned the town, destroyed the Indians' granary, and allowed his troops to pillage what they could. In his post-battle report, Harrison claimed a major victory. For one who saw victory measured in numbers of buildings burned and acres of crops laid to waste, the Tippecanoe campaign was indeed a success.[11] It was a textbook application of the first way of war. Moreover, it sent a clear message to the western Indians: Harrison and the United States would tolerate

---

9   Robert G. Gunderson, "William Henry Harrison: Apprentice in Arms," *Northwest Ohio Quarterly* 65 (1993): 3–29.
10 Harrison to William Eustis [Secretary of War], November 18, 1811, *ASPIA*, 1: 776.
11 Ibid., 1: 780.

no further Indian obstructionism to the American settlement of the Old Northwest.

The Indians heard the message clearly. Warriors from across the Old Northwest flocked to British-held Fort Malden in Upper Canada, where they found the garrison providing gifts "more abundant than usual [with] an intention to attach the Indians to the British cause."[12] In 1807, after tensions between the United States and Great Britain had escalated following the *Leopard–Chesapeake* affair, Great Britain had abandoned its policy of ignoring the Indians of the West. Between 1807 and 1811, however, Tecumseh had hesitated to commit his followers to an Indian–British alliance, showing a caution that had frustrated British Indian agents. Tippecanoe changed that situation. Tecumseh spoke with greater passion for the need for a unified, coordinated, and concerted Indian-led war on the Americans, and the American settlers worried even more that the British would support the Indians' passion for revenge. Indeed, it seemed in the spring of 1812 that all hope for peace had been lost. The commander of the garrison and the Indian agency at Fort Wayne, Captain James Rhea, predicted that the Americans would "have an Indian war this spring, whether we have a British war or not."[13]

Indian war parties swept across the frontier in the summer of 1812. The Indian confederacy took the lead in striking the Americans; the British were too weak to offer much more than encouragement and small gifts of powder and ball. The first days of the conflict were dark ones for the Americans, as Forts Michilimackinac, Detroit, and Dearborn capitulated after their garrisons of regulars offered only minimal resistance. Only Forts Wayne and Harrison stood, the latter thanks to the heroics of young Captain Zachary Taylor. In their rush of victory, meanwhile, the Indians were little inclined to offer quarter. Fort Dearborn's garrison and settlers, for instance, fell in a Potawatomi and Winnebago ambush after leaving the fort under the promise of safe passage. Among the 52 Americans cut down was William Wells. He had volunteered to guide the refugees to safety, but also had painted his "death mask" on his face in Miami fashion to express his cognizance of his impending doom. When the Indians finished with Wells, they stuck his head on a spike and removed and quartered his heart.[14]

---

12 Congressional Report, June 13, 1812, ibid., 1: 797.
13 Extract of a Letter from J[ames] Rhea, March 14, 1812, ibid., 1: 806.
14 Defense of Fort Harrison, John Brannan, comp., *Official Letters of the Military and Naval Officers of the United States during the War with Great Britain in the Years 1812, 13, 14, & 15. With Some Additional Letters and Documents Elucidating the History of that Period* (Washington, DC: Way & Gideon, for the editor, 1823), 61–63, hereafter *Official Letters*. N. Heald to Thomas Cushing, October 13, 1812, ibid., 84–85; *Encyclopedia of the War of 1812*, s.v., "Wells, William."

The early victories emboldened the Indians. In the fall, more war parties fanned out across the Illinois and Indiana Territories to strike American homesteads. Isolated farms and settlements fell one by one, and a new generation of American rangers found scenes of devastation in most places where they looked. Within only a matter of weeks, the Indians had driven thousands of Americans from the frontier. Few settlers were willing to stay on their farms and risk sharing the fate of the men, women, and children whom the Indians massacred at Pigeon Roost north of Louisville and at the O'Neal farm outside Peoria.

The frontiersmen responded to the Indian raids in kind. Upon arriving at Fort Wayne in September with 2,000 militia to raise the Indians' siege of that post, Harrison, with the intent of "avenging his country and saving the frontier," turned the militia loose on Indian fields and villages.[15] General Samuel Hopkins of the Kentucky militia then mustered 2,000 mounted volunteers for a campaign against the Illinois River villages near Peoria. After a six-day march that accomplished little when his militia turned battle shy and deserted, Hopkins returned from the field and disbanded his main force. Back at Fort Harrison, the Americans' sole remaining outpost on the Wabash, he enlisted only those whom he thought had the stomach for hard marching and fighting. By then, however, the frontier had become the no-man's-land typical of Indian wars, as both settlers and Indians retreated to the safety of distant locales. Still, in October, Illinois Territorial Governor Ninian Edwards and Colonel William Russell led a mixed force of militia and three companies of United States Rangers against Pimartam's Town at the head of Peoria Lake. While there, they killed almost 20 Indians and burnt their fields. In November, Hopkins took his reconstituted force and pushed north, destroying deserted Indian villages as he went. Shortly into the expedition, a violent winter storm compelled him and his lightly clad troops to return to Fort Harrison, but not before they had killed several Indians and destroyed some granaries.[16]

The modest successes of their first campaigns encouraged the frontiersmen to press forward with more raids. Lieutenant Colonel John B. Campbell picked up where Hopkins left off and in December 1812 took 600 federal troops and several companies of Ohio and Indiana rangers against the Shawnees' Mississinewa River towns. After destroying three of them and suffering casualties in a firefight, Campbell returned to Fort Wayne. During the winter, Governor Edwards mustered 300 mounted rangers to patrol the frontier, but they encountered few Indians.[17]

15 Harrison to Governor [Isaac] Shelby, September 5, 1812, *Official Letters*, 56.
16 Russell to the Secretary of War, October 31, 1812, ibid., 89; Hopkins to Shelby, December 27, 1812, ibid., 95–97.
17 Robert Breckinridge McAfee, *History of the Late War in the Western Country* (1816; reprint, Ann Arbor: University Microfilms Inc., 1966), 381–382.

True to pattern, the Indian raids began again in the spring, this time originating from the village of Vallonia. In June and July 1813, Indiana's new Territorial Governor, John Gibson, twice dispatched rangers to destroy the area surrounding the trouble spot. In the second expedition, they covered 500 miles and burned several villages but found no Indians. In September, Missouri's Governor Benjamin Howard sent 1,300 troops to occupy the area around Peoria, significantly reducing the raids originating from there.[18] While the rangers could not take sole credit for driving the hostile Indians from Indiana and Illinois, they could at least claim that their raids and occupation of Indian territory had contributed to it.

Meanwhile, the regular Army's field leadership, true to its pattern, saw little need for the rangers. Henry Dearborn, the Army's senior Major General, failed to understand that there were in fact two wars underway in the West: one between the United States and British regular armies, and a second (and more important one) between the frontiersmen and the Indians. Indeed, Dearborn and most of the officers of the Army missed the significance of what was occurring in the West. The most pressing threat to the Americans came not from the British regulars in Canada, who were fighting a European-style limited war. It came instead from the motivated and emboldened warriors of the Indian confederacy, who, for the first time in a generation, believed that they could roll back the American settlement of the Old Northwest.

Everything Dearborn saw suggested to him that fighting solely a regular war was the proper course of action. First, the Army's prestige was at stake. Its pathetic performance in the first six months of the war, highlighted by William Hull's capitulation at Detroit to a smaller Indian–British force, was fresh in the minds of many Westerners. Moreover, the Indians' scalping, immolating, and killing of 30 to 60 wounded Kentuckians at the "River Raisin Massacre" in January 1813 had fed Westerners' demands that the Army avenge those losses.[19] A victory by American regulars over British regulars, Dearborn convinced himself, would go far toward rehabilitating the Army and defusing the growing anti-Army sentiment among the frontiersmen. Perhaps of greater concern, Dearborn feared that allowing Americans to turn to a partisan war would only escalate the scale of the violence. Believing that if the United States instigated ranger operations, the British would retaliate with their Indian allies, he strictly forbade such tactics. Thus, at a time when he had done virtually nothing of merit to advance American interests in the West, he upbraided Major Benjamin Forsyth of the 1st United States Riflemen for taking the initiative and crossing into Canada to procure prisoners and

18 *Encyclopedia of the War of 1812*, s.v., "Indiana Territory."
19 Samuel Williams to John Beckley, February 20, 1813, *Official Letters*, 185.

attack British outposts. To Secretary of War John Armstrong, Dearborn reported that Forsyth's "known zeal for a small partisan warfare has induced me to give him repeated caution against such measures, on his part, as they would probably produce such retaliating strokes as he would be unable to resist; but I fear my advice has not been as fully attended to as could have been wished."[20]

Dearborn thus squandered opportunities to attack the British infrastructure that supported the western Indians, showing a passivity that frustrated even the Secretary of War. With snow accumulations in the winter of 1812–1813 in some places of over three feet, Armstrong observed that regular operations were impossible. But, Armstrong continued, "Major Forsyth's last expedition shows that small enterprises, at least, may be successfully executed at the present season." Nowhere was the potential for "small enterprises" more promising than in the Detroit theater. Armstrong could see from a map in Washington that only a thin logistics line connected the British outposts in Upper Canada and their supply depot at York. Indeed, they were, Armstrong instructed Dearborn, "open to our attacks, on a line of nearly one hundred miles."[21] Rangers or men of the Army's rifle companies could have cut those supply and communications lines. While such operations indeed may have resulted in the loss of Americans behind enemy lines, and perhaps an escalation of *petite guerre*, they offered the only immediate option to complicate the British war effort in Upper Canada. Certainly, the benefits of such raids, especially the dislocation they would have caused in the British efforts to supply their westernmost outposts and Indian allies, would have outweighed the risks. Nonetheless, Dearborn decided to hold off; he simply lacked the will to fight a *petite guerre*.

Harrison, however, understood the value of rangers in both *petite* and regular operations. Upon taking command of the western armies, he welcomed any rangers, particularly the horse-mounted ones of Kentucky, who would join him. He knew that the frontiersmen of the Blue Grass State were the ideal troops for a running brush fight with the Indians; indeed, Harrison willingly depended on his rangers, even at those times when he could have called upon regulars, throughout the war.

In the most effective use of rangers during the war, they led the 1813 pursuit of the British across Upper Canada. Following the American naval victory on Lake Erie, British Major General Henry Proctor realized that his position at Fort Malden was untenable. Outnumbered and outgunned, Proctor chose to retreat eastward. As the British withdrew, they

20   Dearborn to John Armstrong, February 25, 1813, *ASPMA*, 1: 440.
21   Armstrong to Dearborn, February 24, 1813, ibid.

left their Indian allies to follow as best they could. Harrison thereupon turned Lieutenant Colonel Richard Mentor Johnson's Kentuckians and 140 handpicked regulars loose on the fleeing British and Indians. While the rangers were to search out Tecumseh's warriors and kill them, the majority of the regulars would stay behind and garrison Detroit.[22] With a rallying cry of "Remember the River Raisin," Johnson's troops relentlessly pursued Proctor's army and turned what could have been an orderly retreat into a rout. With the American rangers pressing down upon them, Proctor's forces were unable to mount a rear-guard action that slowed the Americans' pursuit. Many of Tecumseh's warriors, sensing that the Redcoats had abandoned them, deserted the British.[23]

Harrison's rangers were instrumental in the American victory at the Battle of the Thames. Proctor's plan was to hold his front with his regulars and use Tecumseh's warriors to turn the Americans' left flank. In the ensuing battle, however, that plan disintegrated in the face of the Kentuckians' hard-hitting attack. Johnson split his forces in two; half of them under his brother, James, charged the British line, and the other half under his direction hit the Indians' ranks. With just one artillery piece bolstering Proctor's front, James's men overwhelmed the demoralized British. On the American left, meanwhile, Richard's troopers charged headlong into Backmetack Marsh to root out the Indians from it. In a half hour of hand-to-hand fighting, they drove the warriors from the field. The battle was a disaster for the British–Indian alliance. Tecumseh had been killed (by Richard Johnson or some other Kentuckian), and the main British army in the West had been defeated in battle. Indeed, few battles in American military history were more decisive. The Indian confederacy and its challenge to American control of the Old Northwest had died with Tecumseh at the Indians' Armageddon on the Thames.

From Tippecanoe to the Battle of the Thames, American victory in the Northwest Indian War can be credited in large part to the frontier rangers and the first way of war. Throughout the conflict, American rangers focused their efforts on subjecting Indian noncombatants and agricultural resources to withering attacks. When they had the opportunity to engage the Indians and British in a quasi-open-field battle, they proved their mettle in that kind of fighting as well. While the regular Army was mired in the better-known struggle outside Niagara and in the Chesapeake, the American frontiersmen of Kentucky, Ohio, Indiana, and Illinois used the first way of war to conquer the Old Northwest.

---

22 General Orders, September 26, 1813, *Official Letters*, 216–217.
23 John Sugden, *Tecumseh's Last Stand* (Norman: University of Oklahoma Press, 1985), 92; Harrison to John Armstrong, October 8, 1813, Brannan, *Official Letters*, 233–239.

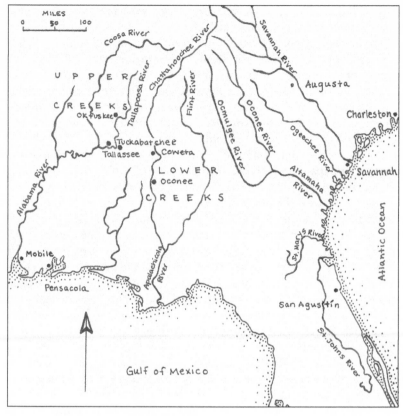

The Southern frontier, 1740–1815

II. The Creek War, 1813–1814

The Creeks stood as the last barrier to American settlement of the Old Southwest. The Americans had already co-opted both the Choctaws and Chickasaws through huge acquisitions of those tribes' lands. With the Americans' effective containment of the Spanish in Pensacola following the War of Independence, the Choctaws and Chickasaws turned to American traders and, in short order, became fully enmeshed in the United States trading orbit. Both tribes subsequently ran up huge debts with United States citizens. Thomas Jefferson's calculating claim that the Indians would always cede lands to pay off their debts proved true in 1805. The Choctaws signed a treaty with the United States that ceded the majority of their lands in return for $50,500; the Chickasaws abandoned claims to all their lands north of the Tennessee River for $20,000. With only slivers of their ancestral lands left, the Choctaws and Chickasaws found themselves forced to return to the old-style and nearly defunct deer-skin trade and, more ominously, found themselves landless participants in the expanding cotton economy. The result, of course, was continued debts and impoverishment.[24]

The rhetoric of the Red Sticks found many willing adherents, exacerbating frontiersmen's deeply held antipathy and fear of the Creeks. As anti-American sentiment, fanned by the teachings of the Creek "Prophet" Josiah Francis and by Tecumseh's visit to Tuckabatchee in October 1812, spread across the Upper and Lower Towns, Americans became more and more wary of the Creeks.[25] The feeling, naturally, was mutual. Even before the outbreak of the war in the North, Red Stick warriors had enlisted in the northern confederacy and joined its armies. Although the Red Sticks did not have a large presence in the North, they participated in the raids on American settlements and in the River Raisin Massacre.

Benjamin Hawkins, the American agent installed at the conclusion of the Creek Troubles of the early 1790s, nevertheless proved tireless in his efforts to forestall the calamity that he knew faced the Creeks if they chose war with the United States. After nearly 20 years among them, Hawkins genuinely hoped for peace between the Americans and his adopted Creeks, many of whom had wholeheartedly embraced American social mores and lifestyles. "What will war bring us?" he asked in early 1813, speaking as a Creek Beloved Man. His prescient answer: "An army, who will destroy our towns, kill our warriors, drive our women and children into the swamps to perish, and take our whole country to pay the expense. If we make ourselves their enemies, their power will destroy us."[26]

Hawkins's efforts were for naught. The frontiersmen had learned the lessons of the Creek Troubles well. Although Hawkins had convinced the members of Creek National Council to suppress dissension within their towns, in 1813 nothing, including Creek accommodation or federal intervention, would stand in the way of the Americans' conquest of the Creeks. Simply put, the frontiersmen wanted the Creeks' lands, and they would no longer tolerate the existence of Creek villages on their borders.[27]

---

24 For the Choctaw and Chickasaw treaties, see <Kappler/cho0087.htm> and <Kappler/chi0079.htm>. Daniel H. Usner, Jr., "American Indians on the Cotton Frontier: Changing Economic Relations with Citizens and Slaves in the Mississippi Territory," *JAH* 72 (1985): 297–317.

25 For Creek nativism, see Dowd, *A Spirited Resistance*, chap. 8.

26 Hawkins to Alexander Cornels, March 25, 1813, *ASPIA*, 1: 839.

27 Besides wanting Creek lands, frontiersmen were concerned that the Creek offered runaway slaves a safe haven. See Claudio Saunt, *A New Order of Things: Property, Power, and Transformation of the Creek Indians, 1733–1816* (New York: Cambridge University Press, 1999), 236–241.

Andrew Jackson decided that, if necessary, he personally would raise an army to "drive the Indians and their allies into the ocean."[28]

Jackson and the frontiersmen received what they saw as the final moral justification that they needed for their conquest of the Creeks in August. A month earlier, at Burnt Corn Creek, Colonel James Caller's militia from the American settlements on the Tombigbee River, accompanied by friendly Creeks, had attacked a Red Stick party under the mestizo Peter McQueen on its return from Pensacola, where it had sought arms from the Spanish. Fearing for their lives after Burnt Corn Creek, American settlers, their slaves, and accommodationist Creeks fled to Fort Mims, located north of Mobile. On August 30, McQueen, the one-eighth Creek William Weatherford (Red Eagle), Josiah Francis, and 750 warriors attacked Fort Mims. Upon hearing their prearranged signal, the bell calling the garrison to the afternoon meal, the Red Sticks rushed the stockade and through the fort's open gate. They quickly overwhelmed the garrison. Only a dozen of the over 250 men, women, and children inside the fort escaped with their lives.[29] In response, an enraged Tennessee legislature called up its militia, and Jackson began his final preparations for the conquest of the Creek country.

After the "Fort Mims Massacre," the frontiersmen unabashedly declared that theirs was a war to extirpate the Creeks. Governor Willie Blount (half brother of William Blount) advised a correspondent that the backwoodsmen would avenge the years of wrongs that the Creek nation had committed. The settlers, Blount reported, had an "ardent desire for the general improvement of the face of the country inhabited by the hostile Creeks, and that they feel too little inclination, after knowing the present and the past conduct of these people, to permit their longer residence thereon." The frontiersmen's expected reward for taking up the sword would be their right to "soon become the cultivators of the rich soil, which they may, in that time, soon become possessed of by their valor."[30]

With their war of conquest in view, the frontiersmen saw little point in stopping to differentiate among the Creeks. The talk of a civil war dividing accommodationist and Red Stick Creeks was "altogether fudge – a mere tub for the whale," according to Blount.[31] Although entire Creek towns professed their fidelity to the Americans and fell to Red Stick sieges,[32] the attitude the frontiersmen took suggested that every Creek must share

28　Jackson to Willie Blount, July 13, 1813, *ASPIA*, 1: 850.
29　Ferdinand Claiborne to Thomas Flournoy, September 3, 1813, *Official Letters*, 202–205.
30　Willie Blount to Thomas Flournoy, October 15, 1813, *ASPIA*, 1: 856.
31　Blount to Flournoy, October 15, 1813, ibid., 1: 855.
32　For the details of the Creek Civil War, see Saunt, *A New Order of Things*, 254–259.

the Red Sticks' fate. The Americans' strategic objective, such as it was, aimed at driving all Creeks from the Southeast. Four separate armies would converge on the nation. Major Generals Jackson and John Cocke would divide Tennessee's 5,000 militia into two columns and strike from the North. Major General John Floyd would advance from the East with the Georgia militia. Brigadier General Ferdinand Claiborne's Mississippi militia and Army regulars marching from the West would strike the final blow. The columns would meet at Tuckabatchee, ironically the place that for years had symbolized Creek amicability after James Seagrove's peace mission in the winter of 1793–1794. Twenty years later, however, Americans saw Tuckabatchee as the heart of Creek recalcitrance, even though the Creek National Council there had refused to hear Tecumseh's call for war against the Americans. On the march to Tuckabatchee, the American armies were to kill Creeks, destroy Indian fields, and establish permanent garrisons to occupy the lands through which they passed.

Jackson's army of Tennessee militia proved to be the most active and, from the Creeks' perspective, the most destructive. Jackson's campaign into the Creek country has been criticized for lacking tactical coherence and being little more than a series of search-and-destroy missions.[33] Jackson, however, lacked neither strategic nor tactical insight. The goals of his operations were simple and twofold: first, inflict as much punishment as possible on the Creeks by destroying their villages; and second, occupy their lands. Thus Brigadier General John Coffee's and his attacks on Tallushatchee (186 Indians confirmed killed and 84 prisoners taken) and Talladega (290 Creeks killed) in November 1813 should be seen as parts of an overarching strategy to destroy the Creek nation.[34] The strategy gradually paid dividends. By January 1814, Jackson's troops had contributed to the death of 1,000 Creeks. Coupled with the Red Sticks' conviction that killing the nation's livestock herds was a first step in purging the Creeks of American influence, famine stalked the Creek towns.[35]

33 James W. Holland, "Andrew Jackson and the Creek War: Victory at the Horseshoe," *Alabama Review* 21 (1968): 243–275.

34 Coffee to Jackson, November 4, 1813, *Official Letters*, 255–256; Jackson to Blount, November 11, 1813, ibid., 264–265. For insight into Jackson's efforts to occupy the Creek country, see Yancy M. Quinn, Jr., "Jackson's Military Road," *Journal of Mississippi History* 41 (1979): 335–350. A major point of contention between the Americans and anti-accommodationist Creeks had been the Americans' desire to construct a road through the Creek county to the Mississippi Territory. Jackson built his road in 1813 to connect Mississippi with the American settlements to the East, as well as provide a conduit by which he could rapidly reinforce and resupply his army on its march against the Creek towns.

35 Saunt, *A New Order of Things*, 257. Saunt quotes one army officer as observing, "not a track of a cow or hog was to be seen in the Creek country" as a result of the Red Sticks' insistence upon slaughtering livestock.

The conquest of the Creeks, however, would take time. The greatest obstacle proved to be not Red Stick resistance but American infighting. First, Jackson began to lose control of his army. Many of the militia chafed under his authoritarian command and nearly mutinied when supplies grew dangerously short. With his army deserting before his eyes, Jackson retreated north to Fort Strother to regroup. Second, Jackson, the most aggressive of the American commanders, received little sustained support from the leaders of the other American forces. Although in November Brigadier General Floyd and William McIntosh's combined force killed 200 Creeks at Auttose, and Brigadier General Claiborne's column cleared the lower Alabama River region of Red Sticks, neither of these materiel- and troop-poor armies could maintain its offensive and press on to Tuckabatchee.[36] John Cocke, meanwhile, Jackson's political rival, feared doing anything that might contribute to the rise of Old Hickory's star. Because Jackson had won a victory at Talladega, Cocke determined that he too needed a battlefield success. His sole positive contribution to the campaign fit no strategic plan, though it conformed very well to the frontiersmen's first way of war: he ordered James White to slaughter 64 peaceful Creeks at Hillabee on November 13, the same Indians who had agreed to surrender to Jackson the day before.[37] Moreover, by the time he reached Fort Strother, Cocke's militia had only a few weeks remaining in its term of service and was of little use to Jackson. Still, by early spring, Jackson had assembled 4,000 troops for his second invasion of the Creek country.

Hard fighting awaited them on their southward march. After moving against Red Stick camps at Emuckfau and Enitachopco Creeks, he met the bulk of the remaining Indian force on the 100-acre peninsula in the "horseshoe" bend of the Tallapoosa River at Tohopeka.[38] The Red Sticks and their allied runaway slaves had built a log and earthen barricade across the neck of the peninsula. They had concentrated nearly 1,000 warriors together with their families behind the barricade. They thought their peninsula stronghold offered safety; in reality, it became a trap in which Creek independence perished.

March 27, 1814, proved the high point of the war for both the frontiersmen and the United States Army. Jackson – with Coffee's mounted brigade of rangers, the 39th United States Infantry, and allied Cherokees and Creeks under McIntosh – attacked the Creeks lined up against him, "determined to exterminate them."[39] While he directed the regulars' assault

36   Floyd to Thomas Pinckney, December 4, 1813, *Official Letters*, 283.
37   James White to John Cocke, November 24, 1812, ibid., 281–282.
38   Jackson to Pinckney, January 29, 1814, ibid., 298–305.
39   Jackson to Pinckney, March 28, 1814, ibid., 319–320.

on the earthwork barricade at the Red Sticks' front, Coffee's troopers cut off the Indians' retreat across the river. McIntosh's Indians then swam the Tallapoosa, stole the Red Sticks' canoes, and set the village on fire by shooting flaming arrows into it. After two hours of ineffectively battering the barricade with his two artillery pieces, Jackson ordered the 39th to take it with a bayonet charge. The head-on assault into the teeth of Indian musket fire and arrows managed to break the Red Sticks' line. The Red Sticks fought bravely in their ensuing retreat down the peninsula, but found themselves within an increasingly constricting cordon raked by the Americans' superior firepower. When others tried to flee across the river, Coffee's frontiersmen, armed with accurate rifles, shot them like fish in a barrel. Jackson's men took five hours to root out and eliminate all the pockets of Red Stick resistance on the peninsula. At the end of the day, Old Hickory was well pleased with his troops' performance: at a cost of fewer than 50 killed and 160 wounded, they had killed over 800 Red Stick warriors and taken around 300 women and children captive.[40]

Horseshoe Bend sounded the knell for Creek resistance. While over the summer Jackson fretted that other bands of Red Sticks might appear to challenge him, only a few holdouts continued the war. Other Red Sticks who still had the will to fight managed to escape and join their Seminole cousins in Florida. While the Seminoles would continue the struggle against the Americans into the next decades, causing the Army no end of frustration, they were simply too few in numbers and too unreliably armed to threaten American control of the Old Southwest.[41] Indeed, Jackson's initial post-battle assessment that the power of the Creeks was "forever broken" was correct.[42] Present-day Alabama and Mississippi lay open to American settlement.

The "principles of national justice and honorable war," the frontiersmen asserted in the surrender instrument the Creeks signed in August 1814, justified American demands for "retribution."[43] Indeed, magnanimity in victory, rarely an American trait exhibited in their dealings with vanquished Indians, was nowhere to be found in 1814. The Creeks, the citizens of Mississippi noted, had visited upon them a war "unrestrained

---

40 Thomas W. Cutrer, "'The Tallapoosa Might Truly Be Called the River of Blood': Major Alexander McCulloch and the Battle of Horseshoe Bend, March 27, 1814," *Alabama Review* 43 (1990): 35–39. For Coffee's view of the battle, see John Coffee, "Letters of General John Coffee to His Wife, 1813–1815," ed. John H. DeWitt, *Tennessee Historical Magazine* 2 (1916): 264–295.
41 For the role of Creek militants in the First Seminole War, and one that contextualizes that struggle as a continuation of Jackson's personal war for imperial conquest, see David S. and Jeanne T. Heidler, *Old Hickory's War: Andrew Jackson and the Quest for Empire* (Mechanicsburg, PA: Stackpole Books, 1996).
42 Jackson to Thomas Pinckney, March 28, 1814, *Official Letters*, 319–320.
43 Articles of Agreement and Capitulation, *ASPIA*, 1: 826.

by any principles, which govern warfare among civilized nations."
"Reparation," they continued, "is thought due for the property which
they [the Creeks] have wantonly destroyed."[44] Thus, few questioned Jackson's bleeding of the Creek nation at the Treaty of Fort Jackson. Indeed,
the only serious question frontiersmen had centered on how they might
take more land from the Creeks. In June 1816, for instance, Thomas Freeman asked what was to become of the area near Tuckabatchee. It seemed
to Freeman that by oversight it had not been included in the Creek cession
and had become a quasi-reservation. He wondered if the few dozen acres
of the town site could be surveyed and tacked on to the 23 million acres
of the Creek cession.[45]

In the end, Freeman and his like-minded compatriots dispossessed
the Creeks of all their lands – a harbinger of the next two decades of
American–Indian relations, in which removal of the eastern Indians to
the lands of the Transmississippi West became the official policy of the
United States government as well as the personal preference of the man
Americans elected to the Presidency in 1828, Andrew Jackson.[46] It was in
those years that the United States, with the Indians powerless to prevent it,
harvested the fruits of victory won in the Northwest and Creek Wars, and
indeed, in over 200 years of American fighting with the Indians. While the
conquered Indian nations of the Transappalachian West descended into
depths of misery that few peoples have known, the citizens of the United
States looked forward to the peaceful settlement of their new domain, an
"Empire of Liberty" secured by the first way of war.

44 Memorial to Congress by the Territorial Legislature, December 23, 1814, *Terr. Papers*,
    6: 481. See also, Judge Toulmin to William Lattimore, November 12, 1815, ibid., 6:
    566.
45 Thomas Freeman to Josiah Meigs, June 30, 1816, ibid., 6: 695. Tuckabatchee was
    perhaps one of the most difficult places for the Creeks to abandon. Long the most
    important of the Upper Towns, it was also the repository of the most sacred objects of
    Creek culture. *Encyclopedia of the War of 1812*, s.v. "Tuckabatchee."
46 After acquiring Louisiana, some Americans began to consider its vast "desert" portions
    as a reservation for the eastern Indians. See Isaac Briggs to the President [Thomas
    Jefferson], May 18, 1805, *Terr. Papers*, 5: 403.

Epilogue

The history of the regular Army predominates in our understanding of the American military heritage and overshadows the ubiquity and permanence of the first way of war in Americans' martial culture. American military history, the conventional wisdom seems to show, progressed through the nineteenth and the first half of the twentieth centuries in a series of more or less orderly wars with European or Euro-American opponents. Indeed, historians have focused on Americans' conflicts between the War of 1812 and the Second World War as little more than regular conflicts that fit nicely within Weigley's paradigm. In those instances when later Americans embraced elements of war that their predecessors would have recognized as their first way of war – whether William Tecumseh Sherman's march through the South in 1864 and 1865 or the dropping of the atomic bombs on Hiroshima and Nagasaki in 1945 – they, the historians point out, attacked civilian populations only as a means to the end of increasing the effectiveness of regular war making. "To fight the enemy armies was immensely expensive, above all in lives," Russell Weigley wrote to explain why Sherman unleashed his armies on the economic and social fabric of the Confederacy. Weigley pointed out that Sherman came to believe that if the Union armies took the war straight to the enemy's civilian population, they would lose their will to continue the war, and without the people's support, the Confederacy would collapse. Sherman therefore designed his marches as campaigns of terror and destruction.[1]

Yet accompanying each of the regular conflicts were campaigns that seem reminiscent of the first way of war. The first way of war against Indian noncombatants on the frontier continued to define American war making throughout the nineteenth century, from the Seminole Wars, through the Sand Creek Massacre of 1864, to Wounded Knee in 1890. Frustrated by continued Indian resistance and befuddled about how best to quash it, the Army looked the other way when either its own men or

1   Russell F. Weigley, *The American Way of War: A History of United States Military Strategy and Policy* (Bloomington: Indiana University Press, 1973), 149.

citizens acting on its name subjected Seminoles, Arapahos, Cheyennes, and Sioux to the same treatment that earlier Americans had inflicted on Abenakis, Cherokees, and even Christian Indians. In the most regular of America's nineteenth-century wars, the Civil War, Americans, the most famous being William Quantrill and his band of Confederate raiders, fought a *petite guerre* in Missouri and Kentucky.

Beyond its sheer military utility, Americans also found a use for the first way of war in the construction of an "American identity."[2] The political careers of Andrew Jackson and William Henry Harrison are only the most powerful examples of the imaginative grip that the identity of the Indian-fighting frontiersman had on American political culture in the first third of the nineteenth century. Similarly, despite modern writers who have termed soldiers like John Gorham of King George's War "Monsters of the Past,"[3] the enduring appeal of the romanticized myth of the "settlement" (not the conquest) of the frontier, either by "actual" men such as Robert Rogers or Daniel Boone or fictitious ones like Nathaniel Bumppo of James Fenimore Cooper's creation, points to what D. H. Lawrence called the "myth of the essential white American." If, however, we are willing to accept Lawrence's proposition that there is something "essentially" American in the frontier experience, then there also seems truth, especially in terms of the centrality of the first way of war and the extravagant violence it engendered in the conquest of that frontier, to his assessment that "the essential American soul" is a killer.[4]

2   Within the recent explosion in identity studies, the identity of the "American soldier" is missing. Indeed, the most recent collection of essays by early Americanists on the "identities" of seventeenth- and eighteenth-century North Americans (see Ronald Hoffman, Mechal Sobel, and Fredrika J. Teute, eds., *Through a Glass Darkly: Reflections on Personal Identity in Early America* [Chapel Hill: University of North Carolina Press for the OIEAHC, 1997]) ignores soldiers and military men. Yet soldiers were ubiquitous in seventeenth- and eighteenth-century America. See John Grenier, "'Of Great Utility': The Public Identity of Early American Rangers and Its Impact on American Society," *War and Society* 21 (2003): 1–14.

3   John Gorham's place in history, for example, was the topic of a heated debate in Nova Scotia in January and February 1998. The Nova Scotia Department of Transportation (DOT) had named a stretch of road between Bedford and Sackville in honor of the ranger captain. The DOT's logic was that Gorham had been instrumental in the *settlement* of the region. In the January 16, 1998, edition of the (Nova Scotia) *Chronicle-Herald*, however, "Indian and human rights activist" and Mi'kmaq author Daniel N. Paul judged Gorham one of the "Monsters of the Past." Paul took note of the activities of Gorham and his rangers, particularly their practice of scalping Indians and Acadians for bounties. He asked: "What is the real difference between the likes of Hitler and Stalin and the likes of" Gorham? Paul's editorial in the *Chronicle-Herald* unleashed a maelstrom of criticism of the DOT and supporters of "Captain John Gorham Boulevard." The DOT quickly abandoned the idea of naming the road after Gorham. See <http://alts.net/ns1625/gorhamj.html>.

4   D. H. Lawrence, *Studies in Classic American Literature* (New York: Albert and Charles Boni, 1930), 92.

For the most part, however, Americans prefer to think that our military culture neither condones nor encourages the targeting and killing of non-combatants. But we no longer use the first way of war perhaps because we no longer need it. Americans have not fought a war of conquest in the past 100 years and have fought only limited wars since World War II. Similarly, the modern American democracy that places such high value on liberal principles cannot condone the means of war making that our early ancestors used to win their wars. Operation Iraqi Freedom – note that it was an "operation," not a "war" – saw the American military accept more, albeit only a few, casualties rather than inflict "collateral" damage and unnecessary suffering on the people of Iraq. In that sense, it seems that the first way of war has become superficially incompatible with the way Americans, both civilians and soldiers, view themselves.

American soldiers and students of military affairs have never officially recognized or sanctioned that aspect of our military past, partially be-cause Americans are bereft of a sophisticated military literature. Students of the first 175 years of American military history generally focus on the War of Independence. It, with the Civil War and World War II – distinc-tively regular wars – are the major landmarks on the horizon of American military history. Moreover, during the period when the United States mili-tary found itself engaged in a distinctly American enterprise – the military conquest of the Indian peoples of the Transmississippi West – its leading theoreticians (Dennis Hart Mahan, Winfield Scott, and Emory Upton, for example) turned their backs on the frontier and sought to align American war making with European models. After that point, the regular Army flourished and dominated military affairs. Little wonder, then, that we have not engaged in a serious philosophical consideration of the first way of war, despite the fact that it undeniably shaped the first 207 years of American history.

From a professional military officer's perspective, American soldiers are notably reluctant to engage in conflicts like those in which our predeces-sors fought.[5] Except for a few specialized units, the overwhelming ma-jority of American military forces today train and fight in army-on-army engagements. Although one of the major challenges facing the twenty-first-century American military will be "asymmetrical warfare," that is,

5 For the American attitude – one fraught with hostility and exasperation – on waging low-intensity conflict, see Max Boot, *The Savage Wars of Peace: Small Wars and the Rise of American* Power (New York: Basic Books, 2002), chaps. 14 and 15. Nearly a decade before Boot published his well-received and highly acclaimed *The Savage Wars of Peace*, Carnes Lord, in "American Strategic Culture in Small Wars," *Small Wars and Insurgencies* 3 (1992): 205–216, made many of the same points. For the place of violence and terror directed against noncombatants in modern-day low-intensity conflicts and the American perception of those methods, see Roger Beaumont, "Thinking the Unspeakable: On Cruelty in Small Wars," ibid., 1 (1990): 54–73.

an adversary's use of nonregular means (turning hijacked commercial airliners into flying bombs piloted by men intent on sacrificing their lives as "martyrs"), comparatively little thought and effort have been devoted to how American soldiers will meet the asymmetrical challenges of the new century. We can only speculate on the role that the progeny of the first way of war will receive in America's "War on Terror" and sure-to-be frustrated efforts to "democratize" Southwest Asia. I suspect they will become crusades in which the military identifies the enemy, despite pronouncements to the contrary, as "radical Muslims" intent on destroying and incapable of embracing the liberties and freedoms that define "Western civilization."[6]

Indeed, today we see others than ourselves as the practitioners of the kind of war addressed in this study. We recoil at the news reports of the killing of innocent men, women, and children in Central Africa and Bosnia. We look with repugnance on the Serbians who drove the ethnic Albanians from their homes in Kosovo and pillaged their land.[7] We judge those as genocidal acts that fall far outside the norm of American behavior. When we look into our military past and see events like the My Lai Massacre, we can rationalize it as an anomaly or the result of an overzealous and deranged junior officer like Lieutenant William Calley, not as a grim waypoint in the evolution of the American way of war.

Coming to terms with what happened at My Lai, or for that matter any other American "atrocity," forces us to the crux of the question this study has attempted to address: where does war waged against noncombatants fit in Americans' martial culture? American soldiers killing noncombatants is nothing new. It is not, as Stephen Ambrose suggested, the "logical development" from the Second World War, what he called "a break with the past" when "the civilian became a legitimate target" through strategic bombing and the use of atomic weapons.[8] Nor is it, as Weigley suggested, the legacy of the Civil War and Ulysses S. Grant's and William T. Sherman's – two men who knew little of Clausewitz's philosophies and nothing of Delbrück's writings – adoption of a Clausewitzian–Delbrückian unlimited-annihilationist synthesis. Rather, violence directed systematically against noncombatants through irregular means, from the start, has been a central part of Americans' way of war. American soldiers

---

6   For the predilection of Americans to see the "War on Terrorism" as synonymous with a "War on Islam," see Sami G. Hajjar, "Avoiding Holy War: Ensuring That the War on Terrorism Is Not Perceived as a War on Islam," *ROA [Reserve Officers Association] National Security Report*, April 2002, 31–32.

7   James M. Dorsey, "Ethnic Cleansing Was Just Business for Well-Paid Paramilitary Units," *The Wall Street Journal*, September 1, 1999, 18.

8   Stephen Ambrose, "My Lai: Atrocities in Historical Perspective," *Americans at War* (New York: Berkley Books, 1997), 200, and Ambrose, "The Atomic Bomb and Its Consequences," ibid., 127.

have turned to it out of military necessity, economic need, and the search for social legitimization.

Over the course of the colonial period, Americans found that what I call the first way of war was the most effective means to wage war. In their numerous wars with Indians of the seventeenth and the first half of the eighteenth centuries, they gradually refined and perfected it. Near the end of the imperial wars of the eighteenth century, they saw it gain acceptance and legitimization within British military culture. During the era of the American Revolution, it continued to dominate military affairs on the frontier. A subsequent generation of Americans carried it into the nineteenth century, and despite the Army's general disdain for it, they made it the engine of conquest in the quarter-century drive to gain dominion over the Transappalachian West. Thus, the 205 years between the first Indian war in Virginia in 1609 and the end of the Creek War in 1814 were the seedbed from which the rest of American military history grew. Indeed, when we contemplate what an uncertain future may hold, we would be wise to recognize all the ways in which Americans have and perhaps again will let slip the dogs of war.

Index